AN
EVERYDAY
HISTORY
OF
SOMEWHERE

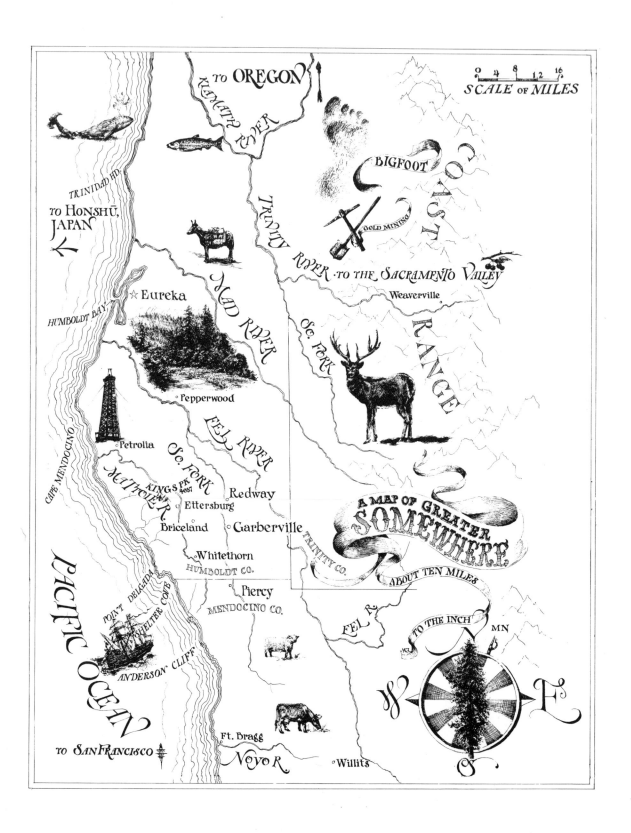

AN
EVERYDAY
HISTORY
OF
SOMEWHERE

BEING *the true ſtory of* Indians, *deer, home-ſteaders, potatoes, loggers, trees, fiſhermen, ſalmon, &* other living things in the back- *woods of* Northern California::

as Written Down by
RAY RAPHAEL

and Pictured from Original Sources by
MARK LIVINGSTON.

561371

NEW YORK   ALFRED A. KNOPF   MCMLXXIV

THIS IS A BORZOI BOOK
PUBLISHED BY ALFRED A. KNOPF, INC.

Grateful acknowledgment is made:
To Suzanne Galliher for use of her photographs of Alden,
Grandma Beerbower, Burrill, Roy and Mabel Cathey, Glen,
Mr. and Mrs. Ernest McKee, and Fred Wolf.

To the Library of Congress for the Spanish Galleon, Prospectors,
Dance House, and the two logging pictures.

To the General Research and Humanities Division of the New York
Public Library, Astor, Lenox, and Tilden Foundations,
for Old Fort Humboldt, Homestead,
and the Eureka fashion and Pacific Lumber Co. advertisements.

Library of Congress Cataloging in Publication Data

Raphael, Ray.

An everyday history of somewhere.
1. California—History. 2. California—Social Life
and customs. 3. Indians of North America—California.
I. Title.
F861.R36   917.94′03′5   73–20742
ISBN 0-394-48736-2

Manufactured in the United States of America
First Edition

FOR HARRY, RONDAL, AND MARIE

CONTENTS

AN
EVERYDAY
HISTORY
OF
SOMEWHERE

INTRODUCTION.

WHAT'S AN EVERYDAY HISTORY?

You won't have a book big enough to write this all down.

—AN OLD-TIMER

"Somewhere" could be anywhere. This particular somewhere happens to be in the coastal hills of northern California. It's just a place, like any other place, except it turns out to have a fascinating everyday history. Actually, every place has an everyday history, and it's all probably equally fascinating. People, however, tend to be blinded by the light of a few special places and a few big events, and so the everyday histories are rarely learned. An everyday history tells of the people, the places, and the times which other books are in too much of a hurry to talk about.

An everyday history starts from scratch; it takes nothing for granted. The sun rises and sets, seasons come and go. Through it all trees blossom and grow, animals eat and mate. People wake up, eat breakfast, do their daily work, and go to sleep. Sometimes there are big events such as wars, fires, or storms. But most of the time, life just goes on, one day after the next.

My interest in everyday histories began, I guess, by listening to fairy tales as a kid. I was never really satisfied with "happily ever after." What, I wondered, was life really like during "happily ever after"? What did people eat? Did they work? Did they go to the bathroom, and what kind of bathrooms were available to go to? As I got older I started going to the movies, where years would pass in seconds as the words "ten years later" flashed on the screen (or per-

3

RAY, MARIE, AND FRIENDS: THE PATH TO THE SEA

The books rarely told much about what life was really like. Historians seemed to follow the same pattern as the Hollywood "star" system: they were interested only in the lives of a few Very Important People—people who "made history." When I learned about the Middle Ages, it was all about a handful of kings and queens and noblemen—nothing about the lives of the serfs. And of course it was mostly about the exciting wars among the nobility, not about the commonplace times of peace. Even "sophisticated" histories tended to focus only on the big events, on acts and treaties, on elections and coups d'état, on politics of all sorts.

There was always considerable confusion in my mind about what people meant when they said Columbus "discovered" America. What about all the Indians who lived here? Some history books, in a sort of liberal exposé to shock the minds of young students, admitted that it was really Leif Ericsson who discovered America. But still nothing about the Indians. How could the Indians, I wondered, not have discovered America if they lived here? It just didn't make sense. Nor did it seem fair to give Columbus himself all the credit and forget about the rest of his crew—people who risked just as much as he did by an adventure onto the unknown seas. Nobody ever seemed to care about anyone but the captains of the ships.

When I think back on the history I was taught in school, there appear to be certain hidden assumptions:

1. History meant human history.
2. Human history meant the history of Western civilization. (Other civilizations were relevant only insofar as they interacted with the West.)

haps the pages of a calendar blew off in the wind). What was life like in those ten years? How did people eat? What work did they do? Again, when I studied history in school, these basic questions never seemed to be answered.

3. Great men shaped history.
4. Some events were more important than others.
5. History showed progress, culminating in the civilization of today.

When stated so simply, these assumptions seem highly presumptuous, but perhaps they can be understood by looking at the function history plays in the human mind. People have always sought a tie with the past. Ancient and primitive societies had legends and various forms of ancestor worship; today we have our history books. History forms a bond between the living and the dead, and reassures us of the continuity of life. Since humans are blessed with the consciousness of their own impending death, it becomes a matter of great importance to each of us to feel that tie between the living and the dead. In this respect history functions in much the same way as religion—indeed, it is only fairly recently, and only within our own civilization, that history, in aspiring to be one of the social sciences, has pretended to be anything other than religion, anything other than the story of how it all began and of the great deeds of our ancestors. Our society, like all others, has certain legends which explain our origins and our past, and it is these legends that we learned in school.

History is legend, and legends tend to deal with the extraordinary rather than the ordinary. Perhaps this is why the everyday histories never get told. Through history we seek inspiration from great deeds of great men. Identifying with historical heroes works much like going to the movies: we can imagine ourselves to be greater than we are. When we go to the movies, we don't like to see some average guy at a nine-to-five job—we see that all day and are bored with

it. We want excitement. History is excitement: most people, for instance, love to witness a fire, or any other event they might read about in tomorrow's paper. We can all remember exactly where we were on the day that John F. Kennedy was assassinated; history was being made, and, however grieved, everyone felt a certain excitement by being part of it.

It's a difficult matter to break away from this human obsession with the extraordinary and focus on the ordinary. It's not easy to break away from the assumptions we've lived with all our lives—like the intrinsic belief that history means human history. Human beings are only one of the many different forms of life that flourish on the earth. We are certainly part of history, but scarcely all of it. An everyday history talks about men and deer and trees and insects and all the life forces as they interact with each other in their daily lives. In this book I'll do the best I can to give a picture of the various forms of ordinary life that have inhabited my "somewhere." More emphasis, I'm afraid, will still be given to human beings than to the plants and other animals—for two reasons: 1. I am shaped by my own human consciousness (if a deer could write this history, it would of course be altogether different); 2. Human beings, particularly in recent years, have played an important role in the way things happen. When people inhabit an area, they tend to leave their mark rather dramatically. An everyday history thus focuses much of its attention on how people shape their environment to make a living in the world, and the effects people have on other forms of life.

I'm not quite sure what type of book this really is. It's sort of like history, sort of like anthropology, sort of like biology, and sort of like ecology. It's history that talks more about

ALONG THE COAST: TABLE - MEADOW & CLIFFS

common people than about politicians and diplomats, as much about the hundred years of harvests as about the one year of famine. It's anthropology that looks at the intimate relation between man and the world in which he makes his living, but not an anthropology that treats people and cultures as pawns in an intellectual game. It's biology that is just as interested in eating the plants and praying to them as in classifying them. And of course it's ecology, which means sort of anything and everything. One wonders which shelf this book will be on in the bookstore, or how a librarian will catalog it. For some strange reason, we just love to break knowledge apart into a million little pieces, into all sorts of separate "ologies," only to try to reassemble it in encyclopedias and "interdisciplinary" courses. An everyday history starts by never taking it all apart in the first place. It's like a true documentary movie. The everyday history of anyplace is just talking about what's been happening there over the centuries—nothing more, nothing less.

A short way north of Fort Bragg, the California coastal highway turns inland. The shoreline cliffs rise quickly to a height of two thousand feet. The rugged terrain of steep hills and deep valleys would make the continuation of the highway difficult, although of course not impossible. In former times the stage route followed the coast as far north as the settlement at Four Corners before turning inland in the face of the formidable Kings Peak Range. Today the stage has long since disappeared, as has Four Corners, which is now nothing more than the intersection of four dirt roads marked by four county road signs.

The expansive hillsides facing the ocean are covered alternately with fields of tall grass and forests of Douglas fir. The deep gorges through which water rushes into the ocean are thick with the moisture-loving vegetation of a rain forest. This dense growth is the result of the ocean fog which creeps up these channels so frequently that the earth never has a chance to dry out, even during the summer months when hardly a drop of rain falls. Ferns and berry bushes grow profusely under alders, broadleaf maples, and California bay laurels whose trunks are covered with moss.

Over the crest of the first ocean-facing ridge, the vegetation changes dramatically. The fir forests become mixed with tan oak and madrone, both hardwood trees whose leaves are not shed during the wet but mild California winters. Since most of the fir trees have been logged, the tan oaks and madrones dominate the hillsides extending several miles inland. The undergrowth is often thick with huckleberry bushes and baby trees, but sometimes sparse because of the extremely rocky soil. The fog occasionally reaches up and in from the ocean and the rain forests to cover these hillsides as well. Where the fog extends into the inland valleys, stands of giant redwood trees dominate the terrain.

On top of the highest ridges, where the fog reaches only rarely and the soil is hard and parched by the sun, only bushes and dwarfed trees can grow. The prominent species in this windswept brushland is a chaparral called manzanita, whose small red berries gave nourishment to the Indians, were thought poisonous by the settlers, and are virtually ignored today. These arid semideserts are sometimes no more than a mile or two away from the thick rain forests, but they are two thousand feet higher.

Overlooking the area from the top of the hills one notices few, if any, signs of human habitation. The wooded hillsides have been logged, but now the loggers have gone. The open meadows are sometimes, but not always, grazed by sheep. The occasional settlements are well hidden in the valleys. The land is virtually a wilderness, although not a virgin one.

Tucked away in these hillsides of "somewhere" is a small wooden cabin which is my home. I have neighbors nearby, but Whitethorn, the closest approximation of a town in the vicinity, is ten miles away. Thorn, as it is called by its inhabitants, consists of a general store with two gas pumps outside and half-empty shelves inside, a post office, a school, and a library, even smaller than my cabin, which is open on Wednesdays from two to six and Saturdays from ten to two. There is one streetlight and a neon "Jesus Saves" sign above the Assembly of God church. "Whitethorn Vol. Fire Dept." is inscribed above a single-car wood-frame garage.

Whitethorn, as it turns out, was not always the simple little town it is today. When the forests were being cleared of fir and redwood trees,

Thorn was filled with five mills to cut the logs, and almost as many saloons to service the loggers. In earlier years, it was the home of several hundred bark peelers, who took off the outside of the tan oak trees to obtain the tannic acids necessary to process leather. Before that, it was a group of homesteads surrounding a large white house that served as a major stage stop on the main road from San Francisco to Eureka. And still earlier, yet less than 125 years ago, the Whitethorn Valley was the home of several families of Indians who had not seen their first white man. In the space of little more than a century, several civilizations have come and gone through this sleepy little town and this seeming wilderness.

My first real insights into the everyday history of where I live came when I met a man named Harry Roberts, part-Indian who had grown up about a hundred miles from my home. From Harry I learned how the Indians used to make a living from the land. Harry talked of his life with the Yurok Indians along the Klamath River, and I soon became interested in what existence had been like for the Indians in my own immediate area. I looked through the anthropological journals and found that the Sinkyone Indians who lived right here had been virtually exterminated within their first ten years of contact with white civilization. From the anthropologists' work with the few survivors, however, it was clear that the Sinkyone and the Yurok shared a basically similar way of life common throughout northwest California. As I learned more and more about the Indians from both Harry and the anthropologists, I began to picture their villages and campsites in the hills and valleys I frequented. A whole new world began to open up. From Harry I learned the area's wide variety of edible plants and started to use them. I tried (with little success, I'm afraid) to walk through the woods with the quiet alertness of an Indian hunter. At night I read the legends of the various California Indians and gained a feeling of kinship with the lively world of animal-people who filled the Indians' imagination.

Getting in touch with the Indians' way of life necessarily involved gaining some familiarity with the plant and animal life of the region. As the seasons passed, I followed the changes in life forces with a new consciousness. As I watched the animals to understand their way of life, I began to feel my own existence as one of the animals; while opening my food box to prepare dinner, I'd wind up thinking of the squirrel going to his cache for his dinner. On every walk through the woods I'd come across a new plant which I'd take to Harry, who would tell me what it was and how the Indians used it. I had never had much interest in biology in school, but this was different.

While browsing through the Whitethorn library one day, I came across some old books on the history of the area—books dating back to the 1880s. Besides noticing the obvious signs of past logging, I had never really thought much about the changes the region had gone through since the time of the Indians. It had just seemed too remote, I guess—too insignificant a place to have a history. In these books, however, I read about elaborate shipping arrangements from the presently deserted beaches, about mill towns that had come and gone, about sheep ranching and the extraction of tannic acid from the bark of the tan oak trees. Again, whole new worlds were opening up. Now when I'd walk through the woods I'd feel the presence not only of the In-

AT HOME

dians and the plants and animals, but also of the loggers, ranchers, bark peelers, teamsters—everyone who had lived on the land nearby, all the human and nonhuman creatures who had shared this space on earth.

Although these old books told something about life in the back hills in which I lived, they focused their attention on the nearest center of civilization—Eureka and the region around Humboldt Bay. I followed the paths of white settlements as they came to Humboldt Bay during the gold rush and then spread into outlying areas such as my own. I saw what had happened in this remote area as inexorably related to what was happening in the rest of northern California and in the rest of the world. The microcosm of an insignificant place somewhere in the back hills reflected the macrocosm of national and world history. In this book, I will try to put the history of my own remote "somewhere" in its larger context by following the course of civilization as it progressed through the Humboldt Bay region and thence into the back hills.

As my fascination with the past grew, I came into contact with some old-timers from around the area. Strange as it may seem, old folks have been virtually forgotten as a source of historical information. In other societies throughout the world, the job of older people is to pass on the knowledge and wisdom of their culture and the history of their people. In our society, however, this is done through books, educational institutions, the mass media. Old folks have been replaced by modern, automated techniques and have thus become obsolete. If the natural "job" of old people is to pass on information, in our country they are now all "unemployed." They have been left behind by a world oriented toward the new, the changing, and the young.

Without exception, all the old-timers I met were overjoyed to talk to someone who was interested in hearing their stories. They spoke of what life had been like in the old days, and of all the changes they had lived through. With each life story, I experienced the history of the area from a different perspective. Bark peelers, loggers, ranchers—these were no longer abstractions but, rather, real people telling of their personal adventures in these endeavors. Just as my experiences with Harry had turned dry anthropological research into a living reality, talking with the old-timers made history come alive.

From Harry and the old-timers I was gaining knowledge that was more practical than academic. My own culture of twentieth-century urbanized America had taught me little about living off the land. I had to fill in the gaps of my inexperience, and this is just where older people can be of such great help. History is not, in my eyes, an abstract affair; from history I was learning helpful insights into my own life. Even as I write this everyday history book, I am intimately involved in the historical process. I am learning from history at every turn—learning how to do things and how not to do them. Much of what there is to gain from the history of this area is, I'm afraid, a knowledge of the mistakes which should not be repeated. Since the advent of white civilization, the natural ecological balance has been drastically changed, even in the back hills. By writing about these changes, and by the way in which I myself make a living off the land, I am involving myself in the shaping of current history.

From the start, then, let the reader be warned that this book is meant more to be lived than studied. I have found learning the everyday history of my home to be a consciousness-expanding

experience which I wish to share. If the reader, after finishing the book, wishes to pay a visit to this particular "somewhere" to see the scene of all the happenings, my whole point will have been lost. There's absolutely nothing special about my "somewhere"—it's just where I happen to live—and gawking tourists are most thoroughly discouraged by all of us who live here. The point of the book is rather to show how anyone can add new dimensions to his awareness of his immediate world by finding out its everyday history. The method is simple: talk with the old-timers nearby; look for the old books in the library; find out about the Indians from anthropological journals (it's better, of course, if there are any Indians around raised in the traditional ways who can teach you directly); look through the old local newspapers, which can probably be found on microfilm in a university or historical society library (for the purposes of an everyday history, you'll probably learn more from the ads than from the headlines); learn all you can about the plants and animals that inhabit the area. As you begin to get the picture of how other folks and other living beings have related to your home environment, you'll probably feel your own life in a new perspective. Each of us is another small chapter in the everyday history of the world.

N.B.: Throughout the text, bibliographical references are indicated by a number in parentheses—(14), (63). These numbers refer to the source materials cited in the Bibliographical Essay at the end of the book.

PART ONE.

BEYOND MEMORY

TARAXACUM OFFICINALE
(DANDELION)

CHAPTER ONE. THE INDIANS

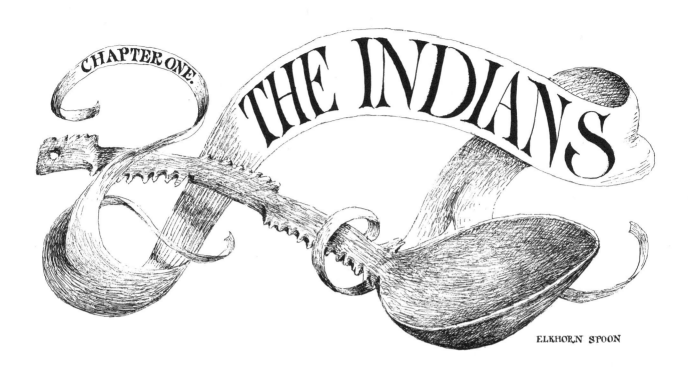

ELKHORN SPOON

The Northern Coast of California was a primeval wilderness, inhabited only by wild beasts and wilder Indians.

—A. J. BLEDSOE,
PIONEER AND EARLY HISTORIAN

One hundred million years ago, the coastal hills of northern California lay underwater. To the west, in what is now the Pacific Ocean, there was a large body of land; to the east, the Sierra Nevadas had just emerged as part of an American continent upon which dinosaurs flourished in a semitropical world of giant ferns and redwood trees. But in this particular "somewhere" the life forms were all aquatic, with many well-developed species of fish living midst a wide variety of oceanic organisms.

Millions of years passed, and the stresses in the earth's crust gradually began to push the ocean floor upward. The Coast Ranges were slowly being formed, but it wasn't until ten million years ago that California took on an approximation of its present shape. By this time the dinosaurs had long since disappeared from the face of the earth, while birds and mammals and flowering plants flourished throughout the world. As the coastal hills surfaced from the ocean, they quickly became inhabited by these relatively new forms of life.

Neither human beings nor any of their close relatives were among the animal species to evolve in this area. Thirty or forty thousand years ago, however, toward the tail end of the ice ages, the ancestors of the modern-day Indians found their way to the Western Hemisphere by crossing the northern land bridge which then connected Asia with North America. The paths followed by the migrating Indians as they spread out across the continent are unknown, but in one way or another many of them found their way to California.

With the advance and retreat of the last of the glaciers, the California climate changed dramatically. Subarctic conditions were followed by periods of intense, dry heat. What happened to the Indians and their way of life during these times is not known; perhaps they adapted successfully to the great alterations in the animal and vegetable life upon which they fed, or perhaps some Indian civilizations died out and were replaced by others at a later date. At one point, the Indians seem to have thrived on a wide variety of large mammals—mammoths, mastodons, bison, and native American horses and camels. As many of these large game mammals disappeared, the Indians apparently turned more of their attention to edible plants, fish, smaller mammals, and seafood. The climate finally became mild and temperate and the forests, fields, rivers, and seas abounded with the numerous forms of life which could support human beings.

SPEARING SALMON

In other areas of the country, Indians were often forced to rely on one basic source for their food supply; the people of the plains would have starved without the buffalo, as would the people of the far north without the caribou. In California, however, if game was scarce there were always fish, and if the fish weren't running there were acorns and a host of other wild plants they could eat. In such food-abundant surroundings there was no real need for the Indians to domesticate the plants and animals that lived around them. Thus an agricultural society never developed, although the standard of living was high and starvation virtually unknown. There was no further need for mass migrations or nomadic existence, and the human inhabitants of California settled down to enjoy the fruits of their environment. It was several thousand years ago that the California Indians developed the civilization that was to continue into modern times.

When the European-Americans arrived in northwest California in the nineteenth century, they found a native human population as large as that in any other area north of Mexico. Yet the Indians they met were living in small, isolated villages, each one being the home of perhaps twenty-five to fifty people. Even today it is easy to spot the sites of these Indian villages—anyplace the wooded coastal hills open into a fairly flat natural clearing near the ocean or a good-sized stream was probably where Indians constructed their dwellings. Such spots are infrequent in this rugged terrain, however, and several miles usually separated the inhabitants of one village from their nearest neighbors. Both whites and Indians seem to have chosen the same few locations as suitable living sites: Usal, Needle Rock, Shelter Cove, the Whitethorn Valley, Ettersburg, and the areas around Briceland

AN INDIAN VILLAGE IN THE BACK COUNTRY

and Garberville. Construction workers building houses in these areas often come across obsidian arrowheads and other artifacts of the previous inhabitants.

To speak of the Sinkyone—the Indians living in this particular area—as a "tribe" is misleading. An Indian of northwestern California belonged first and foremost to himself and his family. There was no political organization whatsoever—no nations, tribes, or chiefs. The people of several neighboring villages might speak the same language, but if an Indian ventured more than about twenty-five miles from home he would be unable to communicate in his native tongue. There were over a hundred distinct languages and dialects throughout California, a linguistic decentralization unparalleled anywhere else in the world.

The first white settlers could make no sense of this anarchistic world. They had to impose their order on it. A much-respected Indian would thus become a "chief," and all Indians speaking a given language were considered a "tribe." A problem arose concerning what to call these "tribes." There were Indian names for the villages and sometimes even for the households, but there were no names for the "tribes" since they didn't exist. Most Indians simply called themselves "the people." Thus when the whites heard some Indians call themselves "Pomo," meaning "people," they applied this name to all the people speaking that language, who then became known as the Pomo tribe. In other cases tribal names came from the language of neighboring Indians. "Yurok," for instance, means "downstream" in the language of the Karoks, who lived upriver from the Yuroks on the Klamath. When the white man heard the Karok

POMO BASKETRY

refer to the folks downstream from them as "Yurok," this was conveniently assumed to be a tribal name. And soon the Karoks, likewise, became known as "Karok," which in their language means "upstream." Similarly, the Yuki received their name from a word in the Wintun language meaning "stranger" or "foe"; when the white settlers heard the Wintun speak of their neighbors as "Yuki," they rather impolitely applied this as a tribal name.

The daily lives of the Indians had some variations from one village to the next, but the pattern was basically the same. All Indians started the day early. Dawn is a maiden, it was told,

who will say of an early riser, "I like that man. I hope he will live to be old. He always looks at me." The first job of the day was to stoke up the fires from the previous night. The men then ritualistically sweated in the sweathouse and bathed in the nearby stream, while the women prepared the morning meal. The basic food, eaten twice a day, was acorn mush served with dried fish, seaweed, or berries on top. The meal was prepared and served in tightly woven baskets and eaten with mussel-shell spoons by the women and elaborately carved elk-horn spoons by the men.

The standard work of the women during the

day was to grind the acorns and weave the baskets. The uses for baskets were numerous, each use requiring a different type of basket. There were large carrying baskets, worn on the back and supported by a band around the forehead; large storage baskets, woven loosely to permit air to circulate and avoid molding; shallow winnowing baskets with which to sift acorn flour or separate seeds from chaff; bottomless baskets to hold acorns in place while they were pounded into flour on a mortar; tightly woven baskets for carrying water, cooking, eating, and drinking; special ceremonial baskets, often decorated with feathers. There were also basket trays, basket purses, basket hats for the women, and basket cradles for the babies. Even animal and fish traps were made with basketry techniques.

The men spent most of their days hunting, fishing, or preparing the tools with which to hunt and fish. In bad weather they would sit in the sweathouse weaving and mending fishnets, rolling iris-string, carving hooks and spears, and working on their bows and arrows. When a hunt was decided upon for the following day, they would spend the night in ritualistic preparation. They hunted primarily for deer and elk. Sometimes several men surrounded a large area in which game were feeding, sometimes individuals would try to disguise themselves as bucks and slowly approach the animals from downwind, and sometimes a hunt consisted simply of setting iris-string snares along well-traveled deer trails. Once an animal was killed, a prescribed ritual had to be followed in butchering it. It was believed that the soul of a deer was reincarnated in another deer, and the hunter had to be careful not to stray from the accepted manner for fear of offending the deer soul. The dead animal was utilized in a number of ways. What meat

wasn't eaten fresh was smoked and stored. Some Indians, when meat was scarce, ate the feet and intestines of deer, but others with a more abundant supply of meat fed these to the dogs (dogs were the Indians' only domesticated animals). The marrow was eaten by pushing a stick inside the bone, then removing and licking it. Thus the bone itself was kept whole so it could later be used for various tools and utensils. Bones were made into spearheads, fishhooks, knives, and hide scrapers. Elk horns, because of their extreme durability, were made into wedges with which to chop down trees and cut wood. The sinews from the deer were made into bow strings and were also used to strengthen the backs of the bows. The hides were used for clothing, moccasins, and blankets. The brains of the deer were used to tan the hides. There seems to be a certain completeness in the use

ACORN GATHERING

19

MALLET AND WEDGE

thanks which essentially said, "You've spent your whole life growing into a perfect tree. You are so straight, so perfect, that now you will become a canoe!"

For both men and women, everyday work included many seasonal activities. Mussels had to be collected in the winter or spring, before the poisonous plankton upon which they fed in the dry season made them inedible. Surffish could be caught only in the summer, when they came in great numbers to the beaches to spawn, and seaweed had to be collected in July before the snails laid their eggs on it. In the fall, berries and acorns were ready to be harvested. The acorn harvest, the key to Indian survival, was actually an elaborate affair spanning several months. In the late summer or early fall, when the first worm-ridden acorns had fallen to the ground, the underbrush was burned. This cleared the ground so the acorns could be more easily gathered when they fell; it also killed off many of the worms that would have turned into moths the following spring, only to lay their eggs in next year's acorn crop during the summer. Then, when the remaining acorns ripened in October, the children would climb the trees and shake them down while the adults gathered them from the ground. A good harvest depended on proper preparation by prior burning, so the Indians were in essence *farming* the forest. An uncared-for oak grove generally yields nothing but worm-ridden acorns; it is like a garden gone to seed or an untended orchard. (Such is now the state of most oak forests in northwest California: in summer there is a flurry of moth activity up in the treetops, and by fall most of the acorns are worthless.) Since the Indians had to tend to the forest carefully, the choice groves were in many cases individually owned, or at least owned by a

of deer sinew in the bow that kills the deer and the use of his brains to preserve his hide. For the Indians, to kill without making full use of the victim's body was deemed sacrilegious. No life was taken lightly and without good purpose. Even plants, it was felt, were alive and had individual spirits. If a redwood tree was to be cut down to make a canoe, this was no casual matter. The cutting was preceded by a prayer of specific village. Harvesting someone else's forest was looked upon much as raiding a garden or orchard would be looked upon in an agricultural society.

The northwest California Indians, although technically nonagricultural, tended several other wild plants. They made their arrows from a shrub variously called arrow-wood, sea foam, or ocean spray *(Holodiscus discolor)*. To get the bush to grow straight, they would cut it in the fall and let the new shoots grow for three or four years, constantly training them in much the same way as we train our beans around a pole. This was called "tame" arrow-wood, as contrasted with "wild" arrow-wood, which was used for "unstraight" objects such as pipes. Hazel and willow shoots, used in basket making, were treated in a similar fashion: they were burned in the fall, and the following spring the new growth was trained to grow straight. It was a cause for tension in some areas when the white man no longer allowed the Indians to burn their hazel and willow patches. The choice areas for basket materials were jealously guarded much as were the acorn forests.

"Work," for the Indians, was not always set off as a separate activity. Many of the jobs to be done required little attention and were often accomplished while doing something else. As the men sat around the sweathouse and chatted, for instance, they would also be weaving their nets and carving their spoons. When someone went for a walk, he or she would nibble at the various greens and berries along the way; this was how the Indians ate their salads. An obstacle encountered along the path would be removed by the first person to come upon it; there was no trail crew to come along afterward. No one would come home without a few sticks for fire-

wood or a few boughs to serve as a sort of carpet to prevent a dusty campsite.

For the children, "work" was both work and play. Their days were spent imitating the activities of their elders, and this in essence was their education. Girls started making crude baskets almost in infancy, and by the age of six or seven their play baskets became real ones. Using scrap materials, they would alternate rows with an ac-

BASKET WEAVING

complished basket maker, thus gaining both knowledge and experience. Each girl had to learn the complicated starting knots, the various stitches, and how to finish the borders. She was taught how to weave a basket tightly enough for it to hold water, and she had to figure out how to produce the complicated designs. When scraps would no longer suffice, she had to learn how, when, and where to gather her own materials, and how to prepare them. By the time of puberty and possible marriage, she was, of course, expected to be fully capable of supplying her family with all the baskets they might require for cooking and eating, gathering and storing, grinding and winnowing, and all the other uses to which her art was put.

Boys, likewise, showed an interest in hunting at a tender age. According to an astonished early explorer: "At this time we saw a child, who could hardly have been one year old, shooting arrows with a bow in proportion to his strength and height; he would hit a hand at a distance of two or three yards, if they offered it as a target." (40) As they grew a little older, the boys would band together to hunt the smaller game. They would surround jackrabbits in much the same manner as their elders would hunt deer. Wood rats were driven from their nests, chased, clubbed, and roasted on the spot. The boys thus learned to be hunters simply by being hunters themselves.

The children's daily activities made the distinction between men's and women's work very clear. But any person, it was felt, should know what it takes to make a living in the world, so all the children received limited training in the basic skills of both sexes. Occasionally, from an early age a person would show an inclination to become, in effect, a member of the opposite sex; such people were regarded as perfectly normal and allowed to follow their inclinations.

At the close of the workday the evening meal was prepared and served. The men then retired to the sweathouse, where they sat around the fire gambling and smoking. Tobacco was much appreciated, being the only crop that the California Indians planted themselves. Their tobacco was very strong and produced dizziness. As they passed around the pipe at night, men would virtually pass out, having smoked themselves to sleep. When visitors came from surrounding areas, the men would have a sort of smoking contest: the pipe would go around until some of the men had passed out, and those that remained stayed up to conduct their business in a somewhat intoxicated state.*

---

* Tobacco was the only intoxicant used along the northern coast of California. Along the central California coast, the *Amanita muscaria* mushroom, a strong hallucinogen, was used, but it was not consumed by anyone north of the Pomo.

22

Both the women in the family house and the men in the sweathouse often spent the evenings telling stories and passing on legends in which Coyote, Lizard, Squirrel, and all the other animals are portrayed as human characters. Each character embodies the personality of his species, but they also live the everyday life of the Indians: they eat acorn mush and hunt deer, they have races and play tricks on each other, they even just sit around and chat. The best-known and most amusing of these animal-people is Coyote. Coyote is a very complex character: he is both foolish and wise, both a mean trickster and a kindly benefactor. Although sometimes he is godlike, the special appeal of Coyote in these stories, I suspect, is that he is so human. He seems to embody the whole range of human folly and wisdom.

NICOTIANA BIGELOVII

WILD TOBACCO

TWO COYOTE TALES

LAZY COYOTE

Once Foolish Coyote wanted to gather some pine nuts. He went to Saykalal, the little gray squirrel, and said, "I'd like to gather some pine nuts. How do you get them?"

Saykalal answered, "First, I look around until I find a tree with many new cones on it. Sometimes the crop fails. Then there are only a few old cones left on the tree. Don't bother with a tree that has just a few old cones left on it. Wait until you find a pine loaded with new cones."

"Yes, yes, I know all that," the old man said with an impatient wave of his hand. "But how do you get the cones down?"

"I run up the tree and cut off the cones with my teeth," said Gray Squirrel. "Then I run down to see where the cones fell."

"But I can't cut off the cones with my teeth," Coyote said grumpily.

"That's true, you can't," said Gray Squirrel. "You'll have to use your obsidian knife. When you have as many as you want, climb down and get the nuts out."

"You're not telling me the truth about the way you get the cones down," said Foolish Coyote, who never believed anything that meant a little work.

"Yes, I am! Yes, I am!" cried Saykalal.

"I don't believe it!"

Saykalal didn't like this, so he decided he'd have some fun with the old man. "Well, since I can't fool you, I'll tell you the easiest way," he said.

"Yes! Yes!" cried Coyote. "Hurry up and tell me!"

"You climb a tree, go out backward on the

"Then I run down to see where the cones fell."

limb with your face toward the tree trunk. Then take out your obsidian knife and cut off the limb where it joins the trunk. In this way you won't have to climb down again. You'll just ride down on a limb loaded with pine nuts."

"That's more like it!" cried Coyote as he hurried away. Soon he found a tall tree full of new cones. He climbed up and crawled out backward on a limb. Then he took out his obsidian knife and began cutting the limb near the trunk. Coyote soon got tired of this work and he bounced up and down on the limb. The jarring loosened it and down it crashed with the foolish old man. Coyote lay on the ground, stunned.

Now Blue Jay was also out looking for pine nuts. He saw Coyote lying on the ground and flew down. He pecked on the old man's forehead, and cried in his piercing voice, "Wake up, Coyote, wake up!"

Coyote sat up and looked around. "I wasn't asleep!" he growled. "Can't you let a great man lie in the shade and rest?" Then he picked himself up and sneaked off home. He didn't want to meet Saykalal, the little gray squirrel, just then. (19)

WHY THE INDIANS ARE ABLE TO GET FIRE BY DRILLING

In the very beginning of things the Karok Indians had no fire. Kareya, the creator, had made fire but he had hidden it in a box and given it to two old hags to guard. He did not want the Karok Indians to get it. Coyote decided to help the Indians by obtaining the fire for them. He called together all people and told them what he was going to do. He then stationed them in a line along the road to the cabin of the hags who

kept the fire. This done, he went with an Indian to the cabin. As he neared the house, he told the Indian to hide under a hill nearby while he went in.

He rapped on the door.

"Good evening," he said, as the hags opened the door to him.

"Good evening," they replied.

"It's a pretty cold night," he said. "Can you let me sit by your fire?"

"Yes, come in," they replied.

So he went in and stretched himself near the fire. He pretended to go to sleep, but all the while he kept the corner of one eye open, watching the hags. The hags did not go to sleep. They never slept, for they guarded the fire night and day. As Coyote watched them he thought of how he would get the fire.

Next morning he left the cabin and went to the Indian hiding under the hill.

25

The hags did not go to sleep.

"You must make an attack on the hags' cabin, as though you are going to steal fire, while I am in it," he told the Indian.

Then he returned to the cabin. The hags had no fear that Coyote would try to steal the fire. They believed only the Indians would try to get it. While Coyote stood close to the fire, the Indian descended on the cabin. The hags saw him and dashed out one door to attack him. Coyote at once seized a brand of fire and ran out the other door. He fairly flew over the road, the sparks from the fire flying about him.

The hags saw the sparks and gave chase. They had almost overtaken him when Coyote reached Mountain Lion, the first person stationed along the road. The hags continued to chase each one. The last one along the road was Frog, who could not run. So when Ground Squirrel, running with the fire, came to him he opened wide his mouth and swallowed the fire.

The hags were almost upon him, so he jumped into the water. They grabbed for him but only succeeded in catching hold of his tail, which they pulled off. That is why frogs today do not have tails.

Frog swam along underwater, holding his

breath so as to keep the fire. Finally, he could hold his breath no longer and had to come up. He spat out the fire into a log of driftwood, and then took a deep breath.

The fire has stayed in the wood ever since, and so now when an Indian wants fire he simply rubs two pieces of wood together and the fire comes out. (20)

THE EVERYDAY LIFE
OF THE COYOTE
(PART 1)

A coyote eats just about anything and everything he can get hold of: squirrels, rabbits, rodents of all sorts, birds, chickens, fish, crayfish, frogs, tadpoles, deer, porcupines, sheep, snakes, insects, and so on. He is as much a scavenger as a predator, feasting both on carcasses of animals that have died of natural causes and on those that have been killed by other predators. He lacks the strength of a wolf, who is about twice his size, and is often subject to severe injury or even death at the hands of his would-be prey. Deer and elk, for instance, can deal mortal blows to the coyote with their swift, sharp hoofs. Although primarily a carnivore, a coyote often eats grasses, nuts, fruits, and berries; indeed, he is notorious for his ability to pick ripe watermelons from the vine. He will investigate almost anything for its potential food value; scientific studies indicate that coyotes have swallowed string, paper, cloth, rubber from automobile tires, harness buckles, and many other seemingly inedible items.

What he lacks in brute strength the coyote must make up for with adaptability and cunning, which is perhaps what led the Indians to an appreciation of his complex character. The tricks in a coyote's repertoire are many and varied, each one fashioned to suit the particular circumstances of his environment. He will build a small dam shortly before a thunderstorm to flood out a prairie dog from his underground home. He will play the clown under a group of wild turkeys congregated on a limb overhead, often causing one of them to lose its balance in bewilderment. He will play dead to nab a buzzard. He will tag along after a bear who has made a catch, nipping at his heels until the bear turns around in anger; with the food thus left unguarded, the coyote will grab it and run. He will follow after an elk who is pawing through the snow to graze on the grass; the pawing often chases out mice, whom the coyote quickly snatches. He will station himself at an escape route of a wood rat's nest or a burrowing mammal's hole and wait patiently as a badger—a better digger than a coyote—invades the home from another side and chases the prey into the coyote's paws.

The coyote's many antics sometimes backfire, causing him unwillingly to play the fool he is pictured as in many of the Indian legends. One fairly recent eyewitness account tells of an incident in which a badger was digging after a prairie dog:

A waiting coyote ran up to the badger and gave him a hard bite on the rump. The badger whirled and chased the coyote off a short distance and then returned to digging. Again the coyote nipped him and again, growling and grumbling, the badger chased him away . . . The coyote kept badgering the badger. I guess he was impatient and wanted the badger to bring something out quick. Pretty soon the badger got the hole he was digging big enough to turn around in. He went out of sight, and the coyote poked his nose in. The badger grabbed it. When that coyote finally got loose, he didn't act like he was on the hunt for another badger. (64)

Coyotes often cooperate with each other on the hunt. They will surround a large area and flush out the rabbits, sometimes running them into a nearby fence. They will set up an effective system of relays to relieve each other while chasing larger game. They will send out decoys to capture the attention of the prospective prey as other coyotes sneak up from behind.

Coyotes mate in the winter, with a litter of five or six pups being born nine weeks later in the spring. Unlike domestic dogs, coyotes are often faithful to their mates year after year, and the coyote male remains a helpful member of the family until the pups are weaned and on their own. During the time of pregnancy, he lives with his mate and brings her food. Just before the time of birth, he usually moves away but continues to hunt for the mother, who must now spend most of her time with the pups. Most of the hunting during this period is done far from the den so the family won't be endangered. When the five- or six-week-old pups are ready to be weaned, the mother regurgitates partly digested food for them, since they are still too young for whole meat. Soon the father returns to live in the family den and helps the mother teach the pups how to hunt. During the summer the whole family hunts together so the pups can gain some experience before striking out on their own in the fall. The first few months of independence are exceptionally trying, for the young coyotes must establish their own territories apart from the family territory, which remains in the hands of the parents. Only the hardiest, or perhaps the smartest, pups in each litter are likely to survive the first winter.

(The everyday life of the coyote is continued in Chapter Seven.)

The fabric of the Indians' everyday lives was, of course, marked by certain special events. Births, marriages, and deaths served as the occasions for appropriate ceremonies. Lovemaking was also a special event. With the women sleeping in the family house and the men, in many cases, sleeping in the sweathouse, some provision had to be made for the men and women to get together. A couple would build themselves a small brush shelter off in the woods where they might spend the night or even several days. Lovemaking was thus not routine, but, for that very reason, probably all the more intense. This arrangement also tended to make procreation somewhat seasonal, with most births occurring in the spring.*

The biggest regularly scheduled celebrations were held in the fall, when all the people from nearby villages gathered at certain spots along the river to take advantage of the salmon runs. The salmon were headed upstream to spawn, and the Indians constructed nets, traps, and dams of sticks which spanned the width of the river. (A few openings were always left, however, so some of the salmon could get through to spawn and so the folks upstream could also make a catch.) It would take several weeks to build the dams and traps, and for the fish to be

---

* Birth control was exercised by the use of fish-bladder condoms. It is said that some Indians also practiced birth control with the use of herbs. This was "women's medicine," unknown to any man, and the last women reported to know the secret have recently died.

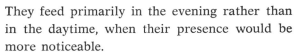

caught and smoked, and the prolonged congregation of so many people made the fall a natural time for festivities. Some villages had world-renewal ceremonies in which dancers would dress up in specially preserved white deerskins. These ceremonies were a celebration of the natural forces which kept the world in balance, and the deer, I suspect, represented all the living beings that gave the Indians life.

THE EVERYDAY LIFE
OF THE DEER
(PART 1)

Deer are browsers, subsisting mainly on leaves, buds, berries, and fungi. In our area, they are particularly fond of Ceanothus, or "deer brush."

They feed primarily in the evening rather than in the daytime, when their presence would be more noticeable.

The doe generally gives birth to twins in the late spring. The fawns are entirely helpless and an easy prey for any predators that can find them—coyotes, cats, owls, whatever. They are protected only by the good camouflage their coats provide and by the fact that they give off no scent when their mother is not around. The mother must frequently go off to eat, during which time the fawns lie motionless in a thick covering of brush. The mother trains her young to stay in place by nuzzling them when they attempt to move about. As the fawns grow older, they are sometimes disciplined for such sins as hogging food from their siblings or failing to stand guard duty. The mother reprimands the offender by nuzzling him harshly, blowing strongly through the nose (a threatening gesture), or even hoofing. She then ignores him for a period of time, while the fawn goes off and sulks. The lesson is over when she approaches him and gently licks his face. This obvious form of communication is easy for humans to understand, but deer also communicate in ways that are incomprehensible to us. For instance, they apparently use the scent glands at the base of their legs to send messages to other deer.

A lost fawn who is still being nursed will bleat in distress until found by its mother or adopted by another doe. The fawns are weaned by fall, but generally spend the first winter with their mothers. Sometimes they are joined by one or two bucks or by other does with fawns. Particularly in areas with heavy snowfall, deer will band together in the winter so they can help each other establish paths—their sharp hoofs fall deep into the snow, making travel quite difficult.

THE DOE WITH HER FAWN

In some cases (but not here) they migrate in the winter to find milder climates.

When the does are about to give birth in the spring, the bucks disappear to their summer grounds, usually accompanied by a friend. The bucks are of little use in feeding the fawns, and would only endanger them by drawing attention to their presence. During the summer the bucks grow their antlers. At first, the antlers are covered with a velvet-like skin, which nourishes the interior with blood. Toward the end of the summer, the blood supply dries up and the skin becomes shriveled. The bucks then rub their heads on tree trunks to relieve the itching and the skin falls off, revealing the hardened antlers. During this time, their necks thicken in preparation for their coming battles. By fall the rutting season is on and the summertime friends become bitter rivals who engage in sometimes deadly battle over the does in heat. After mating is over, the bucks once again become passive and join the small winter bands. The bucks now

THE BUCK DEER

share in the social responsibilities: taking their turn at the watch, teaching the fawns how to fight, and helping to protect the group against predators. If a fawn is in danger, a buck will frequently divert the enemy's attention to himself. During the winter his antlers fall off and are quickly eaten by rodents, who need the calcium.

How can a human being come to understand what the everyday life of a deer is really like? Perhaps he can't. Having felt the magic, how-

ever, of many a brief encounter with various deer—and the almost irresistible lure to their hidden way of life in the forest—I decided to try to put myself in their place for a while and see what it was like. Of course I could only pretend, but even just pretending taught me a lot. Some friends and I went to a totally uninhabited region for a few days with the intention of living off the wild foods available. Each of us became either a man or a deer. Appropriate incentives (requiring some exercise in imagination) were set up: if a man shot a deer (hit him with an orange—a harmless simulation of a bow and arrow), he got to enjoy the deer's meat (a high-energy package of food each deer carried with him). A deer who was shot was required to experience death as fully as possible (lie still for several hours while life around him went on). The incentives were sufficient to make the game somewhat realistic.

The experience of being a deer was dominated by two realities: hunger and caution. To survive off the few greens and bulbs available at that time required an almost unending process of foraging for food. And much of the food was found only in open places, where I was dangerously exposed. I could not tramp doggedly through the woods and fields in my usual manner, but could take only a few steps at a time before pausing to check out the situation. I had to become alert to every noise and movement in the forest and was painfully aware of whatever noise I made. Since my only defense was to detect danger soon enough to escape from it, there was not a moment when I could afford to be unaware of my surroundings. I emerged from the experiment a nervous wreck, but at least I had not been "shot." I retreated home to rest in peace, but for the real deer of the forest there was no reprieve.

(The everyday life of the deer is continued in Chapter Six.)

The basic routine of everyday life for the Indians was also broken by travel and trade. Trade was a social as well as an economic affair, offering a natural excuse for a vacation from the workaday world at home. A number of people from one village would travel to the village with which they wished to trade. The standard meal of acorn mush was replaced during these journeys with pemmican, a highly concentrated food made by grinding up dried fish or meat, dried berries, and dried acorn mush and mixing it all together with a little oil that had been collected by placing shells under meat or fish while it was drying.

The visitors often stayed for days, with much feasting, dancing, and gambling. During this time, they would gather the food for which they had come. Inlanders would come to the coast in July to gather surffish, seaweed, abalone, and other shore life—and to take a vacation from the inland heat. Coastal people would travel to the inland hillsides in the fall to gather acorns, seeds, nuts, and manzanita berries, and perhaps to take a vacation from the coastal fog. The variety of life in the California terrain could thus be taken advantage of by all the villages. Sharing food in seasons of abundance also functioned as a means of storage: when there was plenty of food in one area at a given time, the people could trade their surplus with people from other areas in exchange for money or other nonperishable goods; when food was scarce in that area, they could trade back with areas enjoying a greater abundance.

The most drastic divergence from everyday life encountered by the Indians was warfare. Actually, there were no wars of the type found among Indians elsewhere on the continent, or in Western civilization, in which large groups of people fought each other over ideas, religion, or territory, or for economic gain. The only "wars" were really just extended feuds. All differences, according to Indian law, could be settled by appropriate payments to the aggrieved parties. Warfare could occur only because of some grievance for which there had been no settlement. Perhaps a traveler had been killed because it was thought he was poaching, or a family in mourning was passed by someone from another village who, in defiance of accepted custom, offered no payment to the mourners. In each case, the matter could be settled by mutually agreeable payment: whether or not the traveler had actually been poaching, payment was due to his family; compensation would be made to the mourners by paying the original amount due them and an additional sum for the insult of not having paid them at the time. If settlement was made, all was well—if not, revenge might be sought; but if a man were killed in revenge, payment was then due to *his* family as part of the settlement. If no settlement was reached, an open battle might be announced by a messenger for one of the parties. Often no one was killed in the open battles, but if anyone was, part of the eventual settlement would have to include payment to his family. The "war" was over when a final settlement was reached, to include the return of any property that had been seized and compensation for all loss of life and property suffered during the feud. War was thus a very costly affair, with each party having to pay in full for all the losses inflicted on the other. It didn't pay to win; indeed, there was no concept of a "winner" at all—wars were not won or lost, but simply settled.

However, the Indians eventually were to encounter a civilization with a totally new concept of warfare, in which the winners reaped the gains and the losers really lost. The Indians were ill prepared for this different kind of war, just as they were ill prepared to meet the people who waged it.

CHAPTER TWO.

CONFLICT

BLUNDERBUSS

The people of this county are driven to madness by the red-skin scourge that has so long been preying upon their lives and property and are impatient to have the county rid of it.

—FROM AN EARLY EDITION OF THE
Humboldt Times

In 1854, four years after California had become a state, explorers reported that the Indians in the Whitethorn Valley had never before seen a white man. By 1864, only ten years later, their entire society was destroyed. The Indians here had already been conquered—they were already subjects of a foreign state, of a race of people they had never seen—but they didn't know it yet. For as long as anyone could remember in the collective consciousness of the Indians—perhaps for thousands of years—they had led the life just described. Yet in a few short years their world would be totally shattered by the sudden appearance of a rival civilization.

Before the whites showed up in person, there were signs of their impending arrival. Ships were spotted on the ocean, creating great excitement and causing some Indians to hide in the bushes. Knives from the Hudson's Bay Company, traded by the early trappers, made their way from one place to another, and soon became an integral part of Indian culture in areas untouched by whites. The honey bee, introduced from Europe, spread faster than man, and the first white explorers reported the Indians already gathering wild honey.

Prior to the arrival of "civilization" in the backcountry, its presence had been felt in more accessible areas. First there were the Spanish explorations along the coast and the missions in southern and central California. Then came the Russians looking for valuable furs from seals and sea otters, followed by the American fur trappers seeking skins of inland mammals. Finally, there was the gold rush, which led to permanent white settlements and the end of Indian life.

The first Spanish ships appeared off the coast of northern California in 1543. Starting in 1565, the "Manila Galleons" made a yearly pilgrimage from the Philippines to Mexico via the Japan Current, which brought them off the coast of Cape Mendocino. The main interest the Spanish had in the New World was gold, which was also what Sir Francis Drake and his crew had in mind when they raided the Spanish ships and settlements along the Pacific in 1578 and 1579. None of these ships purposely landed in northern California, although some of the galleons might have crashed in the stormy seas off Cape Mendocino. There's a local legend that one of the ships was wrecked and washed ashore near a place called Spanish Flat. The strange treasure was supposedly taken by the Indians to a cave in King's Peak, the entrance of which has since been closed by an earthquake. Many people—locals and outlanders—have searched in vain for the hidden cave. Sally Bell, a local Indian who claimed to have played with the treasure as a child—before she had ever seen a white man and before she knew the value of the unknown substance—looked for fifty years but even she couldn't find the entrance to the lost cave. Whether there's any truth in the legend is anyone's guess. On the one hand, hidden treasure is a common fantasy; but on the other hand, Spanish goods have in fact been found off the coast nearby.

The first ships actually to land in this area were the *Santiago* and the *Sonora*, in 1775. When the ships anchored in Trinidad Bay, friendly Indians greeted them in canoes. The Indians were eager to trade, showing a particular interest in glass beads and metal knives. The first contact was filled with exhilaration and excitement—

new worlds were opening up, people with no common language or culture were trying to communicate, totally unknown objects were seen for the first time and acquired through trade. Both the Spanish and the Indians viewed each other's mysterious and seemingly incomprehensible customs with great curiosity. The Spanish journals tell of the strange ways of the natives, and the Indians surely found the acts of the Spanish just as baffling. Within two days of dropping anchor, the Spanish Captain Hezata treated the Indians to a gala spectacle of the way things were done in Christian societies by laying claim to the land with great ceremony:

> Coming ashore with the commander of the *Goleta*, the Fathers, officers and armed men of both ships, I set up a cross on the shore and, forming an extended front, we performed the first adoration. Then, in as orderly a fashion as the narrow trails permitted, we followed the path to the top of the hill where the chapel was made, and took possession with the most scrupulous formality, as enjoined by the instructions given me. Mass was celebrated and a sermon was preached by the Reverend Father Miguel de la Campa. This ceremony was solemnized with several volleys of gunfire. Each of us returned to his own ship which, with banners waving, saluted with three volleys of artillery and "Long Live the King." (40)

The Indians, having never before heard gunfire, were understandably terrified, but the Spanish gave them presents to calm their fears.

A few days later, relations became strained when two sailors deserted ship. The captain suspected the Indians of aiding and encouraging the criminals and ordered that their houses be

A ROCKBOUND COAST

searched. One deserter soon returned and was offered a pardon if he gave a full confession. Out of fear he said what the captain wanted to hear—that the Indians had helped him. With his suspicions confirmed, the captain stormed ashore in a fury and brutally beat the first Indian he saw. He ordered the deserter to repeat his confession in front of the Indians, whereupon the deserter admitted that he had not told the truth when he said the Indians had helped him. The captain then apologized to the Indians and had the deserter given two hundred lashes. The captain's second in command, Don Juan Perez, summarized the effects of the incident:

The search was conducted in such a way that the Indians were astonished at what was done to their houses, without knowing the nature or purpose. This turn of events was sufficient to make them change their good opinion of us, as evidenced by their friendly intercourse at the beginning. (40)

The Indians continued to engage in trade, but they soon learned to be a bit wary of the newcomers.

The Spanish, on their part, regarded the Indians as barely human: "They are so savage, wild and dirty, disheveled, ugly, small and timid, that only because they have the human form is it possible to believe that they belong to mankind." (Pablo Font, 57) Such creatures, however, lived on land that the Spanish wanted for themselves, and so the Indians had to be dealt with somehow. In southern and central California the Indians were forcibly placed in missions, where they were treated much like slaves. The Spanish, however, did not establish permanent settlements north of Sonoma, so the Indians in northern California were not affected.

Although the Spanish never followed up their explorations along the northern California coast, other peoples did. The Russians, in particular, were interested in acquiring the thick fur coats of sea otters, which were highly valued in their land of winters. The Russians themselves actually did little of the hunting. They had taken control of the Aleutian Islands, and the Indians there were excellent hunters, depending as they did upon sea mammals for their livelihood. So the Russians imported the Kodiak Indians into northern California and used them as hunters.

THE EVERYDAY LIFE OF THE KODIAK SEA-OTTER HUNTER

The Kodiak Indians hunted in skin-covered canoes called "bidarkas," which were totally enclosed except for two holes for the hunters, who fastened their own clothing to the canoe to make a watertight seal. Waves could thus flow over the canoe, and the entire unit of a bidarka and two Indians could swim through stormy seas without taking on water. From five to fifteen bidarkas hunted together. When an otter was spotted, the hunters approached from the windward, with the stern men steering and the bow men ready to throw their spears. The spears didn't kill the otters immediately, so a line was attached from the spear to a floating bladder; the hunters followed the course of the float and were on hand with their clubs when the wounded otter emerged from his dive.

The Kodiak Indians used their ancient hunting methods, but they were employed by the Russians. Up to one hundred and fifty hunters and seventy-five bidarkas were loaded onto a ship which transported them to various offshore islands. Here they were left to set up camp for a few months, sometimes with the help of some Kodiak women who were employed to take care of the hunters. While on the islands, the Indians lived on the meat of the animals they killed, saving the skins for the Russians. Some hunters were kept on board the main ship which patrolled along the coast, hunting and trading for skins with the local Indians.

The Russians controlled more Indians than they could employ on their own ships, so around 1800 they contracted for the services of some American ships from Boston. The contract was beneficial to both parties, since the Bostonians wanted to get some of the profits from the lucrative fur trade but could not do so without the use of the Kodiak Indians. Everyone was happy, except perhaps the Indians; they had to brave not only the elements but also the wrath of the Spanish, who resented the presence of other nationalities along the Pacific coast and were quick to kill any hunters they could find.

In 1806 the *O'Cain*, one of the ships of the Russian-American Fur Company, entered Humboldt Bay. Most local history books, apparently for-

THE OLD GREEK ORTHODOX CHAPEL ~ FORT ROSS

getting about all the native inhabitants, report that Captain Jonathan Winship "discovered" the bay. The ship also visited Trinidad Bay, where the Indians were eager to trade for the metal knives they had come to value so much.* By this time, however, a handful of encounters with the white explorers and hunters had given the initially friendly Indians of Trinidad Bay much cause for suspicion. They began to resent the crude treatment they received from the foreigners, who searched their houses, took water and provisions from the land without recognizing the property rights of the Indians, and had begun to destroy the entire sea-otter population by launching up to fifty bidarkas at a time. Despite the eagerness to trade, mutual suspicions led to occasional outbreaks of violence in which a few Indians were killed by gunfire, the power of which they were only beginning to compre-

* An early settler reported that he was offered a boat, several beaver skins, and a bow with a quiver full of arrows for a single hunting knife. (12)

hend. The *O'Cain* returned from its voyage along the northwest coast with no fewer than 4819 sea-otter furs, and other expeditions around that time were equally successful. In 1812, the Russians established a settlement at Fort Ross which would serve as a base for the fur trade. But the number of available sea otters had already been greatly diminished. In the same year that Fort Ross was founded, Captain Winship abandoned the fur trade because it was no longer profitable. An indication of how quickly the population of sea mammals was being exhausted can be seen by the following figures of furs taken from the Farallon Islands, where a permanent hunting camp had been established. (The numbers refer to both seals and sea otters—sealskins were taken primarily in later years when there were few sea otters available.)

1809–1812	150,000
1812–1818	8427
1833	54

 The Farallon camp was abandoned after 1833,

OTTER HUNTING KODIAK-FASHION: THE BIDARKA

and the Russians withdrew from Fort Ross in 1841. With no profit to be made, there was no reason to stay.

THE EVERYDAY LIFE OF THE SEA OTTER

Sea otters live off sea urchins, abalone, crustaceans, mollusks, and various small fish such as smelt. Like humans, they prefer a regular schedule of three meals a day, with the night reserved for sleeping. To hunt for its food, a sea otter propels itself underwater with undulating body movements and kicking hind feet. It must rely primarily on its sense of smell and touch, for there is little light under the surface of the ocean. To detach abalone from the rocks and to crack the shells of mollusks and crustaceans, a sea otter employs its powerful jaws or clasps a stone in its front paws for use as a tool. Once the meal is gathered, he returns to the surface of the water, where he spends most of his time quietly floating on his back. Using his large flat belly as a table, he lays his meal out in front

of him and eats slowly. If he needs to crack a shell, the otter places the victim on his chest and pounds it with a rock. After he has finished and licked his paws clean, he usually continues to float or swim slowly on his back. Only when in a great hurry will a sea otter turn over to swim. At night he wraps himself up in a bed of kelp to keep from floating away while he sleeps. The biggest danger a sea otter faces, aside from human hunters, is a storm, which can throw him against the jagged rocks.

Sea otters live in groups. but man knows little of their social organization. There is no special time of year for mating. Courting consists of rubbing cheeks and patting forepaws. A pup is born after nine months and is not fully weaned until it is more than a year old. Such a long dependency period is rare among most animals; the pup stays with its mother in some cases even after she mates and gives birth again. The mother, of course, is devoted to and protective toward her young.

The sea otter's apparent blessing of an unusually thick but soft, fine, and uniform fur coat has proved instead to be its curse. Because of this luxurious coat, man has always been a predator. Not until 1737, however, when white men began hunting for the furs that had been used for centuries by the American Indians and the Chinese, did man's actions affect the well-being of the overall sea-otter population. Today there are only about three thousand sea otters around the Aleutian Islands, and a few hundred off the coast of California. Some also remain off the coast of northeastern Asia, where the Russians are experimenting with raising them in captivity.

Although the explorers and the sea-otter hunters left no permanent settlements, they did leave their mark. In just a few short years the sea otters had been hunted to virtual extinction, and

the population of the seals had been severely diminished. The Indians of Trinidad Bay, who had been so friendly at first, had been turned into suspicious enemies. In the words of seaman Peter Correy, who visited the bay in 1817, "The Indians were ready to receive and massacre us, for they are without exception the most savage tribes on all the coast." (40)

Starting with Jedediah Smith in 1827, an occasional American fur trapper found his way into northwestern California. The trappers traveled a route between the Russian River and the Oregon coast, but no one knows exactly where this route was. Primarily they were just passing through to Oregon and had little interest in the area. The only effect of their presence seems to

FISH SUPPER

have been the hunting knives they traded to the Indians whom they encountered in their journeys.

While the back hills of northern California remained untouched, the rest of the state was going through major changes. Mexico had successfully revolted against Spain in 1821, and in 1833 the new Mexican government ordered the missions to be either secularized or disbanded. Soon American explorers and settlers began making their way in wagon trains over the mountains. By 1846 the newly arrived Americans had reached sufficient numbers to declare their independence from the Mexican government.

Until the discovery of gold, the Americans were simply after new land on which to settle. Picture yourself a back-hills Indian living the life of your fathers, who had lived the life of their fathers, and so on, time out of mind. All of a sudden, seemingly from out of nowhere, comes a virtual stampede of men of an unknown race—men who seem to have no interest in making a living, but spend their time in pursuit of a yellow dust they find in streams. How would you make sense of it? How could you cope with it?

Under normal conditions, settlement starts in the fertile and easily accessible river valleys and moves into the back hills only after the valleys themselves have become crowded. Everything was different when gold was discovered. Land which had been too remote even to explore suddenly became swamped with prospectors. Few if any whites had ever been to the Trinity River, for instance, in 1848. By 1849, however, there were hundreds of prospectors in mining camps along the river. The miners had come from the Sacramento Valley, but it was a major problem to transport enough supplies for the mining camps over the long and arduous trails that connected them with civilization. Food was sometimes so scarce that a hungry prospector might be induced to sell his claim for a square meal.

Some of the prospectors along the Trinity decided to try to find an easier supply route. They had heard of the discovery by sea of a bay which might not be too far from where they were. Sea transport was easier than land transport, so if they could find an adequate harbor and an easy trail across the Coast Range, they could shorten the route. A party of miners was organized to explore the possibilities. One of the members of the party, L. K. Wood, kept a fascinating journal of the trip. The following is based on his account (44, 55).

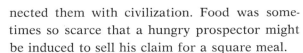

THE EVERYDAY LIFE OF THE EXPLORER

When the exploring party was first organized in the Trinity River mining camps, twenty-four men signed up. The party was to be led by two Indian scouts, but a November storm dropped snow in the mountains and the Indians wisely refused to go. Most of the miners heeded the advice of the Indians and dropped out, but eight of the men were determined to brave the winter and "discover" a port to supply the mines.

The men gathered together a scant ten days' supply of flour, pork, and beans and started across the mountains in the direction the Indians had indicated. At first the mountains were covered with snow and they had to climb up and down numerous ridges which ran crosswise in their path; later, as they approached the ocean, the impenetrable underbrush of the forests slowed their progress to scarcely two miles a day. Winter is no time to go exploring in the mountains, and the men had brought with them little in the way of camping equipment:

Now, "camping" in California . . . consists of nothing more than taking your saddle and blankets from the animal and depositing them on the first convenient spot of Mother Earth (or, as applied to us that night, on snow). To have a choice in ground on which to camp would be deemed fastidious, and to form a hut from bushes a foolish expenditure of time and labor. (55)

The provisions soon gave out, and the men found themselves lost in the wilderness with no food for days on end. Several times they found it necessary to stop their travels, hunt for whatever game could be found, and set up camp for a few days as they rested and cured their meat. There were some times when no game could be found at all and the explorers had to subsist on wild plants, about which they knew very little. They drank yerba buena tea, ate acorns and buckeyes (which more than likely were not thoroughly leached), and tried an unknown "bitter nut" which I suspect was that of the California bay laurel. They found the plant food unpalatable and not sufficient to stave off their hunger. A constant dilemma during such hard times was deciding if the mules might be of more service as food than as transportation. At one point, the men were reduced to soaking deerskins in water, then chewing the hides and even drinking the water so nothing would be lost. The leader of the party, Dr. Gregg, eventually succumbed to starvation.

Occasionally the explorers would come across some Indians. The inhabitants of the first village they came to were so surprised and terrified by the newcomers that they plunged into the nearby river and ran up the hills on the other side. Since their supplies had totally run out by this time, the explorers took the opportunity to help themselves to the salmon that was drying in the vacated village. They had hoped they were safe because of the Indians' fright, but as they started to leave they found they were mistaken: "There came marching towards us some seventy-five or eighty warriors, their faces and bodies painted, looking like so many demons, and armed and prepared for battle."

Needless to say, it was now the explorers who were terrified, but they knew they could impress the Indians with the power of their firearms. Their guns, however, were wet and wouldn't fire, so they had to bide their time. They offered beads to the Indians, who turned out to be more fascinated than furious. When the guns had dried, they arranged a shooting exhibition which did indeed impress the Indians—not so much with the power of the rifle, which was incomprehensible, as with its noise. Throughout most of the journey, the explorers stayed on good terms with the Indians they encountered, trading beads and scraps of metal for food. The Indians gave helpful instructions and provided free ferriage across the many rivers, which by their own custom they were required to offer to any and all passing strangers.

The party finally succeeded in their mission: they reached the ocean and "discovered" Humboldt Bay. The discovery was pointless, however, unless they could make it back to civilization. There was a dispute over which route to take back, and the explorers broke up into two groups. Despite further encounters with grizzly bears and starvation, all the men except Dr. Gregg eventually found their way back to the settlements.

As soon as the good news of the discovery reached San Francisco, companies were formed and ships were supplied with the intention of founding settlements along Humboldt Bay. More than a dozen ships headed for the northern California coast, each one hoping to be the first to find the almost imperceptible entrance to the bay, make claims to the land, and set up townships. The men on the first ship to enter the bay found that before doing anything else they had to deal with the natives, whom they impressed and mystified with the power of their firearms and a display of their compasses:

The compass is placed on the ground, and as the needle trembles and flutters on its pivot the Indians watch it with increasing wonder. The white "medicine man" takes his knife and moves the blade slowly around the dish of the compass. Slowly, with quivering stops like warning fingers pointing at individual braves, the needle follows the knife blade around the circle. Filled with a profound feeling of awe, the warriors see the knife withdrawn and the needle settled to its quiet rest. The white "medicine man" lifted the instrument to his ear, as if communicating with the Great Spirit. The Indians themselves draw nearer, eager to catch a stray whisper from the Unseen World, though it be in an unknown tongue. The "medicine man" withdraws the instrument and gravely endeavors to make them understand that all their secret thoughts and purposes are revealed to him through its agency. (45)

Whatever the success of this magic show, the rest of the ships soon entered the bay and it became clear to the Indians that such a flood of foreigners could not be resisted. The Indians withdrew from the shores of the bay and the whites were left to lay out their townsites. Within a month several towns were established to supply the mines, and prospectors came up by the shipload to seek their fortunes. As it turned out, the trails from Humboldt Bay to the Trinity mines were just as arduous as were the earlier trails from the Sacramento Valley, but gold was soon discovered along the Klamath River, in the nearby hills, and even right on the ocean beach at Gold Bluff.

The Indians didn't know what to make of it all. Since they had never experienced anything akin to territorial wars, they didn't yet understand that the presence of the whites would mean their own demise. For the first few years the Indians simply did the best they could by trading for the desirable articles the whites had brought with them.

The whites, for their part, preferred to ignore the Indians whenever possible. They had brought much of their old world with them and so had little need to learn from the native inhabitants how to make a living from their natural environment. The original settlers along the east coast, by contrast, had been able to carry only a few bare essentials with them on the long voyage from Europe and did not expect to be resupplied with any frequency; thus they were obliged to learn from the Indians how to make a living in the New World. The Indians taught them how to plant corn, squash, and beans, and gave the white men their first seeds. But here the settlers had brought their own seeds, and their own livestock as well. They had no use for the Indians' knowledge of how to obtain food, clothing, and utensils from immediately available materials, for they could easily have more familiar supplies shipped up from San Francisco.

Prospectors in the outlying regions, however,

FACE-OFF

could not easily ignore the Indians, on whose territory they were looking for gold. Making friends with the Indians was necessary both because the prospectors were greatly outnumbered and because the Indians could stock them with food. "Beads, bracelets, and other trinkets captivating to the savage" (58) were thus a standard part of the miners' supplies. These gestures of friendship were generally accepted by the Indians, and many an isolated prospector was saved from starvation during hard times.

In numbers there is security, and when upward of a hundred miners were grouped together in mining camps the cautious attitude toward the Indians was sometimes abandoned. All it took was a few thoughtless deeds by a handful of miners to cause friction between them and their hosts. In 1851 Redick McKee, the Indian Commissioner for Northern California, was dis-

patched to the backcountry to make peace with Indians who had been alienated by the miners. Wearing a red vest as a sign of importance, McKee told the Indians that the "Great Father in Washington" was now their master, and that his "red children" must do as he said. The journal keeper of McKee's expedition described the typical response:

> That figurative personage, the great father at Washington, they had never heard of. They had seen a few white men from time to time, and the encounter had impressed them with the strong desire to see no more, except with the advantage of manifest superiority on their own part. Their earnest wish was clearly to be left alone. (55)

The anarchic social organization of the Indians made McKee's job rather difficult. He often had trouble assembling any Indians at all, and those that he could assemble were usually just from one or two villages that had no political affiliations with any of the other villages. Even within a single village there was no chief, so each Indian could speak only for himself. The idea of a "treaty" made little sense under such conditions, but McKee did the best he could. He offered the Indians, say, two hundred head of cattle for a given piece of land, while reserving other land for the exclusive use of the Indians. The idea might sound good to some of those who heard the proposal, so they'd sign the "treaty." Sometimes McKee's local interpreters would throw in something on their own in the native tongue: a man named Robert Walker got the Indians to run his ferry for him as part of one of McKee's agreements. Since McKee himself knew none of the Indian languages, he never could be exactly sure of what he (and his interpreters) had bargained for.

When McKee returned to the state and national governments with his treaties, he ran into vigorous opposition. Anti-Indian sentiment was widespread, and no one was prepared to pay the Indians with cattle or anything else. The problem in the minds of most whites was simply how to get rid of them. California's Governor Bigler, for instance, maintained that the only choice lay between evacuation and extermination. Previously, Americans had always gotten rid of the Indians simply by pushing them farther west. But this was the end of the line—there was no longer any "farther west"—so the only practical alternative for men like Bigler was extermination. McKee's treaties never got signed, the Indians never got their cattle, and of course whites thought nothing of moving onto land reserved by McKee for the Indians. In 1853, instead of signing the treaties, the government set up Fort Humboldt to deal with the "Indian problem."

THE EVERYDAY LIFE OF THE PROFESSIONAL SOLDIER

To be stationed at Fort Humboldt, in the minds of the soldiers, was to be relegated to a life "out in the boondocks." With the exception of the actual fighting campaigns, there was not an awful lot of excitement in the daily routine.

> The bugle call in the morning would sound the awakening to the duties of the day which began with breakfast, then drill and guard mount. This was followed by more drill, then bugle call for dinner, more drill, the evening dress parade, and the lowering of the flag. Again the bugle or drum would sound for supper and lastly taps. The only diversion was an Indian expedition sent to the mountains. No matter the season of the year, all wanted to go on the trip in preference to remaining with the humdrum life at the garrison. (55)

To escape the monotony of this everyday life the soldiers hunted and fished while on leave and the officers visited with each other's families and played cards, but the main diversion turned out to be drinking. Saloons appeared near the fort, often illegally. A scandal developed when it was discovered that one of the saloons was accepting government-issued clothing in exchange for drinks. The drinking was not limited to the enlisted men; among those who turned to alcohol as an escape from a life of loneliness and boredom was a young officer named Ulysses S. Grant:

> At times Grant had problems getting home from the taverns after too many drinks. On one occasion he fell into the slough. On another his drunkenness caused him to fall off his mule, and he failed to return to the fort, whereupon a party went in search of him. They found him asleep in a thicket, and his trusty mule was browsing close at hand. On another occasion Grant went duck hunting in the south part of the bay. Having forgotten about the ebbing tide, his boat soon became stuck in the mud. The captain was obliged to stay there until the next tide released him. (55)

Grant's case was typical of the depression most soldiers went through at Fort Humboldt. Life was dull, they were not used to the constant fog of the area, and their mail and paychecks were sometimes held up for months, giving them even

Seth Kinman

HE HUNTED ELK FOR THE

FT. HUMBOLDT GARRISON

further cause for complaint. Under such conditions, it is little wonder that several soldiers deserted to seek their fortunes in the nearby mines, and it is also little wonder that the soldiers were eager to take any and every opportunity to go Indian fighting.

Clothing and fighting equipment were of course supplied by the government, but the fort was expected to produce much of its own food. Each company had a separate garden, and the officers and their families often had their own cows and chickens. The gardens were not particularly well tended, however, so most of the food had to be purchased from local farmers and ranchers. Contracts were made with local backwoodsmen to keep the fort well supplied with elk meat. At one point the soldiers were consuming upward of two hundred and forty elk per year.

THE EVERYDAY LIFE OF THE ELK

Elk are members of the deer family: the males grow antlers for the rutting season; they are ruminants; they browse on various leaves, fir needles, berries, fruits, and acorns; and they like to frequent salt or mineral licks. Unlike other deer, elk graze on grass as much as they browse. This brings them frequently out into the open, so they gather in herds for protection rather than trying to hide inconspicuously in the forest. Since they find protection in numbers rather than in the "invisibility" of the deer, they function primarily in the daytime.

Single calves are born in the spring. Within an hour they are on their feet to nurse, and within a week they are running with the herd. During the summer the cows, calves, and yearlings gather in herds, which are organized with a matriarchal leader. The mothers have cooperative baby-sitting arrangements, with one mother watching over several calves while the others feed. The bulls, meanwhile, are off in smaller and more anarchistic herds as they grow their antlers in preparation for the rutting season. When the antlers are fully developed, the velvet coverings which supplied them with blood shrivel up and are scraped off as the bulls rub their itching antlers against the trees. The mating instinct is now strong, and a mature bull will take over a cow herd as his harem by driving off the yearling bulls. An average harem consists of perhaps five to fifteen cows, plus their calves and yearling females. The work of keeping the herd together leaves the bull with little time for relaxation. If a cow starts wandering too far off, the bull coaxes her back by threatening a poke with his sharp antlers—a poke which can be lethal. When a bachelor approaches the herd to challenge the harem master, he must be driven off quickly, for a prolonged battle might result in the loss of the master bull's herd to still another bachelor as the first two bulls are fighting. The strong mating urge of the males results in frequent frustration, and throughout the season they seek release from their tension through their bugling cries, by slashing their antlers against trees, and by wallowing in a mixture of mud and their own urination. Even for a bull who maintains a herd, the rutting season takes its toll: with all his energy expended in keeping the herd together and warding off challengers, he has little time to eat and by the end of the season he is considerably weakened and in poor shape to face the oncoming winter. Rarely does a bull have enough strength to maintain a harem for more than one or two years. Because of the rigors of the rutting season, bulls have a life expectancy far less than that of cows.

When mating is over, elk of both sexes join together in large winter herds. In areas of heavy snowfall, the herds retreat to less rigorous wintering grounds. In the spring, when the cows are about to give birth once again, the yearlings are generally pushed away by their mothers and told to be more on their own. There are cases, however, in which yearlings have been found nursing on the milk produced by their mothers' new pregnancy.

Elk have not fared so well as deer under human domination of the countryside. They are bigger, they are more often found in the open,

their meat is generally preferred to venison, and their antlers are particularly prized trophies. They were so much hunted in the early days of white settlement in California that, by 1873, a law was passed making it a felony to kill an elk, punishable by up to two years in prison. Those weren't times of strong ecological consciousness, but had the law not been passed all the elk in this area would soon have perished. Today, there are fewer than four thousand elk in all of California.

As the white settlements became more established, the Indians began to get an idea of what "civilization" would mean to their old way of life. Cattle and sheep grazed in the fields which

THE BULL ELK WITH HIS HAREM

had formerly provided seeds for pinole. Wild pigs ate the acorns and various roots and bulbs. (It didn't take long for domesticated pigs to become wild. In the words of an old-timer, "You take a sow off in the woods, then her pigs are wild. And theirs, they're wilder.") The deer and elk populations were quickly diminished by the large number of miners, soldiers, and settlers with rifles. Mining practices were affecting the flow of the rivers. Trees were chopped down with unheard-of speed, and whites kept coming in unheard-of numbers. The life of the Indians depended on an ecological balance which was being upset by the presence of the newcomers. The Indians tried to adapt to their new environment by hunting the introduced game, namely, cattle. Needless to say, such a practice was not tolerated by the settlers.

The Indians could not understand the laws and customs of the newcomers, nor could the whites understand the laws and customs of the original inhabitants, and conflicts easily developed from such misunderstandings. A man named Bill McGarvey, for example, hired five Indians to bring supplies from Crescent City to his trading post along the Klamath. The Indians met with rough seas, their canoe capsized, and all five of them drowned. The relatives of the dead men, acting according to Indian law, demanded payment from McGarvey. McGarvey, however, did not feel responsible since he had not told the Indians to risk the rough waters. No settlement was made, and the next step according to Indian law was to seek revenge. Several Indians attacked the store, but McGarvey and two friends managed to hold them off. McGarvey gained a truce by saying he would ask his friends in Crescent City to send him the necessary money. An Indian was dispatched with a letter in hand,

but instead of requesting money the letter requested military assistance. Ten soldiers were sent to protect the store for an indefinite period of time, and what had been a friendly trading post was thus transformed into a small military outpost.

With similar incidents happening all over the countryside, tension began to mount. Violent acts were committed by both sides, and each incident had a snowballing effect because of the custom in both societies to leave no crime unpaid for. If an outlying settler was harmed by Indians, the life of any Indian would often do for purposes of revenge. When a white man was killed near Weaverville in 1852, the enraged citizens massacred 153 Indians in return. If an Indian was killed by a lawless white man or by some settlers seeking revenge, his family could seek no help from the laws of the newcomers, since Indians were not allowed to testify in court. Under Indian law, any life must be paid for by an appropriate settlement. Since the whites didn't understand this custom, let alone abide by it, a settlement was never reached, which meant that the family of the deceased Indian could seek revenge by taking the life of one of the family of the guilty party. Since all whites were seen as related, this meant killing any of the settlers. Such a seemingly random murder was of course never understood in this context, and whites felt that the primitive moral judgment of the Indians was simply incapable of distinguishing between the guilty individual and his race. The settlers, however, were following a similar custom when they formed vigilante committees to get back at the Indians.

Once these kinds of hostilities start, they're hard to stop. Each side becomes enraged by the atrocities committed by the other. Imagine the horror when it was learned that John Briceland (after whom the town was named) was almost killed in the middle of the night by two Indian boys he had generously taken into his household to "civilize." By the mid 1850s, isolated incidents of violence had spread into small wars in some areas, although not all the Indians had yet turned against the whites and there were many cases of an Indian village taking the opportunity to get back at traditional enemies by siding with the powerful settlers. These wars were conducted as much by vigilante committees as by professional soldiers, and in 1856 the California legislature passed an act which enabled any settler to be reimbursed by the government "for services rendered and supplies furnished" while fighting the Indians. In 1857 a large Indian reservation which would stretch along the coast from the Noyo to the Bear River was proposed, in an attempt to avoid full-scale war. The few settlers of the region under consideration, however, vigorously opposed any attempt to take away their land and give it to the Indians (!), and the proposal was defeated.

On the night of February 25, 1860, a secret society of settlers crept ashore at Indian Island in Humboldt Bay, where, in the words of an early historian, the Indians were practicing their "heathen rites" (45), and proceeded to massacre every man, woman, and child they could find. On the same night several other massacres were staged, taking a total of nearly three hundred lives. The incidents, obviously coordinated and well-organized, created quite a stir. Bret Harte wrote an angry editorial in one newspaper, for which he was subsequently run out of town. A grand jury was convened but failed to turn up a single clue as to the identity of the offenders. A typical reaction was that of the people of

Hydesville, a town near the site of one of the massacres: a town meeting was called, at which the settlers agreed on demands for Indian removal; as the superior race, they argued, the white citizens recognized their responsibility to protect the helpless Indians, and this could only be done by moving the Indians far away so further massacres could not be staged.

For the Indians, this was the last straw. There were no more cases of Indians siding with whites against their brothers. Five years of full-scale war between whites and Indians followed. Many of the settlers who had ventured into the back hills had to retreat to safer surroundings. By 1863 the Mad River and almost all of the hill country were under the control of Indians. The settlers indignantly complained of the Indians' violence and of the inadequate military protection they received. As voiced by the *Humboldt Times*, "The people of this county are driven to madness by the red-skin scourge that has so long been preying upon their lives and property and are impatient to have the county rid of it." The citizens formed the Mountaineer Battalion to supplement the regular army. Military expeditions were sent out to conquer the rebellious Indians with instructions to kill the men and take the women and children prisoners. In February 1864, one of these expeditions, led by a Lieutenant Frazier, journeyed to the Whitethorn Valley and raided all the villages it found. The *Humboldt Times* proudly announced the body count: killed, thirteen bucks and one squaw; captured, nineteen squaws and two children. (The use of the term "buck" certainly reinforced the white man's conception of Indians as beast-like savages, thus making their extermination easier on the conscience.) Sally Bell, one of the few Indians of this immediate area to survive the war, described one such raid on an Indian village: *

My grandfather and all my family—my mother, my father, and we—were around the house and not hurting anyone. Soon, about ten o'clock in the morning, some white men came. They killed my grandfather and my mother and my father. I saw them do it. I was a big girl at the time. Then they killed my baby sister and cut her heart out and threw it in the brush where I ran and hid. My little sister was a baby, just crawling around. I didn't know what to do. I was so scared that I guess I just hid there a long time with my little sister's heart in my hands. I felt so bad and I was so scared that I just couldn't do anything else. Then I ran into the woods and hid there for a long time. I lived there for a long time with a few other people who had got away. We lived on berries and roots and we didn't dare build a fire because the white men might come back after us. So we ate anything we could get. We didn't have clothes after awhile, and we had to sleep under logs and in hollow trees because we didn't have anything to cover ourselves with. (2)

Under such conditions, many of the Indians who escaped being killed or captured perished of starvation or exposure. Those captured were taken to temporary prison camps near Eureka and Fort Bragg, from which they were later moved to more distant reservations. As long as the Indians remained anywhere near their home

* The raid described here occurred along the coast, so it was probably not connected with the Frazier expedition to the Whitethorn Valley. This would indicate that there were at least two and perhaps several raiding parties in this area.

territory, there was the possibility that they could escape and fade back into the hills they knew so well. The citizens of Eureka thus felt threatened by the presence of almost a thousand prisoners so close to home and pushed for their removal. In 1864 the Smith River and Round Valley Reservations were established. (The Klamath Reservation had been established by an earlier treaty.) The Indians of Hoopa Valley succeeded in negotiating to make their home territory into a reservation, but only after they had laid down all their arms and abandoned the right of self-government. The settlers in and around Hoopa Valley naturally opposed the reservation, but by this time the government was tired of the war and its expense and so ratified the treaty.

Once on the reservation, the Indians placed their lives totally in the hands of the government. In 1868 the government decided to abandon the Smith River Reservation, and the entire Indian population was moved over rugged mountain trails to Hoopa Valley: "The sick were carried in boxes, packed on each side of a mule, as Californians carry smoked bacon or salmon." (44) The reservations were run much like prison camps. A company of soldiers remained on the Hoopa Reservation until 1892, by which time most of the Indians had never known anything but life under white domination. The Indians were put to work in the agricultural and industrial pursuits of their captors. The young were taught in government schools, where they were punished for speaking their native language. They were given names like Trinity Jim, Klamath Mike, and Lagoon Charlie, since the whites had no respect for the importance attached to a name in Indian culture. A Eureka lawyer who visited Hoopa Valley in 1871 summarized the conditions he found:

SPANISH GALLEON, 1578 . . . THE INDIANS HID IN THE BUSHES.

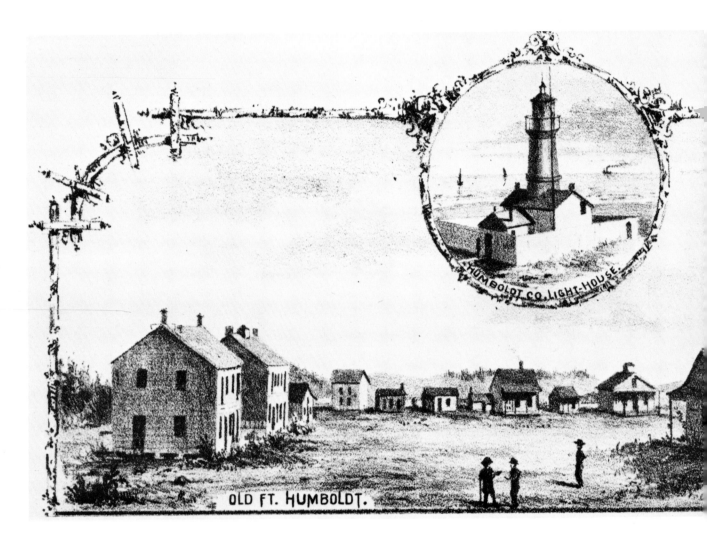

HUMBOLDT CO. LIGHT-HOUSE.

OLD FT. HUMBOLDT.

THE SOLDIERS SETTLE IN . . .

. . . AND SO DO THE MINERS.

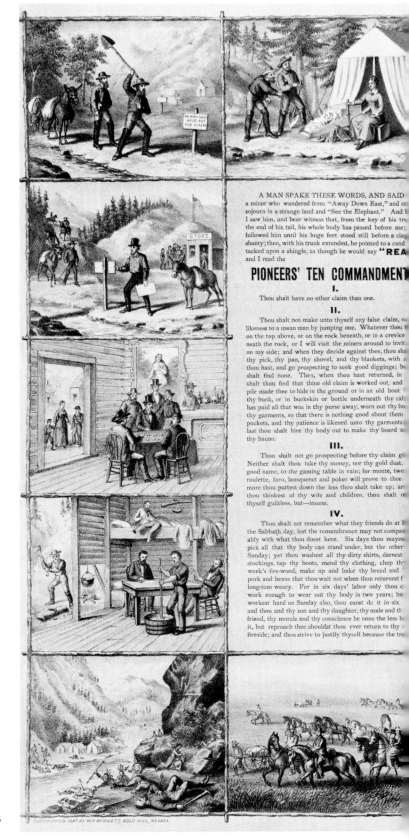

THE MINER PIONEERS' TEN COMMANDMENTS

...cksmith, the carpenter and the merchant, the tailors, ...d Buccaneers defy God and civilization by keeping not ...bbath day, nor wish for a day of rest, such as memory ...h and home made hallowed.

V.

...hou shalt not think more of all thy gold, nor how thou ...ake it fastest, than how thou wilt enjoy it after thou hast ...rough-shod over thy good old parents' precepts and ex-..., that thou mayest have nothing to reproach and sting ...hen thou art left alone in the land where thy father's ...g and thy mothers's love hath sent thee.

VI.

...ou shalt not kill thy body by working in the rain, even ...thou shalt make enough to buy physic and attendance ...Neither shalt thou kill thy neighbor's body in a duel, ...eeping cool thou canst save his life and thy conscience. ...shalt thou destroy thyself by getting *"tight,"* nor ..., nor *"high,"* nor *"corned,"* nor *"half-seas over,"* ...ree sheets in the wind,* by drinking smoothly down ...slings," "gin cock-tails," "whisky punches," "rum* ... nor *"egg nogs."* Neither shalt thou suck *"mint-* ...nor *"sherry cobblers"* through a straw, nor gurgle from ...the raw material, nor take it neat from a decanter, for ...nou art swallowing down thy purse and thy coat from ...back, thou art burning the coat from off thy stomach; ...nou couldst see the houses and lands, and gold dust, and ...omforts already lying there—a huge pile—thou shouldst ...oking in thy throat; and when to that thou add'st thy ...walking and hiccuping; of lodging in the gutter, of ...in the sun, of prospect holes half full of water, and of ...d ditches from which thou emerged like a drown-...thou wilt feel disgusted with thyself, and inquire, *"Is ...nt a dog that he doeth these things?"* Verily, I will ...well old bottle; I will kiss thy gurgling lips no more; ...n, slings, cock-tails, punches, smashes, cobblers, nogs, ...sangarees and juleps, forever, farewell. Thy remem-...hames me; henceforth I will cut thy acquaintance; and ...es, tremblings, heart-burnings, blue-devils, and all the ...atalogue of evils which follow in thy train. My wife's ...d my children's merry-hearted laugh shall charm and ...me for having the manly firmness and courage to say: *wish thee an eternal farewell!"*

VII.

...ou shalt not grow discouraged, nor think of going home ...thou hast made thy *"pile,"* because thou hast not ...a lead" nor found a rich *"crevice"* nor sunk a hole upon ..., lest in going home thou leave four dollars a day ...o work ashamed at fifty cents a day, and serve thee ...r thou knowest by staying here thou mightest strike ...d fifty dollars a day, and keep thy manly self-respect, ...n go home with enough to make thyself and others

VIII.

Thou shalt not steal a pick, or a pan, or a shovel, from thy fellow miner, nor take away his tools without his leave; nor borrow those he cannot spare; nor return them broken; nor trouble him to fetch them back again; nor talk with him while his water rent is running on; nor remove his stake to enlarge thy claim; nor undermine his claim in following a lead; nor pan out gold from his riffle-box; nor wash the tailings from the mouth of his sluices. Neither shalt thou pick out specimens from the company's pan to put in thy mouth or in thy purse; nor cheat thy partner of his share; nor steal from thy cabin-mate his gold dust to add to thine, for he will be sure to dis-cover what thou hast done, and will straightway call his fellow miners together, and if the law hinder them not they will hang thee, or give thee fifty lashes, or shave thy head and brand thee like a horse thief with "R" upon thy cheek, to be known and of all men Californians in particular.

IX.

Thou shalt not tell any false tales about *"good diggings in the mountains"* to thy neighbor, that thou mayest benefit a friend who hath mules, and provisions, and tools, and blankets he cannot sell; lest in deceiving thy neighbor when he returns through the snow, with naught but his riffle, he present thee with the contents thereof, and like a dog thou shalt fall down and die.

X.

Thou shalt not commit unsuitable matrimony, nor covet *"single blessedness,"* nor forget absent maidens, nor neglect thy first love; but thou shalt consider how faithfully and patiently she waiteth thy return; yea, and covereth each epistle that thou sendeth with kisses of kindly welcome until she hath thyself. Neither shalt thou covet thy neighbor's wife, nor trifle with the affections of his daughter; yet, if thy heart be free, and thou love and covet each other, thou shalt *"pop the question"* like a man, lest another more manly than thou art should step in be-fore thee, and thou lovest her in vain, and, in the anguish of thy heart's disappointment, thou shalt quote the language of the great, and say, *"sich is life;"* and thy future lot be that of a poor, lonely, despised and comfortless bachelor.

A new commandment give I unto you. If thou hast a wife and little ones, that thou lovest dearer than thy life, that thou keep them continually before you to cheer and urge thee onward until thou canst say, *"I have enough; God bless them; I will return."* Then as thou journiest towards thy much loved home, with open arms, shall they come forth to welcome thee, and falling on thy neck, weep tears of unutterable joy that thou art come; then in the fullness of thy heart's gratitude thou shalt kneel before thy Heavenly Father together, to thank Him for thy safe return. Amen. So mote it be.

FUN AND FROLIC . . .

. . . AND A LITTLE BIT OF STYLE

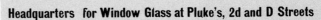

PACIFIC LUMBER COMPANY

SCOTIA, HUMBOLDT COUNTY, CAL.

PACIFIC LUMBER COMPANY'S RAILROAD, FROM SCOTIA TO ALTON

ALLEN A. CURTIS, President

JOHN A. SINCLAIR, Superintendent

"CALIFORNIA WILL FOR CENTURIES HAVE VIRGIN FORESTS, PERHAPS TO THE END OF TIME."
—A FOREIGN VISITOR, 1858

THE TREES ARE FELLED.

If the reservation was a plantation, the Indians were the most degraded slaves. I found them poor, miserable, vicious, degraded, dirty, naked, diseased, and ill-fed. The oldest men, or stout middle-aged fathers of families, were spoken to just as children or slaves. They know no law but the will of the agent. (4)

Many of the reservation Indians succumbed to recently introduced diseases for which they had no tolerance. For those who had survived the ordeals of warfare, removal, and sickness, there was still the difficult task of coming to grips with a new way of life. Each and every Indian was under the extreme shock of personal, cultural, and in most cases geographical displacement. In 1870 a messianic movement originated in Nevada and swept across California, capturing the imagination of many of the defeated Indians. The end of the world was coming, the dead would return to life, and a new world was at hand in which the white race had no part. "Ghost Dances," as they were called, were held throughout the state, with local prophets and dreamers interpreting the new religion in the language and culture of each particular area. But the new world never came, and the reality of the Indian agents proved stronger than the dreams of the prophets. A similar Ghost Dance movement, also originating in Nevada, swept across the Great Plains in 1890, but by this time the reality of defeat was too strong for the movement to be repeated in California.

Not all Indians wound up on reservations. It required great adaptability, but many were able to find their way in the new world that had been thrust upon them. The quickest route to assimilation was by marriage, but this affected only the women, for the idea of an Indian man courting a white woman was highly unacceptable according to the customs of the settlers. Many of the men, however, adapted their knowledge of the land to new occupations such as logging and ranching. But even assimilated Indians had to come to grips with who they were and what had happened to their people. For some the easiest answer was to deny their Indian heritage and throw themselves psychologically as well as physically into the white world. For others there was no answer, and many an Indian found himself eking out an existence on the periphery of white society and taking what pleasure he could in personal escapes such as alcohol. It took a strong yet flexible personality for an Indian to maintain a sense of his own cultural heritage yet still function in the new world.

The path of an Indian seeking his way among the whites was not made any easier by the racism he encountered. At first, when the Indians were still a threat, they had been seen as dangerous savages. In the words of one contemporary: "A great many of these Indians appear to be the lowest intermediate link between man and the brute creation." (57) Once they had been forced into submission, they were seen as ignorant children who needed to be taught the ways of civilization. The former lives of the Indians were never understood or appreciated. They were contemptuously called "Diggers" because they knew no agriculture but found most of their food by digging for roots and bulbs. (The settlers were apparently unaware that much of the digging was done to obtain basket materials rather than food.) Even the historian H. H. Bancroft shared these views:

We do not know why the Digger Indians of California were so shabbily treated by nature;

why with such fair surroundings they were made so much lower in the scale of intelligence than their neighbors . . . They were without houses or dress, with hardly any knowledge of agriculture, and almost devoid of religious ideas, roaming through forest and plain in search of roots and berries, small game and fish, improvident and dependent wholly on the products of the seasons. (57)

The whites, as members of the superior race, had the responsibility of showing the Indians a better way of life. Under the friendly guidance of their helpful teachers, these "children" slowly improved their lives by taking up agriculture:

> There is a striking contrast between their former rude and almost animal state and their present improved condition. Instead of roaming about, listlessly, in the woods, and eking out a precarious life, they are now occupied in agricultural pursuits—have become acquainted with many of the usages and objects of civilized life, and no longer depend for sustenance on the uncertain results of the chase or on the scanty produce of the wild vegetation of the mountains. (60)

The erroneous opinion that the Indians had made a living by "roaming about, listlessly, in the woods" led to a peculiar contradiction in the paternalistic views of the whites. On the one hand, the reservations were justified because they taught the value of useful work to the previously idle Indians. On the other hand, the superiority of an agricultural society over a hunting and gathering society lay in the fact that a better living could be made with less work: "Their exertions for the Reservation are incomparably less than those they had to undergo in their savage state." (60) Despite this doublethink, one thing was clear: the Indians must be put to work. To justify the strenuous labor in which they were employed, the whites conveniently used the myth of the Herculean savage capable of superhuman deeds: "Their physical conformation fits them for labor. They are strong and active; an Indian easily carries a hundred weight for twenty miles over a rough mountain path, or a dead elk for miles into camp." (60) Again, there is a strong contradiction between this image of the super savage and the view that one of the reasons the Indians needed the help of the whites was that they were so small, pitiful, shabby, helpless, and, of course, lazy.

With historical hindsight, these views seem absurd. Looking back a century later, it is safe for us to point out the oppression the Indians suffered at the hands of their conquerors and the contradictory beliefs developed by the whites to justify their acts—safe because the Indians are not fighting for land that we want, because our lives are not in constant danger from a race of people we know nothing about. The perspective of the settlers, on the other hand, was shaped by their intimate involvement in the conflicts of their times, and by a vested interest in the outcome. Few, if any, of the settlers meant any harm toward the Indians when they first came here, but they were caught up in a historical movement which seemed to have a life of its own. The settlers, being human, were first and foremost fulfilling their own needs and desires, while rationalizing their deeds as best they could.

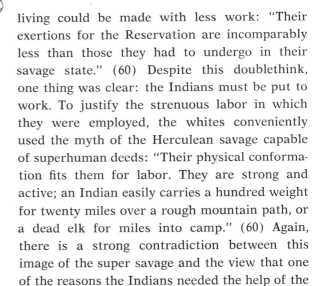

CHAPTER THREE. CIVILIZATION MARCH ON THE

We must take our Bibles, guns, and great New England civilization with us, and act as pioneers of Christianity.

—ADVICE FROM
SECRETARY OF STATE JOHN M. CLAYTON
TO SOME EMBARKING FORTY-NINERS

When civilization finally came to stay in northwestern California, it was in hot pursuit of the most precious of all substances—gold. Perhaps some of the Indians had recognized the existence of the yellow dust, but they saw no use for it. To the salmon, gold was part of the stream bed, and for the deer gold was probably not an element of their universe at all. For Western man, however, gold was the basic measure of wealth and the foundation for all trade; nothing had any economic value except insofar as it could be exchanged for gold. Gold was also the symbol of wealth, a symbol with the power to move entire civilizations; "the stuff that makes men mad," the Indians called it. A person could work hard all his life and never make a fortune, but if he could only get hold of a few pounds of the precious metal he could live like a king forever. When gold was discovered in California in 1848, it is little wonder that people from around the country, even from around the world, left their homes to seek instant fortunes in the gold mines. Drifters from the periphery of society were joined by respectable businessmen, farmers, and professionals who were living out their wildest fantasies. This was the chance of a lifetime, the chance to bypass a life of toil by striking it rich.

THE EVERYDAY LIFE
OF THE MINER

For the average miner, the romantic picture of striking it rich was quickly replaced by the hazards and hardships of a new way of life. Once the last settlement was passed, a handful of miners would find themselves alone in a strange world. Wildcats, bears, Indians—no one knew exactly what was in store for him. There were no roads to the mines, only the trails made by deer and Indians. The miners traveled with mules who carried their tents, bedding, clothing, food, kitchenware, and tools. To the Indians their equipment might have seemed impressive, but to the average miner coming from more civilized ways, it was the ultimate in roughing it. The food they carried was adequate, but the cuisine was not what they were used to back home: pork and beans, black coffee or perhaps tea, and flour made into flapjacks, shortcake, or just baked on a stick over a campfire. The meat from wild animals took the place of fresh beef. Their clothing and bedding were warm enough for the mild California climate, but as often as not they soon became ridden with fleas and lice. In the dry season the miners slept in tents or out under the stars, but a miner who planned to work his claim through the winter did well to build himself a makeshift shack:

> Houses were hardly worthy of the name, being crude and having no floors except the earth itself. The beds were usually made of logs, which were squared so as to be comfortable, and lined with gunny bags or potato sacks. Fern leaves and hay were frequently used to spread over the log and soften it for a bed. The covering was of blankets, and on this the miners were rather comfortable and would have remained so but for the habits of those who did not use sufficient water and precaution with themselves, for which reason many of the camps were infested with vermin. (47)

The actual work involved in mining was quite strenuous. Gold was to be found not in large chunks but in a finely ground sand which was mixed with gravel, dirt, and rock along the stream beds. Holes were dug in the bars alongside the water and the dirt thrown up into a trough called a "long Tom" (a shorter version was called a "rocker" or "cradle"), where it was broken up, washed with water, and sifted until the gold particles settled to the bottom. The work involved at least two and often three or four men, so partnerships had to be formed to work a claim. Once a high-yielding bar had been exhausted, the stream was often diverted into a different channel so the bottom of the stream bed could be worked.

"Good diggin's" were not spread out randomly but were concentrated in particular bars along particular streams. Around each such bar a mining camp soon sprang up, with scores or even hundreds of inhabitants. There was no common heritage, no previously accepted set of laws and customs to bind all these men together. Some laws or customs had to be established to deal with the frequent conflicts likely to develop among eager miners. There could be no recourse to the inaccessible and inapplicable legal system back in the towns. It was a classical "desert island" situation in which a new society had to be created from scratch.

The most important issue to be settled was ownership of the mines. In each camp regulations were set up limiting the size of each claim, a policy that made it possible for newcomers to find claims of their own. A claim could be made by simply leaving a pick and shovel at the site, but this would only reserve it for ten days, after which time the only way to hold on to a claim was to be working it. A violator, or suspected violator, of any of the ad hoc laws and customs was likely to be dealt with severely by his fellow miners. "Lynch law," as it was called, did not always allow full consideration of the rights of the accused before the ad hoc jury, which often comprised everyone present, gave its verdict and sentence. There were no jails; a convicted man could only be flogged, ordered to leave the camp, or hanged.

Keeping the miners supplied in these remote areas was a difficult task. Teamsters would purchase supplies from the nearest town and drive their mule trains packed with all the necessities over the rough mountain trails to the camps. Here they would sell their goods to the owner of the local store-tent, who more often than not had a monopoly and was thus in a position to make a considerable profit off the newly rich miners. By the time the store owner, the teamsters, and the various wholesalers, shippers, and retailers along the way had taken their profits, the prices charged the miners were exorbitant. In winter, when supplies were scarce, flour could sometimes be sold for a dollar a pound and boots for one hundred dollars a pair. The miners might have raked in the gold, but in the end it was rarely the miners who had made the fortunes. Money that didn't go to the merchants often went to the professional gamblers, for the strike-it-rich philosophy that pervaded the gold rush made gambling the most common pastime.

The mining camps were often cut off from all sources of supplies during the winter months. There were many hard times, such as the winter of 1852–3, when the miners in Weaverville had to live entirely off the barley they could get from the livery stable:

> We had barley bread, barley mush, and barley pancakes, night, noon, and morning for about six weeks. No butter, no sugar, a little molasses, no coffee; however, we made coffee out of burnt barley; very little tea, no beans, and very little of anything else in the shape of provisions. Nearly every person lived on barley straight. The first salutation when two fellows met would be, "Hello, Tom," or "Jack," and then, "How is the barley holding out?" (50a)

Sometimes even these scanty provisions would have seemed luxurious. The winter of 1850–1 saw hundreds of men stranded on the Salmon River with no supplies at all. The miners, unfamiliar with the seasonal quirks of the area, mistook a warm spell in January and February for spring itself and flooded into the mines, expecting to be followed shortly by supply trains. A March snowstorm soon cut off all the supply routes, and many of the men starved.

The business of supplying the miners was what lay behind the first permanent white settlements around Humboldt Bay. Within a month of the arrival of the first ship in 1850, there were four different townships laid out along the bay: Eureka, Union (Arcata), Humboldt City, and Bucksport—as well as Warnersville (Trinidad) a few miles to the north. A year later the shops in Union alone did an annual business of a half-million dollars, with a hundred mules carrying four to five thousand dollars' worth of supplies leaving for the mines every week.

Whereas the miners had to create a new legal system from scratch, the townspeople were quick to impose their previous social, legal, and political heritage on their new settlements. Within three days of the arrival of the settlers in Warnersville, an American flag was waving from a sixty-foot pole and an election was held in which one hundred and forty votes were cast. In each new town, the very first job was to divide up the land. Nature's seemingly haphazard distribution of hills and valleys and fields and forests had to be translated into more easily understood terms so that everybody would know exactly whose land was whose. A rectangular grid of lots and sections was superimposed on the landscape. This grid, of course, existed primarily on maps and in legal documents, although fences sometimes gave it a physical expression as well. As time went on, more and more abstract divisions were established: school districts, election districts, road districts, oil districts. The formation of all these local governmental structures helped to give the settlers some sense of security in a land which only a few years before had been total wilderness. The more closely the new society resembled the one they left behind, the safer it appeared to them.

Competition quickly developed among the various towns for prestige, population, commerce, and political authority. It was correctly felt that one town would soon become the focal point of the entire area, and each town wanted to be that center. The rivalry found expression in a series of bitterly fought elections to determine the county seat. Union, being the town closest to the supply routes to the mines, won the first election in 1851. Another election was held in 1854, however, which resulted in a close three-way race among Union, Eureka, and Bucksport. A run-off was held in which there was much fraud: a small precinct with only a handful of voters reported 2136 ballots for Union and none for Eureka—the

figure far exceeding the eligible population for the entire county. The election was declared invalid, and Eureka was later appointed the county seat by an act of the legislature.

The fabric of life in the new settlements was identical to the civilized ways back home: there were flags and politics and elections (complete with the familiar fraud); there were churches and schools; there were houses with picket fences that looked just like the ones in which the settlers had spent their childhood. By 1854, only four years after the initial settlement, there was a local newspaper that advertised the various goods and services available to the settlers: general store, clothing shop, saddlery shop, tinware and stovepipe shop, bathhouse and barber shop, restaurant, hotel, saloon, billiard and bowling saloon, watchmaker and jeweler, gunsmith, flour mill, shipping company, bank, attorney, notary public, physician and surgeon. An advertised list of items available at one of the clothing shops in 1854 gives an idea of how readily the settlers adopted the styles and fashions of the civilized world from which they had come:

Frock, Sack, Business Overcoats; Black and Fancy Doeskin and Cassimere Pants; Satin, Silk, and Cloth Vests; Shirts, Drawers, Cravats, and Handkerchiefs of all descriptions; Boots, Shoes, Gaiters, Hats, Caps, Carpet Bags, Belts, & c.

Also—a variety of Dress and Fancy Goods, such as Black Silks, Merinos, Cobourg Cloth, Alapacus, Muslin Delain; Lawn Muslins; Gingham, Calicoes, Embroidered Sleeves and Collars; Oil, Kid and Silk Gloves, and Mits; Linen Handkerchiefs, Edgings, and Laces; all qualities of Ladies and Misses Gaiters and Shoes; Hosiery, Perfumery, Yankee Notions, & c., too numerous to mention. (43)

DOUBLE-BLADED CIRCULAR REDWOOD SAW

The original human inhabitants of the region had acquired all their essentials from the native animals, plants, and rocks, and had thus become an integral part of a self-contained, balanced ecosystem. For the most part, the new inhabitants did not function within the limits of this ecosystem. They brought with them a new world of plants and animals with which to feed themselves; metal cooking utensils from the other side of the continent replaced baskets made from native plants, and metal tools replaced those made of wood, stone, and bone; all sorts of clothing materials imported from around the globe took the place of native animal skins; temporary houses (tents) were brought in on the first ships; native wood was still used for permanent dwellings, but all the tools used to prepare the wood came from the outside, as did the concrete, metal, and glass materials used in con-

struction. Humboldt Bay had been catapulted out of its self-contained ecosystem into a much larger worldwide network that man had created through travel and trade. This system of trade would soon enable the natural resources of the region to be used anywhere in the world, just as it made the rest of the world's resources accessible to the local population.

By the time the gold rush had subsided, the towns were well established. To keep all the goods pouring into the region from the rest of the world, something of value had to be found to replace gold as a major export. Various natural resources were examined for their economic potential: trees, farmland, fish, minerals, and even oil. The settlers were impressed first and foremost by the vast, impenetrable forests of huge redwood trees growing a few miles in from the ocean and stretching for a distance of

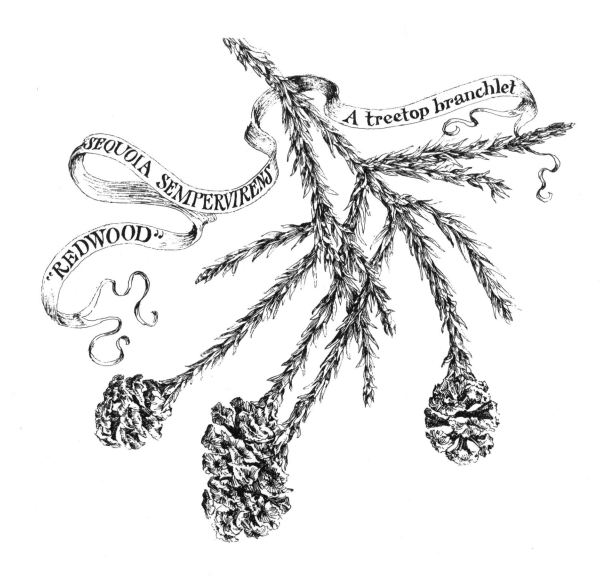

A treetop branchlet

SEQUOIA SEMPERVIRENS

"REDWOOD"

one hundred miles from north to south. The possibilities seemed exciting: redwood has a clear, straight grain that is easy to work with, the wood is particularly resistant to rot, and a single tree can easily furnish enough boards for a house. The availablity of the supply, furthermore, seemed virtually infinite; in the words of an early visitor to the Redwood Empire, "California will for centuries have virgin forests, perhaps to the end of Time!" (60) By 1854 there were six sawmills operating at Eureka alone. A few years later one of the early historians of the region, after describing the majestic size and expanse of the redwoods, proudly boasted that "at every available point for shipment stands a saw mill turning trees to lumber, furnishing employment for labor and investment for capital." (44)

THE EVERYDAY LIFE
OF THE REDWOOD TREE

A mature redwood forest has taken thousands of years to develop. Centuries of decaying matter have built up the rich soil capable of supporting a strong root system. It is not uncommon for the individual trees themselves to be over a thousand years old, while the species as a whole dates back at least 130 million years to a time when most of California still lay underwater. The land at that time was dominated by dinosaurs and giant ferns; birds, mammals, and flowering plants had yet to emerge as prominent forms of life. Thirty million years ago, the red-

woods and their close relatives covered the continents of North America and Eurasia, extending as far north as Greenland. As millions of years passed, climatic changes such as those of the ice ages forced the redwoods to retreat to their last stronghold in California.

The daily life of a redwood tree consists of photosynthesizing the sun's energy and absorbing water and nutrients from the soil. The needles function as leaves, transforming the radiant energy of the sun into chemical energy by combining carbon dioxide from the air with water supplied by the roots to produce glucose and oxygen. When glucose recombines with oxygen, as it does within all living cells, heat and work result while carbon dioxide and water are released back into the atmosphere. Solar energy is thus harnessed for use by living organisms in this everyday activity of the redwood needles.

The food produced by the needles is transferred in solution to the trunk and roots through

AN ISLAND OF REDWOOD: LOWER EEL RIVER

the inner bark. Growth takes place in the cambium, a microscopic layer between the trunk and the bark. New cells are added both to the inner bark, the conductor of food from the leaves, and to the sapwood, the conductor of water and elements from the soil. The outer bark gradually deadens and peels off, while the sapwood gradually turns into heartwood, which is also essentially dead but performs the vital function of supporting the huge weight of the redwood. The thick layer of bark is fireproof, and the heartwood is highly resistant to rot. Since the first fifty or one hundred feet of a mature redwood's trunk are totally clear of branches, a brush fire can occur in a redwood forest which does no harm to the trees. Only its own weight or the concerted effort of man is capable of felling a redwood.

Both male and female cones appear on each tree in late winter. After pollination, the female cones ripen within one season. Many redwood trees begin their lives not as seeds within a cone but as shoots from the base of an old, mature trunk. A redwood that has been felled commonly sends up a half-dozen such shoots, which within only forty or fifty years become themselves towering trees. Each tree benefits from the firm root system beneath it, although it must fight its neighbors to reach the available sunlight. This technique of self-perpetuation, combined with the longevity of each individual tree, makes the redwoods appear almost immortal by human standards. A mature tree in a virgin stand of redwoods today might well have been around when William the Conqueror ventured into England, and its root system possibly well advanced in years when Christ was born.

The needles that collect the sun's rays also take in moisture from the frequent fogs which are a necessary part of the redwoods' world. The moisture is dropped to the ground, which is shielded from the direct rays of the sun by the thick forest ceiling. The earth thus stays damp even during the hot, dry summer months, and the redwoods rarely grow thirsty. During the winter, the warm air from the Pacific generally keeps the temperature well above freezing, but the trees are sheltered from the strong ocean storms by a ridge or two of hills. The delicate balance of rich soil, sunlight, fog, shelter, and a mild climate required by the redwoods is found only along one narrow strip of land paralleling the coast of northern California.

The world of the redwood tree is one of day and night, sun and fog, winter and summer. The

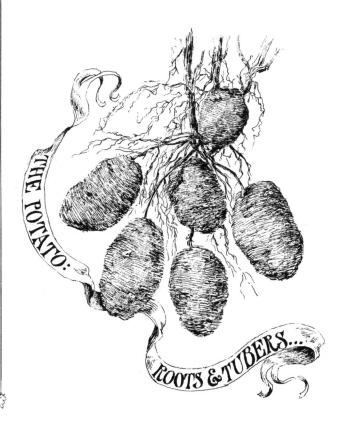

THE POTATO: ROOTS & TUBERS...

weather is its basic reality. Hundreds of years might pass in what seems to us like a monotonous routine, but each year and each day has a life and rhythm all its own. Each day is foggy or sunny; each season is one of growth or dormancy, of reproductive activity or latency. Without self-propelled movement or the ability to alter its environment, a redwood tree experiences history as it is given it in the dance of the elements.

The fields as well as the forests were considered a valuable resource with unlimited economic possibilities: "Both in these woods and in the small meadows there is such luxuriant pasturage that I believe it could maintain an infinite amount of livestock without difficulty." (40)

...AND VINE-SPRAY

Perhaps no one believed that the resources were really infinite, but Americans had always been able to push on to new frontiers before exhausting the forests and farmland in their previous homes, so the idea of natural resources being limited was simply not a reality to them. In any case, large herds of livestock were driven over mountain trails to take advantage of the new pastures. By 1854 there were 1812 head of cattle in the area, and by 1860 the natural growth of the original herds and further importation had increased the number to 19,205—several times the number of settlers at the time. Cattle were used for both meat and milk, with dairy products becoming an important local industry. The rich valleys were also planted with large fields of grain, potatoes, peas, and other vegetables.

THE EVERYDAY LIFE OF THE POTATO

Most potatoes start their lives as the eyes of other potatoes that have been cut up into "seed sets." The soil is plowed into long rows of ridges and furrows and enriched with manure and/or chemical fertilizers; the seed sets are then laid in the furrows and covered slightly with dirt. Since potatoes are purposely planted by human beings, they have little to worry about in the way of competition from other plants—people will see to it that the "weeds" (anything other than a potato) are removed. The potato will be supplied with an adequate quantity of water as it grows and it will probably be sprayed with poison to kill insects that might feed on it, since man wants to save it for his own consumption. The potato's pattern of growth is much like that of any other plant: it sends up shoots and leaves aboveground to utilize the sun's energy, while it develops roots which feed it water and nutrients from the earth. As it matures it flowers and then goes to seed, after which it ends its annual cycle and dies off. By this time large tubers have developed underground, which are dug up, packed together in large quantities, transported for many miles, placed in stores, purchased, kept in houses for a few more days or weeks, cooked, and finally eaten. The starchy tubers are thus transformed into energy which helps support human life, while the rest of the plant is plowed back into the ground.

In order to grow, potatoes have to be supplied with adequate quantities of nitrogen, phosphates, and potash from the earth. They do best when in rotation with other crops such as legumes, which replenish the earth's supply of nitrogen. They prefer well-drained, sandy soil, and a cool climate such as that of Idaho, Maine, or the Humboldt Bay region.

Potatoes were first cultivated by the Indians of South America. The Spaniards brought them back to Europe, where they underwent selective breeding and became a staple food source. English settlers introduced them to North America, and thus they eventually found their way to the cultivated fields of northwest California.

THE EVERYDAY LIFE OF CATTLE

A new-born calf is the product of its biological parents, but it is the property of human beings. It will be nursed by its mother, but its fate will be decided by its master. Its life is not without

purpose, but the purpose is not one of its own choosing. Perhaps its function will be simply to become fat, perhaps to produce milk, or maybe to reproduce more of its own. If the calf were born in 1860, it might also have been required to serve its master by pulling large loads of logs or farm equipment.

The world the young calf inhabits is a structured one. If it is the offspring of a professional milker, its time with its mother might be limited to specified hours each day. As it grows up, it will be taken to fields purposely set aside for its own use. Before the end of its first year, the function of the calf will be decided upon and its subsequent life set up accordingly. If its owner determines that it will be used for beef, it will be castrated or spayed to make it more manageable and to avoid sexual mingling with those members of its herd who maintain their potency. The rest of its short life, in this case, will be spent in luxurious feeding; everything will be provided and nothing more required until the date of its execution. If it is decided the calf will be a milker, it will likewise be fed luxuriously, it will probably live long, but it may be confined to close quarters much of the time. If the calf is one of those chosen for purposes of procreation, it might be at liberty to follow its mating instincts, but only at specified times and with certain partners.

The tie between man and cattle is thousands of years old. Cattle were domesticated in ancient times largely because of the ease with which their immense power could be harnessed to accomplish work that humans were incapable of performing themselves. It was primarily as beasts of burden that cattle made their way to the New World on Columbus' ships, although nonworkers were readily butchered. As mechani-

"PRESTIGE SISKYOU" ~ THE PRIZE DAIRY BULL

cal power took over the functions of animal power, the unemployed cattle were used almost exclusively to convert the energy of the plants upon which they grazed into human food in the form of meat and milk.

Perhaps the biggest single chore in the settlement of the western United States was the construction of fences. Land which was fenced was land set aside for the grazing privileges of a specific herd, and this meant that the land had been effectively claimed for human use. The wild animals—former grazers such an antelope, elk, and buffalo, along with their predators, such as wolves, coyotes, and wildcats—were chased from their homes and, whenever possible, killed off. Cattle had been selected by man as the beasts best able to convert the land into food, and the cattle were protected to the extent that the other animals were destroyed. Not only were they offered exclusive feeding rights to choice pastures, but they were given medical care and winter shelter as well. From at least one perspective, it

can safely be said that the wild animals never had it so good.

Where fencing was impractical, cattle could still graze the land if the local predators were killed off and if some provision were made to determine which cattle belonged to which men. Every head of cattle on the open range, therefore, had to submit to being branded with hot irons, and many also had their ears clipped in distinctive shapes. The fact of human ownership, at branding time, became a concrete reality in the life of each and every domesticated bovine.

For the most part, cattle must accept their subservience as one of the given facts of life. The world of human domination is the only world they know, for it has been thousands of years since their ancestors led independent lives. Although their dependency must certainly be felt when they are castrated, branded, or butchered, or even when the cows aren't milked on time, they probably have no conceptualization of some of the subtler aspects of domestication such as

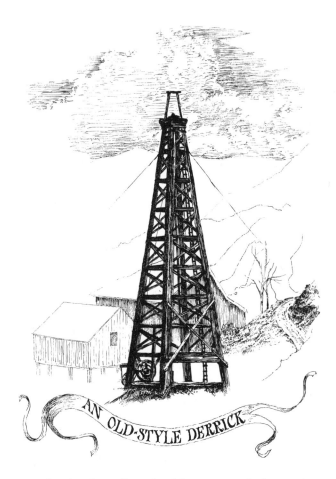

AN OLD-STYLE DERRICK

selective breeding, health care, and the protection they receive from predators they have never encountered. Their fate, like their graze, is given to them; they have been removed from the jurisdiction of the law of the wild, where animals must actively seek their own food and watch out for their own welfare. Is there something gained or lost by the ameliorization of the struggle for survival? Neither cattle nor man, I suspect, can give a complete answer.

Farming in the area around Humboldt Bay quickly became more of a business than a way of life, with each farm developing specialties in grain or potatoes, cattle or sheep. The farms were not self-sufficient units like many homesteads or like the original settlements back east.

The grower or rancher had as much, if not more, in common with the shopkeeper as with the homesteader; rather than produce the means of his own survival, he purchased his necessities with the money he gained by selling his crop. When the previous human inhabitants of the area needed food, they went to the forests or fields to gather some. The perspective of the settlers was altogether different; if they needed food, they went to the store. Their "hunt" had become their "work" or "business"—the activity in the economic world that provided them with the wherewithal to make their purchases.

In a real hunt there are no shortcuts. Certain techniques must be practiced with certain skills if the hunt is to be a success, and the hunt must be a success in order for its participants to live. In an economic hunt, however, shortcuts can be found and are always sought after. The search for gold was one such shortcut but the gold rush was short-lived. The strike-it-rich philosophy soon found a new outlet for the settlers in this region when oil was discovered. In 1865 the first oil wells in California were drilled near Petrolia, and companies were formed to raise the capital to drill more. The oil fields turned out to be not nearly so productive as had been expected, however, and within two years the oil boom, along with the gold rush, had become mostly a memory.

A major problem the settlers faced in their attempts to extract the natural resources was inadequate transportation. The oil drillers had to move both their equipment and their oil over rugged mountain trails by pack horses, and logging activities were limited to areas easily accessible by water. The lack of roads and railroads also had a psychological implication: the settlers felt isolated from the rest of the world, their only

BUILDING THE FORT BRAGG LINE

real contact being by sea. When the railroad was finally completed after several decades and in the face of formidable obstacles, the local inhabitants felt an overwhelming sense of joy and relief:

A hushed and reverential feeling filled the breast of the writer as he stood among the throng of 500 people, watching the golden spike driven by the silver hammer into the last burl redwood . . . Joy came that morning when the link was welded that brought dear old Humboldt into rail contact with the outside. (48)

Road construction began on a fairly large scale as interest developed in logging, ranching, and settling in the more remote areas. Road work was done mostly by hand, so a lot of manpower was needed. Road gangs were recruited from

among the more down-and-out segments of society: "prisoners and Chinamen," in the words of the old-timers. Unable to rely on machinery, overseers pushed coolie labor to its limit. Road workers had an even more strenuous life than the miners, with fewer rewards. Like the miners and the loggers, the crews lived in camps near their jobs, where they were provided with food and shelter. Unfortunately the road workers, mostly illiterate, left few journals, and nobody else recorded their history because they were not thought important enough.

The Chinese had come to California in the gold rush, but they were prohibited from entering most mining camps. Because of this ostracism they worked the "tailings" behind those white miners who had abandoned their old claims for "better diggin's." When the gold rush subsided, some of the Chinese cultivated unwanted swampland, some were hired as coolie labor for the road crews, and some found occupations as servants, street vendors, and laundrymen in the cities. Soon there were slumlike "Chinatowns" for the displaced Chinese, who were generally not allowed to live in other areas. Opium dens were established which were frequented by both whites and Orientals. Almost all of the Chinese were men, and the overcrowded Chinatowns took on a definite skid-row character.

There was frequent fighting among these city Chinese. In 1885 fighting broke out between two rival "tongs" in Eureka. After the first riot, the *Humboldt Times* published on February 5, 1885, an indignant editorial, and a warning:

> It was only a wonder, considering the number of shots fired and the wild manner in which the shooting was done, that some innocent pedestrian was not made to bite the dust . . . If ever such an event does occur—if ever an unoffending white man is thus offered up on the altar of paganism, we fear it will be goodbye to Chinatown.

A few days later just such an event did occur: a respectable white man was killed in the crossfire of a shoot-out in Chinatown. The entire white population was immediately up in arms. A town meeting gave the Chinese twenty-four hours to leave the area for good and all the Chinese who could be found were loaded on two steamers that happened to be in port at the time. Meanwhile, whites erected a scaffold, which was "extremely suggestive." (48) Over three hundred Chinese were shipped out on the steamers to San Francisco, and in the months that followed Chinese in outlying areas were pressured to leave

the county. Humboldt County had adopted de facto a strict exclusion policy for Orientals. For several decades thereafter, whenever a business would try to import some cheap Oriental labor, the citizens would hold mass meetings to protest. In 1906, twenty-three Chinese who had been brought in to work in a cannery were loaded into boxcars and shipped out. As late as 1937, the *Humboldt Times* boasted the distinction of being part of the only community in the state with no Orientals.

Prejudice against the Chinese, like prejudice against the Indians, is perceived more easily with historical hindsight because we are not personally involved. The early white citizens of California saw the Indians as a physical threat to their lives and the Chinese as an economic threat. The coolie laborers accepted far less pay than the whites would have, so in the eyes of the whites the Chinese were stealing their jobs. Although the workers also blamed big business for encouraging coolie labor, they found it easier to attack the Chinese. The Workingmen's Party of California summarized what it felt to be wrong with society:

> The grievances:
> The general corruption of politicians and bad conduct of the state, county, and city governments.
> Taxation, alleged to press too heavily on the poorer class.
> The tyranny of corporations, especially railroads.
> The Chinese. (59)

There were anti-Chinese riots throughout the state from the 1850s on, and in 1879 the people of California voted against further Chinese immigration, 154,638 to 883.

By the time the Chinese were run out of town,

THE WILLIAM CARSON MANSION IN EUREKA

Eureka was no longer a settlement, but a full-fledged, well-established city. The harbor was filled with up to twenty-five ships at a time. Logging had become the major industry, with 40 million feet of redwood cut in the mills each year and sent to such faraway places as Australia, South America, Hawaii, and Shanghai. History books were already being written about the pioneers of the good old days. In 1893, the Humboldt Chamber of Commerce published a book extolling the progress of civilization, with hopes of attracting still more industry to the area. A typical passage describing harbor improvements gives an idea of the great pride most of the citizens took in their advancing technology:

> Up to the time of resuming work the present season, $293,609.66 had been expended on the entrance improvement. From the south end or sand spit, 3,659 lineal feet of jetty structure had been built, and 1,520.7 from the north spit, a total of 5,179.7 lineal feet. To accomplish this 1,206 piles were driven, 31,992.7 cubic yards of brush mattresses submerged, and 101,060 tons of sandstone rock deposited. To carry on the work of improvement requires an expensive plant, comprising wharves, aprons, scow transports, steam tugs, railroads, locomotives, specially designed cars, stationary engines, cables, derricks, and innumerable lesser conveniences. (46)

The settlers competed with the natural forces around them, and they were happy when they managed to come out on top. The old-time loggers proudly posed for their pictures by the "unconquerable" redwoods they had just conquered. When the railroad finally got through to Humboldt, the citizens felt the elation of having won a battle: "The mountains were pierced, hills were leveled and canyons filled. Gorges were bridged.

The primeval forest was cut in twain. Man grappled with nature and man triumphed." (48) The new human inhabitants of the region believed they were part of the unrelenting and irresistible march of civilized man asserting control over lesser forms of life. As an early local historian put it when describing the vast redwood forests:

> Surely Humboldt has something of which she may justly be proud, and from which she is and will continue to receive an ever-increasing revenue until the last is fallen. But they, like the elk they have sheltered, and the poor Indian whose wigwam they built, are doomed to fall before the advance of civilization. (44)

The natural superiority of civilized man over all other living creatures was proved by the fact that he alone was capable of scientific thought. The first party to explore the area left the following mysterious hieroglyphics inscribed in a tree as scientific man's claim to the new land:

> Lat. 41° 3' 32"
> Barometer 29.86"
> Ther. Fah. 48° at 12 PM
> Dec. 7, 1849. J. Gregg.

Were anthropologists of future civilizations to come upon these strange symbols carved on a tree, they would probably assume they had some religious significance—and they would be right. The symbols represent the controlled world that the settlers imposed upon their new home, a preconceived world of science and technology which structured the environment totally according to the needs and desires of the newcomers. Knowing that this was the attitude underlying the settlement of the region from the very beginning makes it easier to understand the exploitation of the natural world that was to follow.

PART TWO.

CICHORIUM INTYBUS
(CHICORY)

LIVING HISTORY

CHAPTER FOUR.

HOMESTEADING IN THE BACK HILLS

Damn near live off the land.

—An old-timer

Once the native populations were removed or destroyed, American settlement of easily accessible coastal and lowland regions presented no major problems. Food, clothing, tools, and the materials for shelter, if they could not be obtained from the local environment, could easily be imported by ship. Thus it was possible for the first lowland settlements to grow into towns and even cities almost overnight. The situation in the back hills, however, was quite different. Without the services of roads, railroads, or waterways, the settlers of the more remote regions had no way of carrying in the wherewithal to

lead a fully "civilized" life. To settle the back hills, people had to be willing to work hard to raise most of their necessities themselves. Nevertheless, as the settlements around Humboldt Bay became more and more crowded, the pioneer spirit led a handful of men and women out into the backcountry to create lives of their own.

When the pioneers first left the lowlands for the back hills, they packed in a few basic articles by mule or horseback: metal tools, nails, stoves, and kitchenware; some clothing, bedding, and footwear; perhaps a few small glass windows (in the early days, settlers always used to take their windows with them when they moved from one house to another). They also brought with them some seeds to plant and a few livestock.

THE MILCH GOAT

After that, they had to find a way of making a living on their own: shelter was obtained from nearby trees; some animals were raised and slaughtered, while others provided fresh milk and eggs; seeds were planted to provide fresh vegetables, grains, and feed for the stock. Every few months, the pioneers might make a trip to the nearest town to replace worn-out tools, clothing, and utensils, and to stock up on certain staples that even the hardiest of settlers found it almost impossible to do without: sugar, salt and pepper, coffee, tobacco, etc. Large quantities of flour were also packed in, for although many settlers raised grain, few had the grist mills with which to grind it. To pay for their staples, the settlers had to raise a surplus of something that could be sold in town. If the herds of sheep or cattle were thriving, some could be driven in to be sold, and bacon and ham were always in demand, as was grain, to feed the folks in town. It didn't take much of a surplus to make a good trade, because the shopping list was not that long.

To make a living off the land in rugged and inaccessible back-hill country was no easy matter. To stimulate the settlement of remote regions, the United States government has always encouraged homesteading. Under the Homestead Act of 1862, a settler could acquire a quarter-section for free (except for a small filing fee) if he could show that he had lived on it and cultivated it for five years. Even before that, homesteaders were offered their land for the token payment of $1.25 an acre. Having just taken over the land from its previous human inhabitants, the government had a seemingly infinite amount to give away to anyone who was willing to settle it. It was through homesteading that this particular back-hills region was first settled on a permanent basis by Americans.

THE EVERYDAY LIFE OF ERNEST McKEE
(PART 1)

Hanging from the wall of Ernest McKee's present home in the Berkeley Hills is an oil painting of a clean white house surrounded by a picket fence in a plush meadow. The picture is of the homestead in which Ernest spent his childhood. The homestead burned down long ago, but Ernest can't remember exactly when.

"When did the fella come in and set the house on fire up at the ranch?" he asks his wife, who's busy in the next room.

As she's figuring it out, she calls back: "Got your foot in the water, Dad?"

"Part of it." Ernest always speaks with poetic conciseness. Never a word is wasted. His succinct statements are wise and gently humorous.

"A little wart on the foot can cause a lot of trouble."

Mrs. McKee comes in to join the conversation. She talks of her father's cattle ranch on the Mattole and the hospitality he gave to passersby: "The latchstring was always out." A man used to come by driving his turkeys to market, and Ernest used to come by on his way to Eureka. That's how they met. "He was pretty sweet on me," she says. "We've been married fifty-seven years, and most people now don't think they'll live to fifty. Quite a while ago, wasn't it, Ernest?"

"Ancient history."

She brings out old pictures of the family and homestead, which are mixed in with postcards of flamingos and buffaloes. We get to talking about life in the old days, but first Ernest warns me, "You won't have a book big enough to write this all down."

Ernest's father came to this area in 1871. He brought cattle down from Petrolia to the hills above Shelter Cove, where he pastured them "on shares" (they were not his cattle). This gave him a start in cattle ranching. Within a few years he drove a herd of cattle down to Fort Ross, sold them, and took the money to San Francisco to buy a sawmill. The sawmill was shipped up to Shelter Cove in pieces and transported inland by wagon. Once assembled, it served to furnish the lumber for the homestead pictured on the wall. Before this, the family had lived in a log cabin, which was where Ernest was born. "Didn't have such a sophisticated name of midwife—the midwife was just the nearest neighbor."

For generations, the McKees of this area have been builders. The house was the central focus of the homestead. There were high ceilings and several bedrooms upstairs, much like the home in Iowa which Ernest's father had come from.

There was a barn for the dairy cows, team horses, wagons, and hay. There was a storage shed next to the kitchen, a smokehouse, a chicken house, and a forging shed. Like most homesteaders, the McKees did their own blacksmith work: shoeing horses, shaping and mending tools, and so on. For fuel for the forge, they made charcoal by banking a large hardwood fire (oak or madrone) with dirt mounds.

With the usual exception of dry goods and luxuries (flour, beans, coffee, sugar, etc.) which were shipped in through Shelter Cove, the McKees raised all their own food. For meat they had beef, pork, or venison: "Never any shortage of food at our table so long as there was deer

SLOW, STEADY, & SURE: A SHIRE COLT

to furnish the meat." From the cows they obtained fresh milk, butter, and cheese. There was a large vegetable garden, enclosed by a picket fence to keep out the animals, which supplied fresh greens in the summer and cold-weather crops such as beets and turnips in the winter. Some vegetables were canned, as were domestic fruits such as plums and wild fruits such as huckleberries and blackberries. Fruit was also dried by placing screened racks in the sun, while apples were kept in cold storage where they would last clear into the next summer. From apples they made cider, from grapes they made wine, and from barley they made whiskey.

Fresh fish could always be obtained from the weekly wagon that passed by the homestead on its way from Shelter Cove to Garberville. But the McKees also did their own fishing with hazel-stick poles. In the summer they'd travel to the coast for surffish, much as their Indian predecessors had done. When the salmon made their run up the Mattole, they'd lay in a year's supply and salt it down for storage.

Although the McKee homestead approached

self-sufficiency, there were many articles that had to be imported. Just in order to do their fishing, for instance, they needed to bring in hooks and lines, nets, and large quantities of salt to store the fish they caught. To account for these and other purchases that were made through the shippers at Shelter Cove, the McKees raised a surplus of cattle and hogs. They drove their cattle to market and the pork they butchered and cured themselves, selling the ham and bacon to nearby stores and lumber camps.

For a child on a homestead, there was much work to be done. Ernest remembers his time being filled with daily chores like weeding the garden, gathering kindling, milking the cows, gathering the eggs. When there was time to play, he didn't wander much in the surrounding hills for fear of panthers. Instead, the children amused themselves with such games as tomball: "It's a good deal like baseball—you just throw the ball and see if the other fellow can hit it." There was no possibility of going to school— it was too far away—so the McKees would hire a teacher to stay with the children during school vacations.

The most exciting holiday, as Ernest remembers it, was the Fourth of July: "You had to go to Garberville to celebrate the Fourth of July." There were giant feasts and a sort of rodeo, which included roping contests and races with ordinary stock horses. And there was the annual swim in the Eel River: "Cut a couple of holes in a gunny sack and put it on for a bathing suit."

When the weather was warm enough to go swimming, bathing was done in the streams. At other times bath water was heated by placing a washboiler over two lids of the cookstove. "Summertime, went down to the creek; wintertime, wait for the snow to thaw—otherwise, put the water on the stove and get all squashed up in the tub." Clothes were washed in the same manner as people, except that the laundry was generally boiled to loosen up the dirt. The McKees made their own soap by boiling up tallow and fat in a large outdoor cauldron and mixing it with lye that had been obtained by pouring water through the ashes from the wood stove.

Before indoor plumbing was installed, the McKee homestead had a rather unique sanitary arrangement: their outhouse was situated directly over the stream. In this way, no holes had to be dug and redug when they were full—the water just carried it all away. The population was so sparse, they reasoned, that there was no sanitary hazard to folks downstream; indeed, the water would travel several miles before reaching the next homestead. In those days, crockery chamber pots were a standard furnishing in most homes, including the McKees'. People felt much more settled, I suspect, if they didn't have to brave the elements to go to the john. The chamber pots were generally pretty elaborate affairs— a touch of Victorian splendor midst pioneer simplicity. For toilet paper, the standard item was old catalogs from Sears or Montgomery Ward.

(The everyday life of Ernest McKee is continued in Chapter Five.)

THE EVERYDAY LIFE OF ROY AND MABEL CATHEY
(PART 1)

Roy started off, "Well, when my folks come in here it was on horseback. There was nothing. They had to raise everything to live on. About 1880, I think, when they first came in here. I was

born 1897. You take up a homestead in them days. And what they call a preemption—another forty—then you're allowed a timber claim. That gives you quite a lot—timber too. And so they build a house—had to split out the rails and shave it all by hand. Built his own house and barn and everything. They had a log barn.

"Them days you had a cow, and raised a calf. You had horses mostly, and you put in the crop. Had to plow and all that stuff. Had goats too at one time. I got cattle here now. I feed 'em every day, all winter long. Winter time you gotta feed 'em. Only got about ten or twelve, that's all, calves and all. I just raise them for meat—for what I eat myself, and I got three sons—raise meat for them and ourselves, see? Butcher six or eight a year. I shoot 'em, hang 'em up, and skin 'em. Hang up down here for about three days, then I cut 'em up. Make steaks out of them."

"We raise all our own meat and vegetables still. Raise our own chickens," said Mabel.

"Geese, ducks, banty chickens," added Roy.

"So we have a variety," Mabel continued. "Have our own eggs. Fresh milk twice a day. We make cheese too. And we churn our own butter still."

"I counted that. I've turned that six, seven thousand times before I got it. That's right, I counted it. Generally about twelve hundred times, but you get it a little too cold in here and you churn and it never comes. But she knows just right. She knows how to do it, see?"

"Back then, his father shoed his own horses and everything, too."

"Had a blacksmith shop. Had to be a jack-of-all trades, in them days, to get by. I heated the old bellows up . . . helped shoe the horses, too. But just helped the old man—I wouldn't want to try it myself."

"His dad did all those things. He had to."

"And wagon wheels. Every year or two you had to dry 'em out and shrink 'em. You had to tighten the tires on them, and that's quite a job. You had to know what you're doing with that, too. Used to be people who make the buggies—buy them, generally. But you had to keep them up with your own blacksmith shop.

"Times was good back then . . . if you could clear a hundred dollars a year and go to town. Might take you three, four days—at least two days and a half going in. I been in with the old man. Take the wagon. Had a hundred dollars in your pocket, go into town, buy a hundred dollars' worth of groceries, come out and live the whole year on that. Be mostly sugar and coffee and stuff like that. Just the coffee beans—had to grind your own coffee. Stuff like pepper and salt . . . and flour. You raise the rest of the stuff.

"Used to camp down there in a hollow tree on the way to town. One night, I remember, it was raining like heck. I went to sleep and woke up and saw my dad standing up there. He had to stand to keep out of the rain, but he let me sleep.

"I remember we were going around there one day coming home. It was a good day then, but the road was muddy, sloppy. Here came an automobile. First one I guess the old man ever seen on the road. Old man said to me, 'You know, if they don't stop, you got a right to shoot them.' First car I ever seen on this road.

"We raised grain seed mostly. When I was a kid . . . well, before that they thresh 'em with a flail. Long stick with a rawhide tied to another little shorter stick, then you flail. Thresh your beans that way too. But when I was a kid, we fill the old house up here about that high—four or five feet—with the stuff and I get in there and ride a horse around on it. Tramp it, see? Then move all the chaff out and go gather it up. Then we had a thing—a kind of a bellows—to blow air, you know. Had a big crank on it—crank that thing and pour the stuff down in front of it and move all the chaff away from it. Anyway, you made enough to try to get that hundred dollars a year. Maybe you make sixty, seventy dollars at that. Then maybe you had sheep around the country. Shear sheep and make another sixty dollars. And that's all the money you needed for a whole year. Maybe you'd do some trapping, too; everybody used to trap in the wintertime. I had a string of traps clear on over to Harris clear on back down to—what's that place above Phillipsville?"

"He'd walk that line everyday."

"I wouldn't walk it—I'd do it on the run, mostly. You get a mink—pretty high price—or otters, fishers. About all I ever caught was skunks. I remember one time up there I skinned a skunk and I got it just right and it squirted right in my eye. Oh, I thought I was gonna die. Dove right into the creek headfirst—batted my eyes around—dove under again—kept doing that and finally worked it out of my eye. Another time a dog chased one down a hole and I peeked down in that hole and he squirted right in my eye again. Lotta skunks. I used to have three pet ones right in the house with me. They used to sleep in front of the fireplace. Had a hole in the door where the cat came in. One night I woke up and he's chewing my skin. I throw him down and wrap up in my blanket and woke up and he's chewing on me again. Third time made me mad and I went and got a poker and killed all three of 'em. Skinned 'em and hung 'em up with the rest of 'em.

"Them days everybody had hogs and they run around the country, and some tame hogs get half wild, you know. And certain times of year people

SHEEP RANCHER'S PRIDE: A RAMBOUILLET RAM & EWE

come round here with hounds and catch dogs. When I was a small kid I go barefooted and fella come down here and my job is holding his catch dogs. And he sends his bay dogs in to bay the hogs, get 'em going in bunches. Then turn the catch dogs loose . . .

"So let me tell you about catching these hogs. I go along barefooted and stubbed my toe. Old Charlie he's in a hurry to get to the dogs before the hogs get away. Didn't ask nothing—just grabbed me and yanked me loose. Skin come off and everything. I forgot about it and run right along behind him. Got to the end and the dogs had the hogs bayed around a stump and I turned this old dog loose to catch 'em. Crawled in there and tied their legs up—tied one front one with one back one. Couldn't get in with a buggy or something, we'd pack 'em out on horseback. That's what we used to do when I was a kid.

"They live on these acorns, you know. Lotta acorns. That's how they live and got fat. For a real good piece of meat, though, you catch 'em and put 'em up for a month or two and feed 'em corn. Real good meat. But when you fry them and it spats all over you, you know you got an acorn-fed hog then."

"You know years ago people never used soap in their dishwater. They'd save that for the hogs. They had big barrels and saved all the whey and dishwater and everything and that would be your pig feed. They never wasted anything."

"So you put the wild hogs in with the tame hogs to fatten them up. But you get 'em in there wild and generally they're too wild so, like I say, we sew their eyes up with heavy thread. You've heard all this, haven't you, Ma?"

"Yea, but that's OK. Go ahead."

"Anyway, one time we had this old sow tied up

and I was gonna turn her loose. I reached down to get hold of the rope and she scrambled up and turned around and came right up at me. Didn't have her tied good. I started running backwards and fell down in a hole and she's there right on top of me. My brother, he's right behind her and grabbed her by the leg and pulled her off, and I jumped up and grabbed on to a log and got out of there.

"Another time we pack one out on a horse and I told my brother, 'You'd better tie his mouth shut.' He said, 'Aw, he won't bite.' He fooled around trying to tie him on and the thing reached out and got him by the finger, just stripped it. So we generally tie the mouth shut.

"Them days when you owned hogs everybody had their own mark. If you owned a hog you were allowed to kill him. But if you came to a

THE FAT OF THE LAND: RAISING PUREBRED SWINE

hog that wasn't marked . . . if you didn't own no hogs and kill one . . . somebody catch you and they're allowed to shoot you and get away with it. I know a party yet who was shot—killed hogs that they didn't own, see?"

"Then when they caught the hogs, they made their own bacon from them."

"Well, first you had a trough made. Put water in it. Someone build a fire and you heat rocks and put the rocks in it till it gets hot—a hundred and forty degrees or something like that. Then you had to throw the hog in there before you cut him up. Put a rope on him. You pull on your rope and the other guy pulls on his and you keep doin' that. Loosen the hair, see? When he starts gettin' that way all over, you hung 'em up, get a knife, and start scraping. Leave the skin on, just scrape him off clean and wash him good. Then you cut him up and throw the pieces right down on the floor. Pack 'em pretty tight and between every layer throw rock salt on 'em—just cover 'em with salt. Then you leave 'em there about twenty days, I think it is, then take 'em up and hang 'em in the smokehouse. Had a wire that bent down—hook 'em in and hang 'em up. And you smoke 'em, I guess, for thirty to forty days anyway. Nowadays they only half smoke it and most of the time you gotta keep it in the refrigerator. You get hardwood. Use oak mostly to hold the fire. Build it up at night and next morning you got coals there—still smoking. Use pepperwood if you want a pepperwood flavor. And cherry tree is good, apple tree is good—anything with a flavor to it. Like I say, it was good pan bacon. We was raised on it. But you get a lot of salt. You gotta parboil it to eat it. Them days the salt come in hundred-pound bags—pack 'em in on a mule.

"Ever make jerky from venison? Take them in strips, salt and pepper them, put 'em behind the

stove, and let 'em dry. In about three days, you get a jerky. Just put 'em behind the stove."

"You can take any meat and dry it like that. They do the fish and the surffish like that too. But you gotta be careful you don't cook it—you just want it to dry."

"When its good and dry, it'll keep forever, practically—if it don't get moist and spoil."

"You know, that's nourishment. You take a small piece of that and it keeps you going for a long time."

"Used to make cider, too. Take apples and crush 'em—get the juice out of 'em—that's all there is to it. Had a place you grind 'em, then you get a press—cider press is what they call it. Boards made like that with holes in them; put them on top of each other and screw a big thing down; the screw presses the boards up tight and the juice keeps going down. Every day you give a little twist or two till you get all the juice out of it. Got a lot of apples here now that I could do it with. Pretty buggy, but I guess they're good to drink anyway. I let the cows eat them now.

THE KETTLE

"You let the apples ferment—leave 'em long enough and they turn into vinegar. Get what you call a 'mother.' When you got a good mother started, all you gotta do to make vinegar is pour cider on this mother, leave it around, and it makes vinegar."

"Years ago they raised prunes here too and dried them, didn't they? Sun dried them."

"You can dry prunes and peaches too. Put 'em in trays and lay them out in the sun. First you gotta put 'em in a vat with . . . what do you call it?"

"Lye."

"Lye. Crack 'em, see? Dip 'em in this lye, then dip 'em in water to take the lye out of 'em. Then they crack so they dry quick."

"The lye cracks the skin so the air can get in there."

"In the night, when there's fog or anything, you take the trays and put them on top of each other. Cover them up that way."

"You put them on the roof. That keeps the animals away, so all you got is your yellowjackets."

"You gotta contend with them!"

"Make a yellowjacket trap. Take a jar, a big jar, and put a nail hole in the top of it. Put meat down in the bottom. They get in, but they can't get out."

"Put one out here, and first thing you know you got a jar full of yellowjackets."

"There's a lot of tricks you pick up."

"She's the expert on all that stuff. Canning too. Anybody in the county want to know something, they call her up and ask her. For years she canned six, seven hundred jars every winter—meat and stuff too. Even yet she's canning—give it to all the kids. We got four or five kids around the country."

"For meat, you can cook it first or put it in raw. If you put it in raw, why, never put no water in it. For a quart jar, take a spoonful of salt and seal it tight. Put it in a water bath and you boil that for four hours. Never let your boiling stop. When you take it out, it's all sealed and everything."

"Think we got some bear meat now we got buried down there. We never liked it too well. Used to bury the deer meat so the warden wouldn't find it, and buried some bear meat with it too."

"We don't care for bear meat, though. Real coarse grain."

"More you chew it, the bigger it gets. Get a young bear is good eating, though."

"We used to make our own soap from fat and ashes. Ashes is what you get your lye out of. You take your ashes and you boil that. Then you pour the liquid off of that, and that's your lye. And then you take fat—all kinds of fat—and you mix it all together and boil them, and when you let it cool, that's your soap. The longer you boil it, the stronger it is.

"You make wax out of fat too. It's different from soap 'cause you have no lye in it. You take sheep tallow, which is really hard anyway. Beef is a softer grease. Then you make your candles. But of course we used kerosene lamps, too."

THE OLD STOVE

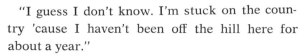

"Everybody had lanterns. Them days, when you teamed, you had to get out and feed your stock before daylight in the morning. Had to go to work with a lantern."

"Tell about the time the doctor rode out here when you was born, Dad."

"When I was born, old man didn't have no money, but he had the doctor in Garberville ride down here. To pay the bill, got an old cow and led her clear to Garberville. They paid the bill *honest*, them old fellas. Had to take something in trade, you know."

"And they never had to go to funeral parlors or anything like that in those days. The neighbors would all come in and built the coffin and took care of it."

"I remember Mother riding on horseback to look after a sick person in the middle of the night."

"They wouldn't think anything of it. It's something people don't do nowadays. Scared to death of their next-door neighbor. It's a shame the human race has deteriorated the way it has—and that's what it is, deterioration."

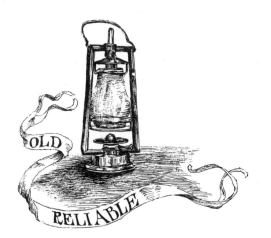

"I guess I don't know. I'm stuck on the country 'cause I haven't been off the hill here for about a year."

"He hasn't been off since last October. I asked him to come to town with me but he wouldn't do it."

"Nothing for me to do. She does all the business. Nothing for me to get off here for. If I wanna take a hike and go couple miles over here to Owl Creek . . ."

"Last time he went off—our son had gone down to the river to get a load of gravel and got stuck. Had to have his dad come down with the jeep and pull him out."

"I got my driver's license, but I don't care about going anyplace. Wanna take a walk and do something, I go up and get me a load of limbs and bring 'em down here and when I get time I bucksaw 'em up by hand. I take my time. I lived up here all my life, except one or two years traveling."

"They weren't ambitious people in those days. You know, you didn't travel very far. You'd just stay home a great deal."

"Tell you a difference between nowadays and then. Guy used to have apples up there then. Make a lot of apple cider. Nobody lived up around there much. One time I come up on the hill here, nobody been there for a month or two and all over the table there's money—two-bit pieces, four-bit pieces, dimes, nickels. You come in and drink cider and leave the money to pay for it. Nobody'd take it. Them days everyone was honest. You never thought about losing it."

"When he was a youngster, they had an old organ. And he can play the violin, sort of, you know, he can chord to it."

"Had dances. Had organs, and used to be a guy who could play a fiddle. Played all night long."

THE BRICK OVEN

"Oh, they'd get all their horses and go a long way for dances."

"Every Saturday night there'd be a dance somewhere or other. Dances all the time."

"They were the square dances, weren't they, Dad?"

"Drink whiskey and fight mostly."

"Those were before Prohibition days, you know."

"I never drank too much, though. During the weektime you worked, mostly. But we was crazy in them days. One time the river was high down there, and he had four bits and I didn't. I wished I had four bits. He said, 'I'll tell you how you make it.' I said, 'How?' He said, 'Dive over.' I dove over and half drowned. Got out and he gave me the four bits. He said, 'Will you give it back if I dive in?' I said, 'Yeah.' And he dove in himself. We was a crazy bunch of kids.

"Another thing, you know, there used to be a peddler come through. Had a big wagon and a canvas over it. And he had everything: sold shirts and overalls and vests and . . . pretty near everything in there. Sweaters. I remember one of these gold sweaters. I was gonna get me one when I got old enough to buy one. And he had dresses and shoes and frying pans and stuff and . . . he came through once a year, that's all.

"Used to be a religious guy come through— hold meetings down here. For a week at a time. Everybody used to go to that, too. Call it 'camp meeting.'

"Another thing kinda funny. My grandmother used to run the stagecoach hotel there at Miranda. Used to be a drummer come through there. Them days you never see much money. And every time he'd go to pay his bill, he'd pull out a twenty-dollar piece."

"They were gold pieces then, weren't they?"

"Yeah. And she couldn't change it. Said, 'Never mind.' Let it go, see? And so her husband died and eventually she married this other fella. And he's a stingy old fella, ya know. Lot about him I won't tell, but . . . Anyway, he was there, this drummer come by and stayed there day or two and went to leave and pulled the twenty dollars out again. This time he took it and said he'd change it, but he took it and kept it."

(The everyday lives of Roy and Mabel Cathey are continued in Chapter Five.)

THE EVERYDAY LIFE OF FRANK
(PART 1)

The early settlers came from varied backgrounds, and each group brought elements of its own heritage with it. Frank's family was from Italy, so for them making a living in the backwoods of America took on a distinctly Italian flavor.

"Damn near live off the land. Everything you can think of: potatoes, tomatoes, beans . . . even made our own salami. I've made salami right on this table here. This is a salami table. Used to dry tomatoes—make paste out of them. Mushrooms, string beans, most everything. Didn't have no town to go to. You had to grow your own."

When Frank's family did go to town, they brought back fifty-pound bags of spaghetti in addition to the usual sugar, coffee, salt, oil, and three-hundred-pound barrels of flour. The oil was used for canning: instead of going through the elaborate sealing process, they merely poured olive oil on top of the food in the jar. The oil formed its own seal and didn't freeze in the winter, so there was no problem with expanding or contracting. The jars were kept along with the wine and sausages in a storage cellar. Frank proudly shows off the hand-hewn beams of the storage cellar at his current home, but since the days of easy household refrigeration the cellar has not been in use.

Bread was made not in a wood cookstove, as was the usual manner, but in an outside brick oven. A fire was built with hardwood (fir would have too much pitch). After a good bed of coals had developed, the extra wood was removed and the bread placed in the oven. A loaf of bread could be baked in an hour or an hour and a half. Cooking and eating bread in those days were entirely different from today, and Frank would prefer it the old way: "So goddamn lazy, people can't even slice bread no more. I never seen the likes of it."

(The everyday life of Frank is continued in Chapter Six.)

CHAPTER FIVE.

MAKING A LIVING IN THE DAYS OF THE TANBARK BOOM

TAN OAK
ACORNS

It looks just like my people lying around, lying around with all their skin cut off.

—NAGAICHO, THE SINKYONE CREATOR

The homesteaders in this area were never entirely self-sufficient. At first the little money they needed was made by selling their surplus food or stock. Soon, however, a local economy developed around splitting redwood bolts into shakes, fence posts, grape stakes, and railroad ties, and peeling the bark from the tan oak trees to obtain the tannic acids used in processing leather. The homesteaders then found it feasible to make their "spending money" by putting in a few months of paid labor outside the homestead. In the words of Lon McKee, a cousin of Ernest's, "They'd work about three to four months in the tanbark and make enough to buy a winter's supply of coffee and flour and those things—sugar too. They still raised their own meat and vege-

tables and they lived better then, I believe, than they do now."

In the days before automotive transportation made long-distance commuting possible, when a man found a job in the backwoods it meant that he'd have to leave his home and live near the place of his work; his wife and children, meanwhile, were left to take care of the homestead. The woodsmen generally lived in small camps of ten or twelve men apiece. They were paid about $2.50 per day, plus room and board. Board was usually provided by a couple who had been hired for the express purpose of keeping the men well fed; apparently camp foremen always recognized that good food was a necessity for both the health and morale of the workers, because none of the old woodsmen I've talked with have ever complained much about it. Room in the bark-peeling camps often consisted of no more than a place under the stars, since all the peeling was done in the warm dry summers when the sap was flowing in the trees.

THE EVERYDAY LIFE
OF ERNEST McKEE
(PART 2)

After leaving the homestead to spend five years in San Francisco as an apprentice shipbuilder and machinist, Ernest returned to Whitethorn to run a small sawmill, split-stuff, and bark-peeling business. During the summer, he'd hire a dozen or so men and get a contract with a leather company to peel bark. In the winter, it was mostly split-stuff work. The shakes he made were shipped to places like Los Angeles to build houses—"that's quite a problem in L.A. and San Diego." The eight-foot railroad ties were bought up by the Northwestern Pacific, Southern Pacific, and Santa Fe railroads, and the six-foot ties were shipped to Hawaii to be used on the big sugar plantations. The stakes were sent to the various vineyards throughout California, and the posts were used to enclose some of the millions of acres of grazing land that was part of the settlement of the West.

To get the logs out of the woods, Ernest and

CUTTING TIES

his crews used bobsleds pulled by horses. Once the logs were cut and split, they were loaded onto wagons to be taken to Shelter Cove or Needle Rock. A four- or six-horse team would pull two wagons at a time. The lead wagon was sixteen feet long, or the length of two railroad ties; the trailer wagon could carry a single load of ties or a double load of the four-foot slabs of bark. I ask Ernest if he ever spilled any of his cargo. "Oh, no. That was a loss. Nobody could afford that."

After the tanbark boom, Ernest made a living by buying and selling cattle. He also engaged in a little buying and selling of land. "Any way to pick up a few dollars," he says. His real vocation, though, is building. His present, rather plush house (which he refers to as "the cabin") in the Berkeley Hills he built when he was sixty-seven; a summer house up in Petrolia he built when eighty. All the McKees of this area, it seems, age slowly and build profusely.

One can't help but wonder why Ernest left the back hills to move into Berkeley. His girls were going to school and his wife preferred a warmer climate, and this partly explains the shift, but he sees his move as part of the larger picture: "Getting a bit old-fashioned to live up there anymore. I don't know whether we could live or exist the way we used to. Nowadays it's pretty hard to live without electricity or running water."

By the turn of the century, the tan oak bark had become the basis of a major back-hills industry. Scores of camps were scattered throughout the woods around Briceland and Whitethorn. The trees were felled and the bark was stripped off in four-foot slabs. The slabs were left to dry for about a month and then packed by mules to the nearest roads, where they were loaded onto wagons and taken to the processing plant in Briceland. They were stored under sheds to finish drying, and then ground to pulp and placed in huge vats, ten or twelve feet square. ("To get in there, all you had was a breechclout and a pair of wooden shoes.") Here the pulp was boiled to extract the tannic acids. The extract was then stored in barrels, hauled by wagon to Shelter Cove, and shipped to such places as Benicia and Redwood City, where it was used to tan leather.

THE EVERYDAY LIFE OF THE TAN OAK TREE

The tan oak begins its life as an acorn. In midsummer, the large male tassel drops its pollen to the inconspicuous female flower at its base, which develops into an acorn the following spring. By fall the acorn is mature and drops from its cap to the ground, but it's a rare acorn that gets any farther along than that in the path to becoming a tree. Squirrels and other small animals rely on the acorn as their staple food source and gather large caches of them when (and even before) they fall. But even the squirrels are generally beaten to the punch by the oak moth, which drills a hole in the shell of the developing acorn and lays its eggs in midsummer. The acorn then provides both shelter and food for the developing larvae throughout the winter, and if all goes well a new moth will emerge in the spring.

If a seed does manage to germinate, it faces a tough struggle for survival. An acorn falling in a recently cut forest or brushland faces intense competition from its neighbors, and only after a young tree has won a sufficient space for itself can it settle into the regular business of being a tree: photosynthesizing the sun's energy, gathering water and minerals from the earth, adding new growth each spring, and, after a while, producing acorns. A healthy tan oak can expect to live from fifty to two hundred years before it succumbs to heartrot, a fungus disease that eats away the inside of the trunk. Mature trees often perpetuate themselves indefinitely, however, by sending out suckers from the very base of the trunk. When the parent tree finally falls, the suckers can often develop into successful heirs.

The tan oak tree has served as the basis of two human civilizations. First, the Indians used the acorns as their most reliable food source, gathering large caches in the fall in much the same way as the squirrels. Much of the Indians' energy was devoted to the tan oak tree: competing with the oak moths through controlled fires, gathering and storing the acorns, and preparing them for human consumption. Later, when the land was taken over by the whites, the acorns were neglected but the bark became coveted as the best known natural source of tannic acids. Whereas the gathering of acorns had done nothing to harm the trees (indeed, the Indian practice of burning the underbrush and the worm-ridden acorns helped to insure a healthier forest), the bark could only be obtained by their destruction. Within the first twenty years of this century, practically all the mature tan oak forests of the area were cut down, and for the most part only the bark was utilized. A small portion of the wood was used in stoves and fireplaces, but most of it was left to rot. One of the three local Indians to survive into the days of the tanbark boom told of a visit from Nagaicho, the Sinkyone Creator. Nagaicho had looked at the area around Briceland and remarked sadly, "It looks just like my people lying around, lying around with all their skin cut off."

The plant in Briceland, operated by the Wagner Leather Company, processed over three thousand cords of bark a year, and over $100,000 worth of extract was shipped from Shelter Cove in each of the boom's peak years. In addition to this, several other companies shipped out the bark itself to be processed elsewhere. Within a few years, the settlement of the area was no longer limited to a handful of isolated homesteaders. Briceland grew into a town with a population of over two hundred and various bars, hotels, stores, dance houses, stables, and blacksmiths to service the local inhabitants. Whitethorn grew from a single stage stop on the mail route to become the home of several hundred bark peelers. The establishment of a saloon at a place called Gopherville just outside of Whitethorn marked its rise. In the words of Ernest McKee, "Gopherville was quite a town. It was a saloon, and that was always necessary." Coming into the area half a century later, however, no one would ever guess that such an industry had once flourished here. Before the most recent influx to the area started five years ago, not a single place of business was left in Briceland, and Gopherville was nothing but a handful of rundown shacks.

Backwoods industry was made possible in this area by its proximity to the ocean. All up and down the coastline, small harbors were built up to take away the natural resources and bring in supplies to the local population. At Usal, for instance, a sixteen-hundred-foot wharf was built in 1889, along with three miles of logging railway and a mill that employed three hundred men. The road connecting Usal with Rockport to the

GETTING THE TIMBER OUT: THE CHUTE

"A mill in every gulch & a chute or two at every landing..."

south and Whitethorn to the north was at that time the main land route from Fort Bragg to Eureka. Today, the same dirt road is traveled only by an occasional summer tourist, and Usal is now

inhabited only sporadically by beach campers and permanently by a few grazing livestock.

At Needle Rock there was no wharf, but ships were loaded and unloaded through the use of a cable rig known as a "slacker." The cables were attached to the shoreline cliffs on one end and extended out about one thousand feet into the ocean to a place where ships could safely anchor. On top of the cliffs, the open meadow was terraced to permit loading cars on tracks to circulate through the stockyard. Around the stockyard a small town flourished which included a store, hotel, school, dairy, and living facilities for the numerous teamsters and teams that hauled the split products and the bark out of the hills. Today, only a single house and an old barn remain in the overgrown fields, but beneath the tall grass one can still see that the gentle slope was terraced. An isolated leafless eucalyptus tree, spreading its branches like an old oak, stands as the only other sign of a civilization come and gone, for eucalyptus trees are not native to California.

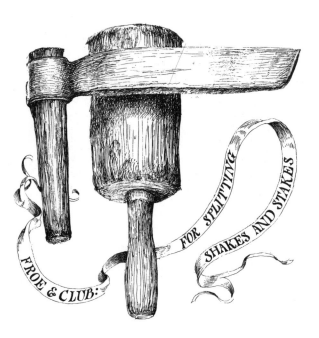

FROE & CLUB: FOR SPLITTING SHAKES AND STAKES

The main industry around Needle Rock was split stuff. All the splitting, of course, was done by hand in those days. Russian Finn immigrants came to the area in large numbers and quickly established a reputation as experts with the broadax. Mostly single men, they lived in camps and were paid by the piece rather than by the hour. Up until just a few years ago, old-timers like Roy Cathey were still making a living by selling the posts, stakes, and shakes they had split by hand.

THE EVERYDAY LIFE
OF ROY AND MABEL CATHEY
(PART 2)

Mabel continued her reminiscing, "And he helped build Highway 101. Built it with a wheelbarrow and pick and shovel, didn't you?"

"Yeah," Roy agreed. "Well, they had a Swede camp, maybe fifteen to twenty men, and an Italian camp, fifteen, twenty men, and an American camp. Had dozens of them off on the road—just small jobs, you know. Take a year or two to finish them. Did it all by wheelbarrow. I was seventeen then. Worked over a year on that job. I got two hundred and eighty-five dollars paid off in gold pieces—thought I was rich."

"All that length of time with just a wheelbarrow."

"My old man got a job as the county road man from here to Dyerville. He had to keep that road up. His team and him made four dollars a day. Figured two dollars for his team and two dollars for him. That was late, though—not them early days. Before that there wasn't no road."

"Then after that when he got older he used to

THE SEASIDE PASTURE: WHERE A TOWN ONCE STOOD

make those railroad ties. Made thousands of them. Took a lot of muscle."

"That's what we did—make ties and stakes and stuff. My job mostly was to get them out of the woods."

"He's a perfectionist with an ax. You oughta see what he can do with an ax."

"I thought I was an axman till I started chopping in the woods with these old-timers. Found out I didn't know nothing. They learn you right there. Learned all about falling then. Before that I thought I knew how to fall, but I didn't even know how to chop. That's a nice job when you're learning. It's hard work but you get used to it.

"You had a left-hand chopper on one side of the tree and a right-hand on the other. And you get so you can saw together. But I used to fell

them alone. Rig up a dummy with a spring pole. Take a long pole that's limber, so you could pull it, and nail it on the other side of the tree and hook a line to it. Hook it into your saw. You pull your saw like this, and the spring pole pulls it back. Lotta different ways, but that's the way I did it.

"You had to fell your own trees and then buck them too—had to buck them all by hand, then. Then split 'em and hew 'em. Used to snake 'em out by horse. Had what they call bobsleds. Put one end on the sled and let the other end drag on the ground. After the horse had made about a dozen trips, you wouldn't even have to go with him. Had a man out there to unload him.

"Used to snake them from here clear out to the highway over there. You see that little cut by the creek—that's where we used to load them. This

THE WHARF AT SHELTER COVE

forty below me, and all up here, I worked this all off myself. I been working up to couple of years ago. Prices got so high for logs in Japan—I sold off. So now I just fool around with fences and putting in gardens and stuff.

"I used to make a lot of shakes, too. You have a mallet and a froe. Hit 'em and drive 'em out. Twenty-five in a bunch then tie 'em up. Standard shake was three foot, made two foot two. I wished I'd saved some trees so I could make some more.

It takes good trees, though, to make shakes."

"What he did during the Depression, he cut wood. All the schools around here used wood."

"I had twelve, fifteen men cutting wood."

"A dollar a cord."

"Oh, I had about two dollars a cord. I was the busiest guy in the country during the Depression, but we got by."

"Do most anything to try to survive in that time."

96

"We didn't know there was a depression on, hardly. Too busy. Didn't have time to use your head. Just had to keep working. Never had time to use my head; had to make some money. Funny how things happen . . ."

The main port servicing the area was Shelter Cove. A wharf almost a thousand feet long was built in 1885, but even before then goods flowed in and out, with skiffs coming in to land on the beach. Wagon roads built by Chinese laborers connected Shelter Cove and Needle Rock with points inland. At first, it was mostly the surplus products of the homesteaders that were shipped out: butter, ham and bacon, wool, etc. But when the tanbark industry became prominent around the turn of the century, Shelter Cove became an important commercial port.

From the beginning, Shelter Cove has served as a harbor for small fishing vessels seeking protection from the prevailing northwesterly winds during the summer fishing season. There used to be a fish-processing plant at the end of the wharf in which the catch was cleaned and placed on ice before being sent to distant population centers, and at one time there was also one that processed abalone. Several hundred boats per night would sometimes anchor in the harbor. The fishermen supported a local hotel, where they could enjoy all the comforts of home. According to Lon McKee, who at one time ran the hotel, they were absolute suckers for lemon pie.

Other backwoods commercial ventures included ranching and trapping. The steep meadows interspersed throughout the extensive woodlands were used as pasture for sheep, while cattle grazed in more accessible areas. There was a butcher in Garberville to service the surrounding ranches. No matter what one's summer occu-pation might be—rancher, bark peeler, shake splitter, teamster, fisherman—almost everybody did some hunting and trapping in the winter. Venison was the cheapest available meat, yet good money could be made by trapping martins, fishers, otters, minks, and raccoons and selling their valuable fur coats in town. Deer hides also found an easy market, with fifty cents per skin being paid in 1880. In a single year, one company purchased 34,000 deerskins from the hunters of this area.

There was little specialization in those days. Most men who lived in this neck of the woods tried their hands at all the available occupations at one time or another. Talking to the old-timers who were around during the tanbark boom, I've been impressed by the incredible adaptability one needed just to make a living.

THE EVERYDAY LIFE OF FRED WOLF
(PART 1)

"As you go into Four Corners, you know that house that sits over there? Well, I was born in the inside guts of that house. It's been added on to, but the inside part of it is part of the old cabin. In them days when they built something, they built it to stay. My dad run a saloon right there at Four Corners. But before he was married, he worked in the woods out there, driving teams. The first morning he came out to San Francisco, he got shanghaied and was out on a whaler for ten months. When he got back, he came up to the mines in Trinity County. He was working with an old miner learning to be a powder monkey—use dynamite and what have you. But this old fellow was crippin' dynamite caps with his teeth, and one of them blew the top of his head off. So Dad got outa there and he come to work at Needle Rock—he was gettin' as far away as he could.

"Old Sally Bell, the old squaw with the hundred eleven on her chin,* she brought me into this world in 1901. They had another cabin over there at Four Corners. The doctor had to come from Garberville in a horse and cart; well, the doctor didn't get there and old Sally delivered me. It was three o'clock in the morning, and I was a blue baby. Well, she mumbled something to old Tom in Injun, and he took off. He come back, Dad said, with a bunch of roots about like that and she had a pot of water goin', she threw them roots in there and steeped it up, whatever it was. Dad said just as quick as I took it, I commenced to perk up. Now what it was, I don't know.

"There was eleven of us—nine kids and the folks made eleven. Dad worked out in the woods from April to September for thirty dollars a month, and we lived *good*. On thirty dollars a month, and there was eleven of us! But you had a big winter garden, you raised your own meat, and for extra money you did a little trappin' during the winter, and what you got outa your furs, well, you was that much ahead.

"Up to about 1922–3, we got our groceries twice a year. Come in by boat. You put in your order in April for your summer supply; in September you put in for your winter. You had to stop and figure, because you couldn't go to the grocery store every day. So you had to guess

* All Indian women in northwest California had three lines tattooed on their chins for decoration.

how much flour and sugar that you was gonna have to have for the winter. You bought coffee green, roasted it yourself, and you bought salt in fifty-pound sacks. That was the main staples that you had to buy; meat and everything else you raised.

"It was in the twenties that the boats stopped running, because then they got trucks and what have you to haul in. After they stopped, I hauled in two seven-ton loads of flour from Eureka to Briceland by truck to last through the winter for the store. The speed of your truck in them days was twelve miles an hour in high gear. Old hard-tire trucks. In them early days, if you owned an automobile, in April you could generally get out on the road. In October you set it in the barn and it stayed there, 'cause mud was tit-deep-to-a-nine-foot-Injun going out of here.

"Dad started ranching out here in 'fifteen. Of course you didn't have freezers and what have you, so if you had any beef, that was generally sold. My brother was sixteen years old before he ever eat a beefsteak. But he had lots of venison, he had goat meat, he had plenty of pork and bacon, and all that stuff. Myself, one time I made a ton of ham and bacon that my father sold, and five hundred pounds of lard. He got, I think, twenty cents a pound for ham and bacon. He sold it to the Wagner Leather Company; they used it in their cookhouse and in their bark camps. Lotta hogs that never seen a white man or an Injun, they weighed two to three hundred pounds, and we'd catch 'em and sew their eyes shut. You'd work 'em into the bunch. You'd get 'em over into the corral and cut them two pieces that you had their eyes sewed shut with, and you had the hottest-headed hogs that you ever seen. All he thought about was gettin' the hell outa there, but you could handle him. Not only

A SHEEP FEEDER

that, but we drove turkeys from here to Scotia. No other way to get 'em outa here, so Thanksgiving or Christmas time, you drove 'em. It was quite a chore keeping them birds moving the right way. But unless you could get four, five, six of your neighbors to take part of your beef, you sold it and bought something else. But you had plenty of chickens, turkeys, and smaller stuff. And of course in the wintertime the salmon come up and you get your fish. Game warden didn't bother you too much, unless you got to be a hog or got to selling it, and then some of your neighbors generally squeal on you. But everybody was doing it. Then, if you wanted a piece of meat, you butchered your neighbor's hog, and your neighbor done the same thing. If your hog got over there, he'd butcher it and sell his own. Tit for tat, but that's the way it goes.

But then after the tan oak was all out, there was no acorns to carry your hogs through. For summer feed we used to plant a field of barley or wheat and then let the hogs thresh it—just turn 'em in, and that was it. Then the acorns come along in the fall, and in the spring, when they had a little grease on 'em, that's when you moved them out. But then as the tan oak went out, the hogs had to go, because there was no feed for 'em.

"So then we gradually shifted over to sheep and cattle. But at one time here at Ettersburg, hell, there was two thousand head of milk goats in here. Hogs and goats work pretty fair together. They had a cheese factory down here, but the reason they couldn't make good cheese is that a goat'll eat anything and everything; they eat this and eat that, and it tainted the milk, and

99

when you got tainted milk it's gonna taint every-thing else, so the cheese factory went—kerplunk—on account of the tainted milk. One day they'd be eating peppernuts, which tainted it, and maybe the next day they'd get a manroot, and then the poison oak tainted it to something else. And even a cow: I used to have one cow here, you feed her turnips in the morning and you had turnips in the milk that night, and turnipy milk ain't worth a damn. So then of course everybody around here went into the sheep business, and that's the way it is now to the present day.

"For entertainment, I've seen right in this room here, believe it or not, two sets of qua-drilles dancing. The fiddler'd be standing in that door and the caller'd be standing in that door. People'd start comin' in 'bout four o'clock in the afternoon. Well, the first ones that got here put their horses in the barn, and then as the others come they'd tie 'em up to a fence or a post and start feeding 'em. Everybody'd bring some stuff, cake or what have you, and they'd eat. When the kids wanted to go to bed, they'd just lay them across the bed like cord wood. Then the next morning, some of 'em would have hot cakes, some of 'em would have hot biscuits, a big pot of gravy, fried potatoes, and you always had your venison steaks—you generally always knew you'd have a house party and you'd go out and kill a deer. Then, after breakfast, everybody'd go home. In maybe two weeks, three weeks, some-body else'd give a house party; everybody'd go over there. But now, Christ, you go to a house and: 'What the hell is he after? He must be lookin' for a free meal or somethin'.' But them days, you never thought anything about it. Some-body'd come here: 'Come on in, sit down, have something to eat.' A lot of times, if you come in

about dark: 'We can always find a spare bed—come in and stay for the night.' Now it's a differ-ent story . . . I wonder sometimes . . . it's a hard story. I'm about at the end of my line, so I ain't worrying about what takes place from now on.

"Years ago, there was schools everyplace. There was a school at Shelter Cove, a school at Whitethorn, a school down at Needle Rock, there was a school in here [Ettersburg], and all the way around. Now, there's only a school in White-thorn, and the next one is in Redway. Garberville ain't even got a school. They bus them all around.

"Most of the work that you got here was in the spring. If you was lucky, you could start in the latter part of April and May to building roads into the woods to get your tanbark. Then if you was lucky you could get in there and go to work in the camp, and they generally run to the latter part of September. All of that come out by teams, wagons. Then they had the extract plant in Briceland, they'd haul it in all summer to there.

"At that time, everything was abooming. Safely to say, there was better than a thousand men working in the woods in split stuff. Most of that come out of Needle Rock and Bear Harbor. They had tracks to take it all down that incline. Dur-ing the war years, World War II, all the steel was taken up from those tracks; all the junk, steel, iron, or what have you was all hauled out for war purposes. They had a car and they started at the Piercy end, and they'd take up the rails and all the steel and load it on the car and towed it out to the landing and away it went. When they wound up, they burnt the old flatcar up for the steel that was in it, and they loaded it on too.

"Down at Shelter Cove, they had a big pier. They weren't too big a boats that come into the

GRANDMA BEERBOWER

BURRILL

MR. AND MRS. ERNEST McKEE

ROY AND MABEL CATHEY

GLEN

FRED WOLF

ALDEN

PETER

NANCY AND THE KIDS

cove but they were a fair size. But now, them bluffs has slid off and washed out into there and there ain't near the deep water that there used to be so a good big fishing boat can't get in too close. The pier got done in by storms and what have you. There'd be a bunch of drift come in there, and an old log would commence to get in between the pilings and just pull it to hell. That's the reason them eucalyptus is planted there at one end of Shelter Cove. The torpedoes, they're a worm that eats piling up, and there's enough scent in the eucalyptus that the torpedo won't touch. But fir—they'll go through fir in about, well, they gotta be replaced about every three years, 'cause they eat 'em up. The redwoods will last a little longer.

"The last big year that Shelter Cove had was 1929. There were five hundred fishing boats laying in the bay there at Shelter Cove. I put in five years there on the ranch, and at night I'd come down when they had a big run of fish and work till midnight helping them take care of the fish. They processed, well, they mild-cured. All that stuff, all the fish, went out by boat. The pier was still arunning. They had a dairy down there at one time; they made butter, cheese, what have you, and that was all shipped out by boat, but all the beef there was drove down the coast to Fort Bragg. That one year at the cove, the big one, there was five bootleggers and three whore-houses operating out there for all them fisher-men.

"I seen a lotta funny things happen there at Shelter Cove. To get down to the small boats, they went down through a hole in the wharf. I seen one guy startin' down there with two five-gallon cans of oil in his hands, down this ladder. Well, you know what happened: he didn't have nothin' to hang on to and he hit the ocean—

kerplunk. And I seen guys fishing out there—they'd be drunk and they'd rock back and forth and pretty soon over they go, headfirst. When they come out, they was sober.

"Then everything passed out till the late thirties when the sawmill came. That's when Thorn Valley boomed the last time; that's when the timber went out. It was in the forties, the late thirties or the early forties, that they come into Briceland and started taking this fir timber, and then these other mills sawed fir timber, along with redwood in there. But the fir timber's gone, so now everybody's sittin' and waitin': what's gonna take place now?

"In the thirties, that's when the Okies come in. Well, anybody who come in with a southern drawl was called an Okie. Then after the timber and the logs is gone . . . now they say the hippies are takin' over. So from the Okies to the hippies, well, how long are they gonna last? Time is gonna tell. But I think most of them is here to stay 'cause they's buying property, which the Okies didn't. They'd come in here in the spring when the woods would open up and the mills would get agoing with a beat-up car and a dozen kids and what have you, they'd work the summer out, and then the mills shut down for the winter and they'd go back to Oklahoma or Arkansas. But, as I say, times change.

(The everyday life of Fred Wolf is continued in Chapter Seven.)

THE EVERYDAY LIFE OF GLEN

"There was eight of us boys born that night in Glen County. We was all born on April 27, 1891. One Indian. And we all met in 1915 in Orland. We was all alive then. We had to go up to the rancheria to get the Indian. He couldn't go into the saloons, of course. He'd stay in the back alley. We'd go from one saloon to the other, and he'd be at the back door and we'd hand a drink to him. It was a felony to give an Indian a drink of whiskey. So somebody'd hold a glass of whiskey out there and it was gone—he didn't see who got it. Now I'm the only one left out of the eight. The Indian—he's dead too. They're all dead but me. I'm the last one. I got a birthday coming up —be eighty-one pretty quick.

"They always called me Glen 'cause Glen County was formed the year I was born. I really don't know whether it was my first name or not. They didn't have no birth certificates when I was born—not until 1907 here in California. I heard them argue it when I was a kid; my mother'd say my first name was Glen and my father'd say my first name was Frank (that's an uncle of mine). Damned if I knew which it was: G.F. or F.G. I grew up and I didn't know the difference. I had to establish it myself.

"We was on a homestead when I was young. Hell of a life. Christ, we'd never see nobody for months. It wasn't too well settled in that county at that time. Back in the nineties, you know. It was twelve miles to town, and I had to go to town once a week. That's a twenty-four-mile ride on horseback. Get the mail, and took a weekly paper. Had to get that weekly paper. It was 1897 when I can really remember it. The Spanish-American War was agoing on, and also the gold strike in the Yukon was on. They was all excited about the war. I didn't give a damn about the war, the Yukon was what I was interested in.

"My father used to run steam engines out in the valley—thrashing grain with them thrashing machines. Sometimes he'd have a sixty-, sixty-five-day run out there in those days. And we

lived up on the homestead. Of course we had horses and wagons to go anywhere we wanted to go. But that was a great life for a kid. I killed deer when I was seven and a half years old. With a rifle. It was pretty near a must: if you want some meat to eat, you had to go kill a deer, or else kill a critter. I was a tough little kid, let me tell you. Sometimes it was catch a jackrabbit or no breakfast. Didn't butcher our cattle much. No way to keep it, except only jerk it. Sometimes there'd be three or four families, and then we'd butcher one. Each take a part of it, and get along pretty good that way.

"Dad never did have over a thousand head of cattle. But that was quite a little bunch itself. Never sold them till they was four-year-olds— big steers, you know. Raised them right off the graze—never fed them a mouthful of nothing. It was a profitable way. You didn't get too much for cattle; nevertheless, it didn't cost you much to raise them. Just your time—taking care of them.

"It was about a four and a half or five days' cattle drive to the railroad. We sold to a local butcher there. There was a big butcher outfit: Snow, Bush and Wineridge—I'll never forget them as long as I live. They had the first gas engine I ever saw. Run their ice plant. That was back in the nineties. They'd light a match to start it. They'd keep lighting matches and keep turning it over and it'd fire and pop and snap and bang and pretty soon it would run. And that kept their refrigerator room—they had a big walk-in refrigerator. It was a big outfit. Old-time Germans, you know. Old-country Germans—they knew how to handle meat.

"And we put in . . . oh—probably six months in the mountains every year. Hair clear down to here when we'd come back. We always tried to get all the cattle out of the mountains by Thanksgiving. We'd put them back on the winter range then. They winter down there, and next spring when it begin to get hot and when the flies get bad in the valley you'd have to fight them old cows to keep them out of the mountains. They'd go up there themselves. If you kept them down there in the winter range, they'd eat all the feed up and you wouldn't have no feed for them next winter. Had to let the new grass come up. Those days they didn't overpasture the land. When you pulled your stock out, there was always plenty of feed left. It wasn't nothing to move four, five hundred head of cattle. Thought nothing of it. We had dogs. Dogs did seventy-nine percent of the work.

"Up in the mountains, we had to guard the stock from bears and cats. Our dogs would tree the cats, then we'd come by and shoot them. Bears were a big problem. Bear would come by and chase a whole herd of sheep and gulch them: the sheep would run into a gulley faster than they could get out. Ran the wheelers on top before the leaders* could get up the other side. Sheep'd just pile up and smother themselves. So we'd hunt the bear and eat the meat. We didn't know nothing of that trichina bug. Made mighty good jerky. You take a bear and skin him, though, and he looks almost human.

"When we was up in the mountains, me and the old man built ourselves a log cabin. I was just a kid and old Ferrerra, he done all the hard work, you know. I just went along and . . . well, I was only seven years old. Of course, I was a lot of help to him because he couldn't get around

---

* The various horses and mules of a team were called "wheelers" (those close to the wagon), "leaders" (those at the head), and "stretchers" (those in between).

and I could. And then there's a lot of work I couldn't do and he could. So building the cabin, we went up in the timber and cut the poles and then I had a mule and I'd sled them down and set the long ones on the sides of the cabin and the short ones across the ends. We cut them and peeled them first, then he measured them off and notched them and then we rolled them up. As soon as it got too high, we put up skids. Put the rope around the logs and then pulled them up with the mule when it got too high for us. We couldn't lift them—they was too heavy so we pulled them up with the mule.

"We went and cut down a big sugar pine and made the shakes—they was about thirty inches long—and put the roof on. Chinked it all up with mud and moss. Took the moss off the trees and made a muck out of it. When you put the poles up you lay the moss in there and that stops the breeze from going through—a lot, anyways.

"We built two cabins facing one another, and left a porch between them—about twelve feet— so there was a dry place to saddle your horses. You kept your saddles and equipment and everything in there. We built a fireplace in each end out of country rock or slate rock. Packed in windows, and we packed in a big range—took it all to pieces and packed that in and put it up after we got there. Had a good stove to cook on and didn't have to cook in the fireplace. We had a very nice, comfortable place up there. We didn't have much to do till it was time to get the cattle out of the mountains—we could just build that cabin.

"We had a big garden. Had a big spring up above and took poles and took a round-nosed chisel and gutted them out. Laid one pole on top of the other—oh, it was a hundred yards or so— run it right down to the cabin and had a barrel setting right there on the porch. It kept the barrel full all the time, and it run over and run out into his garden. He was quite a gardener.

"We had lots of horses, too. We had maybe thirty, thirty-five head of mares. Stallions run right with them. In the spring we'd let them run for a couple of months, then pick them up. We'd keep the stallions for a couple of years, then we'd trade with somebody. So we wouldn't inbreed our horses, see? We always had lots of saddle stock to ride. All you had to do is go out and run 'em off the range and put 'em in the corral. Take out what you want and break it. I was riding horses when I was ten years old. Break them. Sometimes I'd get throwed off, but I'd stay with them. Get up and get on again. That was quite a life . . .

"Mother raised six, seven hundred head of turkeys a year. Just at daylight they'd leave the roost. There was so many coyotes . . . if you wasn't there every day, you just didn't raise no turkeys. The coyotes'd eat 'em. You stayed with them till they'd go in the shade till about four and then they'd take off again. If they was heading away from home, you had to be there to head them back towards home. There's nothing, 'less it's a sheep, that's crazier than a turkey. You take a turkey come to a fence: he'll walk up and down that fence all day, back and forth, trying to get through. Night comes, and he'll fly up on top of the fence and roost. But he ain't got sense enough to fly up there in the daytime to get over. Just keeps looking through the cracks in the pickets, trying to get through. That was Mother's project, this turkey business. They used to get maybe three dollars and a half a bird.

"In 1900 we moved to Lake County. Dad got himself a stump puller. Lake County was all a big growth of timber when we came. He could

TOM-FOOLS

pull a stump four foot across. There was so much pasture to clear around there, he done all right. Made a living for the family that way. He was quite a guy—always taking contracts.

"I went to school in Lake County, and after I graduated from ninth grade, then I took off. I went to the Orient and—hell, I'd been to the Orient and back when I was fourteen years old. Shipped out of San Francisco on a transport. Took about three months roundtrip. We went to Philippines and China and Japan and . . . Hawaii, Guam, Midway—all through there. Worked as a waiter for thirty-five dollars a month. Worked in the second cabin. Pack suitcases aboard for them officers, you know. Sell the boat if you can—any way to make money.

"I came back and went into rice over here in Sacramento Valley. Lost all my money farming

104

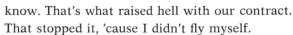

rice 1919–20. Never got it in the warehouse, even. It started raining and never did quit. I wasn't alone—there was thousands of them went broke same as I did. Of course it was during its infancy then; people didn't know how to raise rice. We was just learning. They couldn't get the ground dry enough to get on the ground to work their grain. Too muddy. Afterwards, they got to planting it earlier and draining their fields better and cutting it with a combine. But the weather is what done it to me. That whole valley was a sheet of water clear across it, like a lake. It was before they got their drain ditches in good so they could drain their rice.

"After the rice I went to shooting ducks for the market. Me and two other fellas. I made five thousand dollars in two months shooting ducks. Sell 'em in San Francisco. Take a load of ducks down and bring a load of whiskey back. Get 'em going and coming.

"I put in eighteen months down in South America after that—Peru. Building a railroad across the top of that wild rubber forest. On the west coast of South America, there's wild rubber forests in there. Thousands and thousands of acres. Worked for an English outfit. Twelve and a half thousand feet up that railroad was.

"I been to Guatemala, too. I met a guy who had a contract with Folger's Coffee Company. We was gonna fly that coffee from inland out to ocean where they can get it on the boats. They used to pack it out; Christ, it would take them three weeks to pack a load out from them plantations. We was gonna make an airport out there. This fella was a good aviator, but he got barnstorming—looping the loop, you know, and doing a lot of stunts—and once he came down looping the loop and he never did come out of it. Stuck it in the ground. Whatever happened, I don't

know. That's what raised hell with our contract. That stopped it, 'cause I didn't fly myself.

"First time I come up this way, I was only a kid. Dad and I was the first ones come through on this road. The road wasn't quite connected down here by Squaw Creek, but we drove through anyway. We was just ahoboing; he just wanted to go on a trip. Dad said he was hunting a job, but he kept his eyes shut. He didn't look for no job—he just wanted to see old Uncle Bill.

"In 1909, I came up here. Peeling tanbark. We cut all the tanbark out of this country. They had a plant over in Briceland that took the extract out of the bark—just like syrup. Put it through a distill and took it out and put it in hogsheads and shipped the hogsheads to Stockton. They were big wide barrels like that, but not too high. Wagner Leather Company. Instead of hauling the bark down there, he moved his plant up here where the bark was and just hauled the extract.

"I'd haul the hogsheads over the hills to Shelter Cove, and I'd haul groceries and hay and everything else back there. Boats would come in and unload—there was a big warehouse there in Shelter Cove. You was loaded both ways: haul extract over and haul hay and grain back. They had a hundred and fifty head of mule here had to be fed—you know, to pack bark out of the rough canyons where they couldn't get at it with a sled. They had these bark hooks to keep the load on the mules. Turn the mule loose and he'd go for the bark pile to get that load off his back. Some of 'em get lazy and lay down. Then you have to unload him and kick him in the ass and make him get up and load him again. I could show you old pack trails out there now where they packed bark for a mile or more. But mostly, where they could, they'd sled it down to where they could get to it with a wagon.

"It was all horses back in those days. No roads —just horses and mules. You could pack anything on a horse if you make up your mind to it. But I prefer mules, for packing and for teaming too. I had some good horse teams too, but take it all the way through I prefer mules. Had one pack mule followed me everywhere I went—no rope or nothing. We'd drive ten, twelve head of mule with just one line—what they call a jerk line. Jerk that line and say, 'Gee, gee.' Line is attached to the leader, and when he feels that pull he turns. The teams all had these hames, the ones with the bells on 'em, and they'd be ringing in time with the steps. You'd hear the other fella's bell acomin', and you'd pull off to the side soon as you could. Then they started coming in with automobiles on the wagon roads. We used to spend most of our time back in those days leading horses and mules past them automobiles.

"I seen that whole country out by Briceland piled with bark just as high as they could pile it. They had sheds over it, because the rain'd ruin it. Wash the tannic acid out and you lose most of it if it rains on it all winter. They had sheds down there with driveways through it so they could drive the teams in and unload it. Then they ground it and put it in a vat and cooked it to a certain extent. Then they'd pitch it into a big distill. Christ, that distill was ten feet across. Just the same as a whiskey still. And they'd put a fire under it and chase this tannic acid out and trap it. There's more tannic acid in this tan oak than in any other kind of bark. They use birch back east, but it's nothing compared with this tan oak. And it's easy to peel, too, if the sap's up. Hotter the day the better the peel.

"Five years I come up here. Work only in the summer when the sap's up, so they could peel the tree. Peeled with a poleax. You fall the tree and then ring it at four-foot lengths, ring it around both ways, take off sometimes a whole ring without ever breaking it. We chopped all our trees down with an ax. After you got broke in you'd walk up to a tree and chop it down without ever stopping. You had a partner, of course—two of you generally peeled together. Generally a right- and left-handed man. Never got in a jam that way.

"You lived out in camps. They had contracts. Like if you could savvy that bark peeling and you could handle men, and the company got confidence in you, they'd give you a contract to peel a forty or eighty or one-sixty. They furnished everything and give you so much. It was up to you to figure it out. You hired the men and kept them fed and everything. If you handled it right you could make good money.

"They had camps for the split stuff, too. Ties, posts, shakes, stakes—just about everything. Used to make seven-foot posts. Used to get fourteen cents apiece. Six-foot posts are just too damn short to make a fence. By the time you put two feet in the ground, you ain't got nothing above. Seven-foot posts, you put two feet in the ground and you still got five feet above and that makes a pretty fair fence.

"I made lots of shakes, too—twenty-five in a bunch. Split just like a ribbon, some of them trees. Three sixteenths of an inch thick, split clear through thirty-six inches, come out on the other end three sixteenths of an inch. Perfect all the way through.

"I drove teams from out of Indian Creek to Needle Rock two different years. Six horses and two wagons down that old road from Low Gap. All the ties and bark and shakes and pickets came out of there and went down to Needle Rock and was loaded onto boats. I run that slacker down

PACKING OUT THE TANBARK

there, too. You put that line on the mast and put your load on it, but you had to stop it somehow before it took the mast off the ship. Lots of split stuff they shipped from Needle Rock. Stewart and McKee operated it.

"We'd leave Needle Rock at two thirty in the morning. Be off in the woods by daylight. Make two trips a day sometimes. For amusement we'd . . . buck ties. Handling bark and splitting stuff, that's the amusement. But I did have a gal up at Shelter Cove once. Went up on Saturday night after quitting time and be back Sunday night. No sleep—just dogging around.

"In those days, you didn't drink very much. You couldn't. Christ, it was too hard to work. You haul a hundred and seventy-five to two

hundred ties, you load it up and unload it twice a day, and take care of that team—you didn't want to chase around. You was plenty willing to go to bed, because you didn't get through till ten o'clock and you was on the road again the next morning at two thirty. You didn't hardly sleep—might as well trade your blankets off for a lantern. I don't know how you lived, but you did. I never was sick.

"There never was a saloon in Needle Rock to my knowledge, but fella had a saloon out in Gopherville. Old Bill Hamlin made several fortunes right there in Gopherville. Had a hotel woman—she run the hotel. Two bits a meal, all there. Old Bill run the saloon, and he had a you could eat. Good food, too. Man never went by old Bill's hungry and dry. He'd always feed you, regardless. Even if you was broke, he'd always feed you and give you all you wanted to drink. Of course when you got paid off, you was supposed to spend a little money with him, too. He made several fortunes there, and lost it all playing poker. Died in a poorhouse up in Eureka.

"They had a big fire out there by Needle Rock in . . . I think it was 1913. Damn near burnt my dad and I up. We just did get out. We come north towards Four Corners—fire was just coming over that ridge. Bear come up out of that canyon that runs down to Needle Rock. All fire and smoke. He run right across between the wheelers and the leaders—right across the stretchers. Jesus, did that scare them mules. They doubled their speed after that bear went across there. Lots of deer come up out of there— wild hogs, quail, everything. Burned up lots of quail, grouse. It laid the woods off about three or four weeks before they got the road open again. Seems like a long time ago. Seems more like a dream than it does in reality. Think back on it now . . .

"Later on we used to fish out of Shelter Cove. I fished two years for the market. During Prohibition, so I hauled whiskey most of the time. Made lots of money hauling whiskey. Three or four boats laying out there twenty-five miles— you just go out, get a load, and bring her in. They had big stills working on the boat. Label it Canadian Whiskey. They had labels for everything—any kind you want. Go out there and bring it in—it was a cinch you could sell it. Went down one time and got a load of tequila. Nine dollars a case down there, brought it up and sold it for ninety-six dollars a case. Four days and four nights on board ship. That was good times then. When I was gonna go out and get a

load of whiskey, I'd fish all day with no hooks on the line—just go round and round. Finally I was the last boat, I'd go out to the mother ship, get a load of whiskey, and come on in. Wouldn't even tell my brother when I was gonna do it. Them hijackers was pretty bad. They get you and knock you in the head and take your load of whiskey and scuttle your boat and sink it. They was dangerous. I wasn't scared of the Revenue— it's them hijackers I was scared of, 'cause they kill you for a load of whiskey. We had a Lewis machine gun—when we'd get a load, we'd always set her up. We never had to use it, but we always had it set up.

"During the Depression I had a sheep ranch. Had a thousand head of sheep. Couldn't sell no wool, but I just stored it and after the Depression was over, I sold it. It was thirty-five cents a pound, and in two months it went to six bits a pound—after I had held it for three years. And I worked for the Forest Service, too. Built lots of roads for them when they had the C.C.C. camps.

"I worked for W. P. Fuller, the paint man. Used to go out with his boy—taught him to hunt and fish. Give me ten dollars a day for that. All during school vacation, I was with the kid.

"And I had lots of hunters, policemen mostly, would come up from Oakland and San Francisco to my place to go hunting. I had eighteen head of horses; I could pack them anywhere. If they had the money, I could pack them anywhere. Or kill them a buck if I had to. They'd come up and stay with me a week or two on their vacation, and, hell, I'd get a hundred dollars apiece out of them before they got away. No, I never felt the Depression.

"That was a good deal up there. The sheep were more or less velvet to me. Oh, you had to take care of them. The old lady stayed on the ranch most of the time, and I had a couple of nephews stay with her, and they took care of the sheep. One year there came a big snow. I always was prepared for it—had lots of hay and grain, you know. Five foot of snow. If I hadn't had a barn full of hay, I'd have been out of the sheep business that year. But I brought 'em through. Raised ninety percent lambs, too. Lambed in January, five below zero. Sonofabitch, if that wasn't a winter! I worked one shift and the old lady worked the other; I worked the night shift and she worked the day shift when we was lambing. You had to be right there because the lamb would freeze that quick. I raised the barn up seven feet, put a false floor in, and when I put the hay in I put it on top of that. I had my lambing shed underneath all that hay. Then when the snow banked up around the barn, why, it was warm as toast in there. But between there and the house it wasn't warm, by a hell of a lot. Chopped wood to keep the old fireplace going.

"It was thirty miles to a store. When the snow got on top of the mountains, you didn't get out till spring. We was three thousand feet up. Buy groceries twice a year, spring and fall.

"During the winter, I'd trap. One winter my brother and I trapped and we had eight hundred dollars' worth of fur in the spring. Foxes, cats, 'coons, mink, fisher, mountain lion, bear, everything. Of course the bear hibernate 'long about the first of December, and you don't see any more of them till spring. They're just about coming out now. A few sunshiny days in April, that brings them out.

"In those days, it was pack trails. There was no roads way up there at all. That's what I had all those horses for—to pack these hunters. Pack their game out and pack their whiskey and pro-

visions in; they always had a few provisions, but mostly whiskey. During Prohibition, they had their own bootlegger used to come up there with them. Cops, from Oakland. They sure had it fixed.

"It was all right, I guess. At the time it was all right. But I just got tired of being out in that brush. Why sometimes it'd be three, four months before you ever saw anybody.

"I used to go north harvesting. I was clear up into Saskatchewan one year. Used to go to Calgary to the stampede every fall. It's a rodeo, really, is what it is. There's a big buffalo feed: butcher buffalo and barbecue them. It was a nice trip. One year I met a schoolmate of mine up there. He was gonna go moose hunting. Christ, it was twenty below. I wouldn't even get out of the house. I stayed in the house with the old man. 'You fellas go moose hunting if you want to. I'm not. I ain't lost no moose.' They went, and they killed one.

"Been up to Alaska, too. Used to get salmon bellies for free up there. I'd pack them with salt in a five-gallon can and solder it up. They'd keep forever that way.

"I worked for the railroad for five years. C.W.R.N. California Western Navigation Railroad. From Willits to Fort Bragg and up in the woods. I'd run locomotive up there: freight, passenger. Run everything, logging too.

"Later I come up here and got into logging. Been in logging ever since. Christ, I done everything: I'd run a loading machine, run the Cat, run locomotive. Everything. I built all them roads for years—all up and down the Mattole and where you turn off up there by China Creek —I built all them logging roads. Wore out three Cats. All new Cats, too, to start with.

"Guess I done most everything. Doesn't seem

like much, though, just one thing after the other. There's a lot to do out here."

While the men were out peeling the bark, driving the teams, splitting the shakes, hunting the deer, catching the fish, trapping the 'coons, and running the whiskey, what were the women doing? Mostly, it seems, they stayed at home and kept things going.

THE EVERYDAY LIFE OF GRANDMA BEERBOWER

"I was an orphan. My mother died when I was eight and my father died when I was twelve. After that I just lived around wherever anyone would let me. I went to work for a woman in Eureka to take care of her baby. I had my room and board and three dollars a month.

"When I was fifteen I starting working for real wages. I worked here in Garberville in the old Exchange Hotel. Before that I came to Briceland and worked in the hotel there. And in Briceland there used to be a bark plant, you know. I worked in the cookhouse there.

"I was only seventeen when I got married. My husband was thirty-two years old. Every time I mention that I have to laugh, because it was so funny. His mother was an old lady, you see. Oh, she was in her seventies, and that was considered pretty old them days. We couldn't get no license to get married because I was underage. I had to get somebody to sign the paper. Nobody wanted to be responsible for it, you know. So anyway, we were walking down the road, before we were married, my husband and his mother and

I. So he wanted his mother to sign this paper so we could get our license to get married. She always called him 'Hickey Boy.' I always have to laugh when I think about it. She says, 'Why, Hickey Boy, you don't want to get married yet— you're nothing but a boy!' He was thirty-two years old.

"But he got her to sign it, and we got our license and got married. She was an awfully nice old lady. We moved on the home ranch up there, and she lived with us.

"It was horse and buggy or horseback back in those days. There was no automobiles here then. Hitch two horses to a big wagon, you know. Put the kids in the back. My husband and I'd sit up on the front seat. We'd throw the blankets in the back and the kids could lay down and go to sleep if they want to or sit up and play or fight or cry or whatever they wanted to do. They had the whole back part of the wagon.

"We'd meet somebody else coming with a wagon and team and the men'd stop and put on their brakes and wrap their lines around and sit there and light their pipes and have a nice conversation. The kids'd all jump out of the wagon and be climbing up trees and be having fun. Men had a visit right in the middle of the road. There wouldn't be anybody come along that way; maybe we'd meet two or three people between here and Eureka. We'd get ready to go and we'd find the little boys up in the trees.

"My son owns the old ranch where we lived first, where my first husband and I lived. My children were all born up there. It's been in the Marshal name ever since it left the government. My father-in-law and his sons took it up as homestead, see? I always wanted to see the old ranch stay in the Marshal name as long as possible, so I gave my son the clear deed to it and

GRANDMA BEERBOWER'S HOME

he has it now. And he's got a son and his son's got three sons so it can stay in the Marshal name for a good many years yet."

"Did you give birth to your children right up there on the ranch? Did you go to a hospital?"

"No, we didn't go to no hospital. A woman come to take care of us when we had a baby, a midwife. No, I never had no doctor; I don't have none yet. Never had much use for a doctor."

"When did you move to this ranch?"

"Well, after my husband died. I guess he was dead two or three years. Beerbowers owned this place. Couple of bachelors. Men, you know.

Neither one of them had ever been married. My husband and one of these Beerbowers used to work together all the time on their ranches. So a couple of years after my husband died I married Mr. Beerbower. He was a good friend of my husband's and a good man so I married him. I was with him for several years, and then he died. Don't know exactly how many years it was that we were married. I married older men both times. I never liked boys; I always thought they was crazy. They talked silly. So that's why I'm an old widow. If I married a younger man, maybe I'd still be married. I'm eighty-six now.

My family wants me to go to a rest home, but I want to rest right here in my own home.

"I would have liked to see this place here stay a ranch. The airport and all in through here used to be part of the ranch. But when the county wants something, you know, they just take it. They bought it and paid us what they wanted to, not what it's worth. We had cattle and horses and sheep and big gardens and cornfields and a big orchard. Where that airport is, there must have been seventy-five or eighty fruit trees right out there. And on up further was a big grainfield and corn. We raised all that kind of stuff. But it was the only level land around here for an airport and they wanted it and they just took it."

"Did you grind your own flour from the grain?"

"Oh, no. All that corn and grain and stuff, we fed it to the animals. And sold some of it, too. We had about four horses and we always had cows to milk, you know. So we used to sell our milk. Lots of milk. A big barn right out here back of the house and another one on over further, they'd fill them plumb full of hay. An old corn crib, they'd fill it plumb full of corn. And they feed that out in the wintertime. Just a regular ranch."

"What did the women do out on the ranch?"

"Oh, they just kept house. That's all I ever done."

"What did keeping house entail? What did you do? Did you can food and—"

"Why, sure, we canned fruit. I still can fruit. I just canned five or six quarts of applesauce yesterday. And I canned some plums and peaches about a week ago. Canned about twenty-five or thirty quarts already. I'm looking for some pears now."

"What other kinds of work did you do?"

"Oh, we just kept house and raised our kids and canned fruit and vegetables and stuff to eat in the wintertime and just took care of our house. Same way we do now."

"Did you used to make your own clothes?"

"Oh, yes. I made all my children's clothes. My own, too. I still make clothes for myself a whole lot."

"Did you make the material?"

"No. You bought the material and then made 'em yourself."

Grandma Beerbower likes to show visitors what's left of the old ranch. It's only a couple of acres, but many of the outbuildings are still standing. There's the greenhouse, which used to be headquarters for the roadside garden that Grandma Beerbower ran several years ago. Then there's the bunkhouse: "This is where the hired men stayed when they came in here to shear sheep and cut the hay." The milk shed: "We had a separator and everything. Had enough to run our own little dairy." The corncrib: "We'd back the wagon right up and fill it full." The pump house: "You can't see the tank, but it's up there somewhere." The woodshed: "My son comes down and leaves me some wood now and then." As we walk around, we notice some men working on the other side of the fence, over by the airport. We go over to investigate.

"Whatcha cutting down my fig tree for?"

"We had complaints from people who couldn't see the sign."

"Well, that tree's given us lots of figs." Grandma turns to me. "The county owns it now, so there's nothing to do about it."

We return to the house, where Grandma Beerbower shows us her kitchen. "I've cooked for lots of men on this cookstove. Used up lots of wood. Of course, there's this little electric stove now that I use just for myself." Hanging on the wall over the stoves is a china replica of a teakettle with the inscription: "Caution—Woman at Work."

Grandma Beerbower has a scrapbook, or rather a scrap box, filled with pictures and clippings she's collected over the years. As we're looking through the snapshots, I ask, "How many grandchildren do you have?"

"Well, I'd have to stop and figure. I got some greats and some great-greats, too." The photos range across so many generations that it's hard to keep them straight. We come across a picture of a young woman standing by a horse, and Grandma Beerbower becomes puzzled; "You know, I really don't know whether that's me or my daughter."

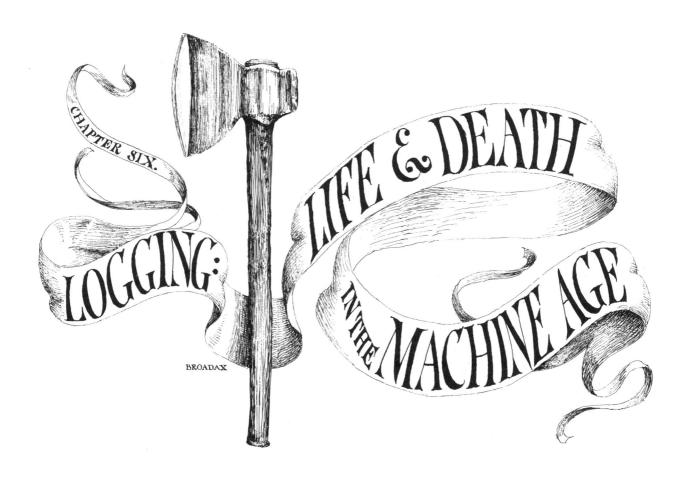

CHAPTER SIX.

LOGGING: LIFE & DEATH IN THE MACHINE AGE

BROADAX

Nagaicho made this world and patted it down
so everything would stay in place. But bad men
were not satisfied and tore it down, tore up
the trees, tore down the mountains.

—From a Sinkyone legend

The bark-peeling industry was particularly well suited to the back hills, where the only arteries of transportation were mule trails and infrequent wagon roads. No matter how remote the region, a mule trail could probably be carved out without too much trouble and connected to the nearest road. The mammoth first-growth forests of redwood and Douglas fir, however, presented a much greater problem.

THE EVERYDAY LIFE OF THE EARLY LOGGER

In order to turn the trees into lumber, men had to find a way of transporting the gigantic logs out of the forests. At first, teams of oxen hauled the logs to the nearest mill, river, or railroad; later, around the turn of the century, horses

THE BULL TEAM

gradually replaced the oxen. But neither horses nor oxen could slide logs over the loose dirt and mud on the forest floor, so skid roads had to be prepared by laying out small logs side by side and adzing off a smooth surface. The "bull-whacker" or "bullpuncher" (the name varied from place to place) then connected several logs to each team by cables and drove the teams out on the wooden roads. The job of swabbing oil on the skids to minimize friction was usually reserved for the youngest boys in camp.

Before a tree was even cut, a path had to be cleared where it was expected to fall. The "fell-ers" then wedged springboards into the trunk several feet off the ground so they wouldn't have to cut through the broader base of the tree. Standing on these springboards, they chopped out large undercuts and then sawed through from the opposite side, using saws up to fourteen feet long. Particularly large trees took several days to fell, and sometimes even a little powder was used to "tip the balance." Once a tree was on the ground, the "buckers" sawed it into thirty-two-foot lengths and removed the branches. Clearings, chutes, or even separate skid roads had to be made to guide the logs to a place where they could be attached to teams. Jacks and peaveys were used to turn the logs over and start them rolling downhill, but the logs might spring loose at any time and the loggers were in constant danger of being crushed.

The transportation of the logs was facilitated in the early years of the twentieth century by the invention of the "steam donkey," a steam-driven engine that replaced the horses and bulls. With the added power of the machine and a bit of Yankee ingenuity, the loggers soon discovered it was possible to lift the logs up off the ground, thus eliminating problems of mud and friction. An elaborate cable network was set up to raise the logs overhead, using the trunks of still-standing trees as anchors. With time, these "stump rigs" moved higher and higher up the trunks to achieve greater leverage. The method was perfected with the "spar tree" system that is still in occasional use today. Using spurs and a rope, the "topper" boosted himself up the most formidable tree around and cut off its top. The "high lead" was then fastened to this spar tree, which had been trimmed of all its branches. A complex system of cables extended down from the high lead and eventually reached the ground, where the "choker setters" fastened the cables to the logs. When everything was ready to go, the "whistle punk" pulled the whistle line to notify the "donkey puncher" that it was time to hoist the log away.

Even in the early days, logging was an elaborate affair requiring the coordinated efforts of several men working at different jobs. In addition to the loggers themselves, there were also the "saw filers" (whom no one could afford to antagonize for fear of being stuck with a dull-bladed saw), the "donkey doctors" (mechanics), the "woods boss" (foreman), and, of course, the cooks. Up to two hundred men at a time lived together in the logging camps, where they received both room and board. The food made up in quantity what it lacked in quality, with flapjacks and meat served in abundance to keep the loggers' work energy at a high level. If there was a railroad near the logging area, the camps consisted of special bunk and dining cars which could be moved from place to place on the tracks. The camps were sometimes shut down during the winter months when logging became too difficult, leaving the men to find homes in shanty towns that sprang up around the skid roads near the mills. This, it appears, is the origin of the term "skid row."

Logging operations of this sort were limited to areas in which a railroad could be built or water transportation was easily accessible. There were a few mills along the coastline in the 1800s, but other than that there was little large-scale logging in this immediate area until easier methods of transporting the logs were found. Thus, although the tan oak forests in the back hills were for the most part destroyed in the early 1900s, the large stands of redwood and Douglas fir were left virtually intact. Some of the redwoods, of course, were cut down for split stuff, but this was a small-time operation compared with the logging that was going on in the lowlands.

It was the introduction of automotive transportation, and in particular the Caterpillar or bulldozer, that opened up the backwoods to logging. A "Cat" could build almost instantane-

250 FEET UP~

TOPPING A SPAR TREE

ously roads that formerly took a crew long days of hard labor with picks, shovels, and wheelbarrows. The logs could simply be "snaked" out behind the powerful Cat, which didn't require a log base on the skid roads to minimize friction. Once out of the steepest hills, the logs could be loaded on trucks and easily driven to distant mills. With instant roads, mechanized power to drag the logs, and trucking, no forest became too remote for extreme logging operations. The back hills no longer enjoyed the safety of inaccessibility.

After the introduction of Cats in logging operations, it was only a matter of time before the first-growth stands of redwood and Douglas fir were exhausted. The forests had always seemed so extensive, so impressive, and often so remote, that no one had ever really given much thought to the possibility of their exhaustion. In the 1890s, logging operations in Humboldt County turned the redwood trees into 200,000,000 board feet of lumber each year and scarcely a dent was made in the seemingly limitless forests. At that rate, the first-growth redwoods would have lasted another two centuries—and nobody even bothered to touch the Douglas fir. Indeed, children were sometimes paid a penny apiece to kill fir trees by ringing their bark so the land could be used for agricultural pursuits.

Logging in this area got under way in a serious manner toward the end of the 1930s, stimulated by the pre-World War II economic boom. Timber was in high demand. Several years before that, new synthetic tanning processes had closed down the tanbark industry. For about a decade there had been little economic activity to speak of around here, and the population had correspondingly dwindled. The new boom saw more people than ever before flood into the area to work in

TUCKED INSIDE THE GULCH:
THE SAW MILL

the woods, to drive the Cats, to run the mills. At one time, five mills were operating in Whitethorn alone, and others were scattered throughout the area. At the peak of the boom, there were perhaps a thousand people living in the Whitethorn Valley. Whitethorn itself, like most logging towns, became something of a hot spot, with several saloons and brothels to service the loggers.

Many of the newcomers were Okies—dispossessed Dust Bowl workers who looked for jobs wherever they could find them. The Okies survived as best they could, often taking advantage of the free and abundant wildlife they found in the woods. The land furnished them with both jobs and food, and they took what they could get from it as long as it lasted.

For the more settled inhabitants, automotive transportation had revolutionized their lifestyles. Cats and trucks had made the new logging boom feasible, and now private cars made it possible for the men to live at home while working in the woods. No longer was it necessary to leave home and family for months at a time; each night the rigors of work in the woods could

THE PEAVEY ~ FOR PRYING & ROLLING TIMBER

be balanced by all the comforts of home. Commuting had come to the back hills.

In the slow-moving time of forests that have been growing for centuries, the logging boom was over almost before it began. It took only twenty years to exhaust enough of the first-growth stands of timber to make further logging unprofitable. By the end of the 1950s, the boom had begun to fade. Just as the tanbark boom had come and gone, the logging came and went.

Today there are a few scattered mills along

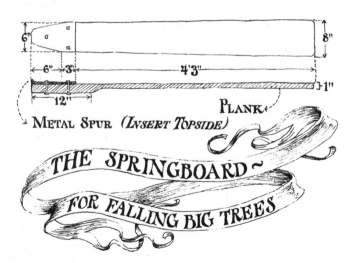

METAL SPUR (Insert Topside)   PLANK

THE SPRINGBOARD ~ FOR FALLING BIG TREES

Highway 101, but all the mills off in the back-country have been abandoned for several years. A concrete slab covering several acres of land where a mill used to stand, a caved-in shack at the bottom of a steep canyon, rusted cables in the underbrush, an old automobile abandoned by the side of a road that has long since become impassable—signs of the short-lived logging era can still be seen throughout the countryside. The forests themselves are now brushland criss-crossed with logging roads, dotted with stumps, and lined with fallen logs that for one reason or another were left behind. Also left behind were the loggers themselves. For those who were too old to move on to more lucrative areas, the excitement of work in the woods has been replaced by the routine of collecting pensions. Every day at eleven o'clock the mail is put into the post office boxes in Whitethorn, and every day from ten thirty to eleven several of the old-timers drive into town and wait around to see if perhaps something new will come into their lives. I approached one of the old-timers, hoping to strike up a conversation. He was practically deaf, however, and the extent of our conversation was his repeated proclamation: "I don't work." Some of the other old-timers elaborated on his theme.

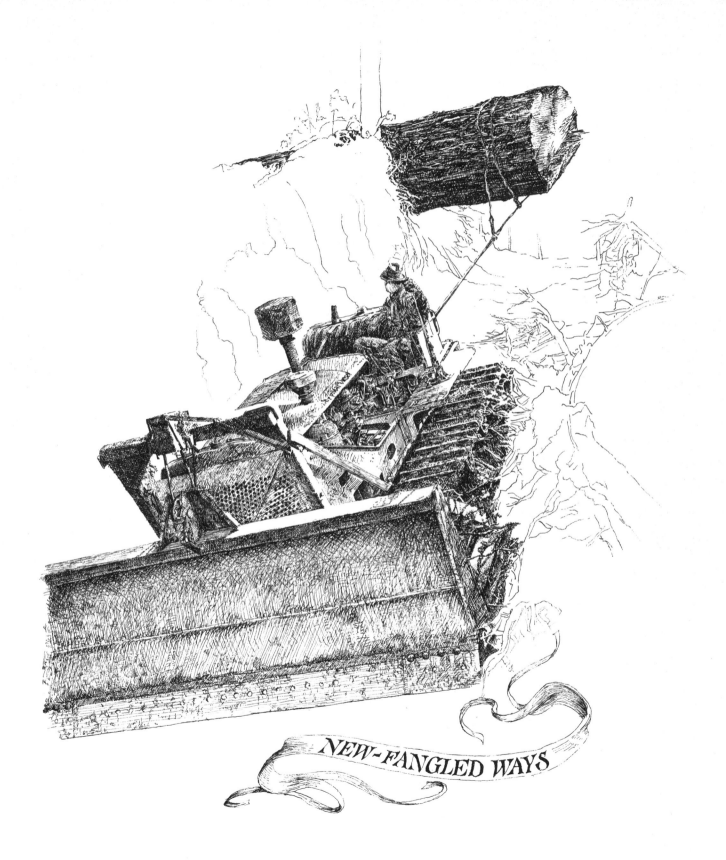

NEW-FANGLED WAYS

THE EVERYDAY LIFE
OF FRANK
(PART 2)

"Machine age now. Workingman is done for. Six Cats do more work than all the Chinamen in China. No manpower now. Don't need men no more. When the machine starts taking a man's place, what can a man do? People gone crazy with nothing to do. Damn it—I'm going crazy too!

"All these young folks around, and no work. Then there's all these snags messing up the streams. Government should give them work cleaning up the country. Not twelve or thirteen hours a day like I used to do, just four or five.

"Government's gotta change. We fought Hitler, now we got Hitler. Sitting down in the White House smoking big cigars and making the poor people fight—and making money too!"

Frank left home at the age of fourteen to work in the woods. Like most old-timers, he's proud of the tough nature of the work he had to do: "Had to swing those logs by hand. Had to be a man in those days. I've done pretty near everything in the woods." But like many workers, he objected to the inhuman conditions under which he was forced to work: "Two, three hundred men in a camp. Sleep in cabins and eat in the cookhouse. Cabins was nothing but holes. Wake up and your clothes was wet as hell. Man gets killed, they throw him outside. Shit, was just like war. Talk about dogs—hell, they treated us worse than dogs. Like pigs. Sometimes had to sleep in sawmills. I been through more hell and poverty, you couldn't believe it . . ."

Like the rest of the old-timers, Frank has been around. He peeled tanbark and split railroad ties; he's worked as a carpenter and a pile driver. At one point, he doubled as a bootlegger and potato grower: "Raised ten tons of potatoes. People couldn't go hungry. Gave 'em all the potatoes they want, but sold my whiskey. Had to make a living." From bootlegging to poaching deer, Frank has often had to work outside the law to scrape together a living. In 1925, he was jailed for catching fish without a license. During the Depression, things got really bad: "Had to steal to make a living. Couldn't do otherwise. I was hungry and would've robbed a stage. If they caught everyone who stole, ninety-nine percent of the country would be in jail. Even the cops oughta be in the jailhouse. They're human like we are. But there's one thing: no one's as bad as a stool pigeon."

As we talked, another old-timer came by with a six-pack of beer. I asked who he was. "Just a piece of humanity who was born and raised in this country that never amounted to nothing." And, half-jokingly, adds, "I got so much against me I never tell my name." This, it turned out, was a reference to his recent arrest for "cuttin' corners" on the road near Briceland.

Taking the cue that the subject of conversation is life in the old days, Earl (his reluctance to divulge his name was soon broken down) pitches in a few memories from childhood: "We had to keep the home fires burning while my dad rode sheep clear over in Nevada to make a living. We used to play with bars of opium. Didn't know what it was—it looked just like an old bar of

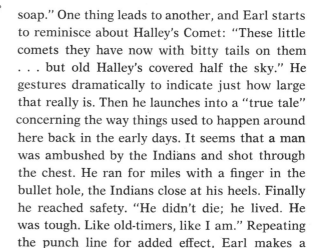

soap." One thing leads to another, and Earl starts to reminisce about Halley's Comet: "These little comets they have now with bitty tails on them . . . but old Halley's covered half the sky." He gestures dramatically to indicate just how large that really is. Then he launches into a "true tale" concerning the way things used to happen around here back in the early days. It seems that a man was ambushed by the Indians and shot through the chest. He ran for miles with a finger in the bullet hole, the Indians close at his heels. Finally he reached safety. "He didn't die; he lived. He was tough. Like old-timers, like I am." Repeating the punch line for added effect, Earl makes a dramatic exit for more beer.

I asked Frank to describe what logging operations were like before mechanization. "Impossible to explain," he says. "Altogether different in those days. Impossible to explain." After much insistence, I get him to attempt an explanation anyway. He unleashes a torrent of technical jargon describing the various cable rigs and chutes. The exact meaning of the terms passes me by, but it suffices to leave me with the impression that he was right: things were altogether different in those days.

Another thing very different in those days were prices—particularly land prices. "Back in 1936 you pay a dollar-fifty an acre, timber and everything. Now it's a thousand dollars an acre. Then I pay ten dollars taxes, timber and all; now it's four hundred dollars taxes—no timber, no nothing. I'm not paying taxes—I'm paying rent! I worked for four bits an hour years ago. Even if I saved it, where would that leave me now? I worked the hardest and got the least . . . But anyhow, I made it. I made it all the way through life. And what a life! I seen the whole thing."

THE EVERYDAY LIFE
OF A DOUGLAS FIR FOREST

The daily life of a fir tree is much like that of a redwood. The needles, with the aid of the sun, combine water with carbon dioxide from the air to make food which is transported throughout the tree by the inner bark. Each spring and summer the cambium adds a new layer of growth to the trunk, new needles shoot forth from the twigs, and seeds mature within the cones. Each winter, the tree becomes latent, but the needles are not shed and food production continues.

The growth pattern of a Douglas fir differs from that of a redwood. Most fir trees begin from seed, not from new shoots on an old trunk. The baby trees do better with a little shade, for when totally in the open they use their energy to grow outward instead of upward. Young fir trees grow much more slowly than young redwoods. After the first few years, however, their growth picks up, and within a century a tree is large enough, by human standards, to be cut down. The mature trees are old and tall, but generally a few centuries younger and a few feet shorter than the redwoods.

Plant life in the fir forests is in a constant struggle for available space. The towering trees provide a ceiling which keeps the direct rays of the sun from reaching the ground, while at the same time they serve to collect moisture from the frequent fog and drop it on the forest floor. The result is a heavy undergrowth of shade- and moisture-loving plants: salmonberries, thimbleberries, huckleberries, salal berries, redwood sorrel, wild violets, wild ginger, Oregon grape, trillium, sword ferns, etc. Douglas firs are more tolerant than redwoods of competing trees; a mature forest has tan oaks growing beneath the

fir and a sprinkling of madrones twisting their red trunks and branches toward the available sunlight. Along the stream beds, bay trees, alder, and maple can be found. Each plant tries to survive as best it can by photosynthesizing the sun's energy (even shade-loving plants need a little sunlight now and then) and gathering up water and nutrients from the soil. Year after year, each plant uses its energy to flower and fruit, or to bear spores. There is a feeling of constancy in these forests, with most of the groundcover plants being perennials and most of the trees overhead having been around for centuries.

When a forest is logged, it is not just the trees that die. The whole forest is altered beyond recognition. With no forest roof to shield the ground from the sun and collect the moisture from the air, the earth quickly becomes hard and parched. Few of the plants constituting the old forest ground cover can survive in the new environment. An entirely new plant world better suited to the new conditions begins to develop. Bracken ferns and various grasses and weeds spring up everywhere. The upper level of the forest, which is now only a few feet off the ground, is dominated by tan oak shrubs and various types of Ceanothus, such as whitethorn and blueblossom (also known as deer brush or wild lilac). A gradual process begins which will result, centuries later, in another mature forest. The tan oak and Ceanothus provide some shade for the slower-growing young fir trees, while the Ceanothus also help to enrich the soil with the nitrogen-fixing nodules on their roots. At this stage, the brushland is particularly susceptible to fires. If the land escapes fires long enough, the tan oaks will eventually take over from the short-lived Ceanothus and provide a safe environment for the Douglas firs. Then, some of the previous

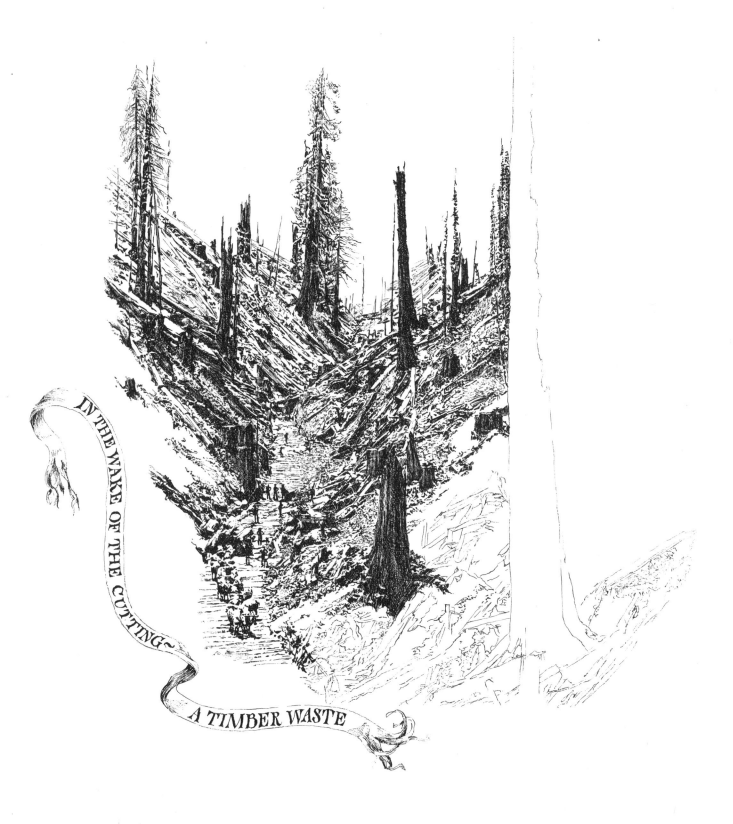

IN THE WAKE OF THE CUTTING~

A TIMBER WASTE

forest ground cover will return: Oregon grape, redwood sorrel, sword ferns, huckleberries, and salal berries. Within a century or two, the mature tan oaks will gradually fall from heartrot and the Douglas fir trees will begin to predominate once again in a mixed forest of oak, fir, and madrone.

THE EVERYDAY LIFE OF THE RIVER

Perhaps it is their constant movement that gives rivers and streams the appearance of life. Their activity is simple: the transportation of water from the earth to the sea. Their motive force is basic: gravity. Yet rivers and streams, like plants and animals, are highly sensitive to the changes of the seasons and to the acts of man.

Along the northern California coast the temperature variation between winter and summer is relatively small, but the seasons are pronounced nonetheless. In the winter, storms blow in from the southwest, dropping over one hundred inches of rain each year in some locations; in the summer there is no rainfall for months on end, but ocean fogs sometimes extend inland for several miles. The rivers and streams, as one might expect, are significantly larger in the spring than in the fall, although it is in the summer and fall that water is most needed by all forms of life in the region. Since there are few lakes here, it is through the flowing bodies of water that the winter rains must be preserved for use when they will be in greatest demand.

In their natural state forests play an important role in storing the water. During the winter, the extensive vegetation and root network of a mature forest help the land absorb moisture from the heavy rains; during the summer, the vegetation shields the ground from the sun, while also collecting moisture from the ocean fog and dropping it on the dry earth. In a cutover forest, the winter rains quickly run off the surface, the summer sun parches the land and dries up the springs, and the fog passes by overhead without releasing its moisture to the ground. The result, of course, is larger floods in the winter and shallower rivers and greater fire danger in the summer. The two largest floods of recorded history in this area—those of 1955 and 1964—occurred in the wake of large-scale logging activities in the back hills. Surely there were extreme winters in earlier years, but now the land could no longer hold its water.

The extensive road building during logging operations only makes the situation worse since it pushes much of the topsoil into the streams, which, after a few heavy rains, also become filled with eroded earth and fallen trees from the hillsides. As the stream beds become shallower, the likelihood of floods is still further increased. Frank remembers what the Eel River used to be like near Pepperwood, where he was raised: clear water up to seventy-five feet deep, and navigable up to Scotia. Then came the roads, the railroads, and the logging operations, in which entire hillsides were plunged into the river. "Them bulldozers ruined the whole thing. All those creeks are shot. Just pitiful. Bulldozers done all that. Just pitiful."

With the yearly cycle of floods and droughts now more extreme, dams are built to exercise more control over the water levels of many of the rivers, as well as to answer the need for water and electrical power in large metropolitan areas. But with the rivers no longer flowing freely from headwaters to the sea, the lives of many creatures that depend on them are altered.

THE EVERYDAY LIFE
OF STEELHEAD AND SALMON

Scarcely under the surface of the clear stream at the headwaters of the Mattole, two salmon lay motionless. The ripples from the moving water which surrounds them give the impression that the fish might still be alive, but they are not. They have completed their life's mission: to reproduce more life. These particular fish have had to travel only about fifty miles upstream from the ocean to reach their spawning grounds; others have to travel several hundred miles. These particular fish have encountered no dams or insurmountable snags on the way; others are not so fortunate. Still, the beating they have taken during their heroic struggle against the rapids has made their flesh half rotten even before they died. Now their huge carcasses stretch

out like fallen logs across a stream that can barely contain them. Where had they gone for the few years which separated their birth from their death? How did they know where to come back?

Man knows little about salmon. We know that the young steelhead and silver salmon spend approximately a year in the streams of their birth before migrating to the ocean, while young king salmon swim down to the ocean shortly after hatching. All species grow rapidly during an ocean life of one to three years and then return as adults to their native streams to spawn. But we don't understand their uncanny ability to return to the very place of their birth, nor are we able to follow their migration patterns in the ocean. The final life-and-death struggle to reach their spawning grounds leaves us bewildered or awed, and the best we can do is pass it all off as "instinct."

Both steelhead and salmon can only spawn in gravel beds of clear, free-flowing streams. When the gold miners changed the courses of streams and filled them with the residue from their

KING SALMON

activities, some of the fish could no longer reach the headwaters of their birth while others, having arrived, found the gravel beds covered with silt. In recent years, the destruction of the spawning beds has increased dramatically. Logging activities and road building have filled many streams with enough silt to bury the gravel beds for years and even decades. Snags in the smaller streams prevent the fish from completing their journey, while the pollution of the larger rivers also takes its toll. A sample study of Redwood Creek in 1966 conducted by the Department of Fish and Game concluded that sixty-four miles of the eighty-four-mile stream bed had been "severely" damaged by poor watershed management, thus depriving the steelhead and salmon of much of their spawning and nursery habitat. As Fred Wolf tells it:

In years past, salmon go up the river here, and a lot of times, when you cross horseback, you gotta chase the fish off of the ripples and get 'em out before the horses cross. Now, since they've logged, wash and fill and stuff that came off of the hills with poor logging, it's practically wiped the salmon out. You won't find as many fish now in five miles of river as you used to find on one ripple. The salmon come up to spawn, and there's a big heavy wash and gravel moving down and covers the eggs so deep they don't get to the surface. That's where your fish went. This little creek at the forks of the road, the first culvert going towards Thorn—I've seen salmon go through that culvert. One time when I was doing the mail I seen a steelhead run in there and I stopped and when he come out the other end I chopped his head off with an ax. But you won't see 'em anymore.

The migration patterns of steelhead and salmon have also been hampered by the construction of dams. Even if the mature fish are helped over the dams, the younger ones have a difficult time making it back through the generators on their journey to the ocean. More than a score of dams in the Sacramento–San Joaquin Valley have reduced the available spawning grounds from their original extent of several thousand miles to less than three hundred miles today.

The net effect is a sharp decline in the population of steelhead and salmon. For three decades, the Department of Fish and Game has counted the adult fish returning to their spawning grounds along various creeks on the northern California coast. The steelhead runs declined from 293,299 in the 1940s to 100,669 in the 1960s; silver salmon declined from 147,000 to 53,000; king salmon from 255,000 to 91,000. Thirty years of mechanized manipulation of the environment have reduced the population of steelhead and salmon to roughly one-third its former size.

THE EVERYDAY LIFE OF BLACKIE AND THE ANIMALS

"I first come out here 'cause of a friend. He was working in the redwoods making what they call split products, you know, grape stakes and fence posts and all that. I started in with him, and we buy the stumpage off of these big redwoods back in this area here about seven miles. We worked it on commission; at that time it was better than any kind of wages you could work for. I still didn't like the idea of cutting these trees, but they're gonna be cut anyway, so I figured I'll get with it—I'd just as well make it as someone else. I was a blacksmith at heart, and when they started building them sawmills, I went to work on construction. I worked at that for fifteen years doing these sawmills; I went from blacksmith on into millwright work and from there I became crew foreman. But then they stopped building sawmills, and within three years they start tearing 'em down. The last millwright job I worked on was tearing down a mill. After that, I went to work on bridge construction on the freeway. Once I reported on the job and the insurance man saw me with my white hair, and he talked to the business agent about it. I worked about three weeks longer, and they had a little slump in the work, and they laid me off, and I never got back on. So I dropped out and went to work for myself back in the woods where we used to make grape stakes and posts. I go back in there and make shingle bolts; I do that, and now I'm building a home for this guy down here at Briceland. I can do any of it: carpentry work, plumbing, steam fitting, welding, blacksmith; anything that comes along, I can do it, but I'm at the age where I can't get on big production. But I still got a lot of hard work left in me.

"When it started, it was the early part of 1945, rumor came in that they were going to build fir sawmills in this area, that the fir timber was going on the market. Then there was such a demand for lumber, after World War II. Pretty soon there was cruisers in, and buyers, even before they built the first sawmill. They were cruising all these acres in here, you know. By middle of the summer, forty-five, there must've been, oh, six or eight sawmills under construction in this area, and by December there were some under production. They were paying seventy-five cents a thousand on their stumpage, from that to a dollar and a half. As time went on, why the price kept going up, and within three years the stumpage price was around ten dollars a thousand. It just kept on and on, and it looked like the more they cut the higher the price went—there was that big a demand for lumber. The stumpage on the fir that was selling in 1946 for seventy-five cents to a dollar and a half a thousand, it's selling now anywhere from sixty dollars to one hundred and ten dollars a thousand. The same type, only it's actually not as good a timber; what they're gettin' out of here now is more or less a relog.

"I don't know for sure, but from what I can find out there was twenty-five sawmills operating in this Garberville area at one time, and I think seven shingle mills. Now these mills wasn't only cuttin' fir; some of 'em was cuttin' redwood and fir. So the price of redwood kept going up along with the fir.

"The labor in the sawmills in 1946 was a dollar an hour—that was top wages in the sawmills at that time. In fact, this dollar an hour drew people in here from Oregon and Washington; it was a premium price for labor. And they were paying in the woods seventy-five cents to a dollar a thousand for falling and bucking the timber. Now they're paying as high as five dollars a thousand for falling and bucking, and the average wage in the sawmill now is three-ninety an hour.

"But you can see where there's such a differential in the price of the product and the price of labor. The timber is jumped, we'll say, from a dollar a thousand to a hundred dollars a thousand; labor is gone from a dollar an hour to three-ninety an hour. That's quite a differential, ain't it? So that leaves the workingman with . . . he just handles more money than what he did before, but, after all, he doesn't have much more than he did twenty-five years ago.

"This piece right down the road here that they just logged—I hated to see it go. It was such a beautiful place down there. It was one of the very few stands of timber left in here. Of course we've known all along that eventually it would be taken out. I could see it if this fella was in a bind for money, if it was his last chance or he was about to lose some of his property or something. But he's a quick-dollar man; he bought that place cheap, he knew he could make a lot of money, and that's what he did. That made me sick. Now we're sitting on a powder keg. We get a fire in there this summer, and if they're not really quick we could burn out up here very easy. That stuff burns just like it has gasoline on it. The brush is real dry; it starts in places like that. It forms a vacuum: it goes up and starts pulling this wind in, and you just can't imagine how fast it goes. If they happen to be off on a big fire someplace, with the equipment tied up, and this catches down here, then we've had it. A good fire after he gets this timber off here would still be in his favor, because he wants to use this land for ranching, for grazing land. So he wouldn't like anything better than to have a good fire in there. But I look for him to get a control burn on this down here soon. When he's got a control burn on it, at least I'm insured then, so I'd much rather have a control burn than somebody set it afire without any permit.

"In California we had a forestry service, but they didn't have any teeth in their laws. There was more slack than any state in the union, I guess, on their loggin'. They absolutely just let the loggers tear this country to pieces. They had a few rules and regulations and you had to get permits at times: there were times in the summertime like this when we're having a heat wave that they'd shut the operations down. But they paid no attention to what they were doin' to the country. They could take these bulldozers and cut all kinds of roads around the sides of these mountains. They had no restrictions. They could push as much stuff into the creeks as they wanted to, and go off and leave them. Which they did—they left it. This went on for years and years. So, over a period of time, after they had logged and gone, didn't put in any water-breaks or anything . . . well, in 1955 we had a heavy rainfall, it just kept raining and raining and raining, and all of a sudden—slush! All these roads around the hill were holding water, just like little dams, and finally one would break open, and it'd bring the next one over, and the next one over. Where'd they end up? In the creek. They get into the creek with all these tops and things in there, and what'd they do? Filled 'em up solid, see? Silt and water rushed out into the river, and flooded the river. The river couldn't take it. There was so much mud in the bottom of it, and the

THE RACCOON

130

water kept raising, raising. The water got so high, and here come these big logs down and knock the breakers out. Then in sixty-four another flood came along. They were still logging a lot here then, and they still didn't have any teeth in their forestry laws.

"Before then, even on this creek right here in front of this house, we used to go down there and catch steelhead weigh up to ten pounds. All kinds of nice trout. But after this, they can't even get away from Redwood Creek down there; there's one fall in this creek, right down close to the county road, that drops eight foot—just big logs in there. It'd be very simple to take out, if the Forest Service or someone would just come in there this time of year with chain saws and break these logs up into short pieces, and the next flood, see, would take them right out. But I have talked to everyone that I know of in this area about it—the game warden and different people—and they say, 'You have to write your senator. We can't do this without permission; there'd have to be a law passed to that effect, to clean these creeks out.'

"We've got to help the fish get back in here to spawn, see? We've lost our fishing industry; there's no more fish in the Eel River, not like it used to be. Even out here at Shelter Cove we don't have the salmon we used to have. Very poor season every year. The salmon are gone, because they can't get in here to spawn in their old spawning beds. They have to have sand and gravel, good clear stuff—they can't spawn in the mud, and that's what we have.

"Before they started falling the timber, this time of year when it's dusty you could walk down this road from here to Briceland and you couldn't lay your hand down on the road without putting it over a 'coon track. That many, big ones and little ones, you never saw anything like it. You start down the road after dark, and here they were, right in the road. They're not a wild animal, you know; they'll just sit and look at you like these guinea hens here—they won't hardly move. I had to stop and herd those 'coons, mama 'coons and babies, out of the road to keep from running over them. These little fellas would be blinded, and the old mama 'coon couldn't get 'em out. OK. But I haven't seen a 'coon track on this road in five years, not one track, and I'm on this road every day. They're gone. There may be a few left down on the creek, but they don't get up in here. Nobody knows just what happened. I don't believe it was the timber itself as much as it was the creeks. You know, when they take the fish out—a 'coon eats a lot of fish. They can still live off of vegetation and bugs and things; they live kind of like a hog. But they do like fish. And a 'coon likes to stay on the creek, because a 'coon is great for washing his food. Did you know that? If there's any water anywhere close, he'll go to it; even a nut or anything, he'll go and wash it. They're great for that. If you have a pet 'coon, and if you have a water pail in there for him to drink out of and you hand him something to eat, he'll go over and dip it in that water.

"The deer population hasn't changed any. If anything, they're thicker because the undergrowth is so thick that you can't kill as many deer now. Right after they logged it, everything was open, you could see so far. There used to be hunters back through here; every year, dozens and dozens of people hunting back in here. Now, they don't even try to, because you can only see what you can see from right here. If they don't find one in the road, they don't have any deer.

"There was quite a few bear then. It wasn't anything to find a bear track on this road two or three times a week. And on the creeks—just about any time you went down there you'd see them. Then they disappeared. For several years I didn't see a bear track anyplace, or any sign of a bear anywhere around here. The last three years, I begin to see bear tracks again. In fact, last year we saw a big track up here several different times. I had some fish in a hole near there, some catfish that I brought up from Clear Lake to put in this hole of water to see if we could save them. So I happened to think one day, 'He might be fishing in my hole,' and I went down there and, sure enough, there was the carcass of the biggest one of 'em laying out there. He had gone down there at night and caught him out in the shallow water and just flipped him out. But the bear disappeared right after the logging 'cause it was open country. A bear has to stay in brush, you know; they're just too wild to stay out in the open. Now, as the growth is coming back in, why the bear are coming back in. This one I saw the track of last year, last time I saw her tracks she came off the top of the hill and had the little fella with her, a little track about that long. She had this baby back up here somewhere. But she went around here and robbed one of my bee trees. So she got one of my bee trees and one of my catfish.

"Years ago we had one little pet deer up in here. My wife was going to Shelter Cove fishing one morning, she found a little fella out there on a bluff on the side of the road. He had diarrhea, you know. She didn't think he'd live, but she picked him up and wrapped him up and put him in the car. She came back home with him and parched some flour and gave that to him and he straightened up, and the last time we saw him he was a three-point. He'd see me in the woods and he'd follow along behind me and I'd stop and he'd get behind a tree. We don't know what ever happened to him, if he got killed or whether he lived his years out in the woods.

"I was thinking the other day and I counted up that we got forty-six mouths to feed, and that's not including my family. I was countin' all these guinea hens, see, and seven cats and three dogs, five goats, and I don't know how many chickens. It seems like every time I go to town I got to buy feed for something. It hasn't been too many years ago we decided to go out of the chicken business —we had about thirty big laying hens. But in this area up here the laying hens molt about three times a year, and they will not lay when they're amoltin'. I tried raising horses, too—had seven head here at one time. But horse feed kept going up and up, and the price of horses was coming

BEAR!

down. Right now, a hundred and fifty dollars is top price for a good horse, and it don't take long for a horse to eat up a hundred and fifty dollars' worth of feed.

"Last week we had a little chipmunk we saved out of a cat's mouth. He was getting along just fine, but we found him dead one morning—he must've been hurt internally somewhere when that cat caught him.

"But these goats, you can't turn them loose—they'll just eat anything and everything. They ring the bark off of your trees, ruin the place. Most mischievous things I ever seen in my life. There's lots to be thought about when you're out in country like this and you start wanting to have a lot of animals around you."

THE EVERYDAY LIFE
OF THE DEER
(PART 2)

Deer, it seems, have benefited by man's removal of the thick forest ceiling that had prevented the sun's energy from being used by plants the deer could reach. A towering redwood is of little value to a deer, who much prefers more accessible foliage. The deer in this area are particularly fond of Ceanothus (deer brush), which grows up quickly on land that has been logged or burnt. Thus they flourish in cutover forests, where the thick underbrush provides them with both food and cover. Because logging activities and fires often prove beneficial to the deer, they are the only large mammals in this country who have successfully adapted to man's domination of the environment.

Deer, however, have been affected in more ways than one by the rapid advance of white civilization into the backcountry. Most of the deer's natural predators—wolves, coyotes, bobcats, panthers—have been killed, and now men themselves, along with their domesticated dogs, have become the deer's worst enemies. The previous predators played an important role in the health and well-being of their prey: they kept the deer population in line with its food supply; they helped ensure the natural selection of the deer who were best fit for survival; and they were instrumental in eliminating disease before it spread by feeding primarily on the sick, the elderly, and the disabled, who were not quick enough to escape. Man, however, fulfills only the first of these three vital functions of a predator. The modern hunter and his powerful rifle kill indiscriminately, and the strong and healthy are stricken just as easily as the weak and sickly. Indeed, the many-pointed antlers of a healthy buck are sought after as a valuable trophy. Many deer, furthermore, are wounded but not retrieved; even if they survive, they may be permanently injured and prone to disease in their weakened state.

The deer have survived, but they no longer play a vital role in the ecosystem of the forests. In former times, the carnivorous canines, felines, and Indians all relied heavily on the deer to convert plant energy into animal food. Today, most deer hunting is done primarily for sport, and even the dogs who go off hunting independently of their masters often kill largely for the fun of it, leaving much of the meat to rot as they return to their bowls of kibble at home. None of the deer's previous predators, human or otherwise, ever failed to follow up his hunt and make full use of the dead animal.

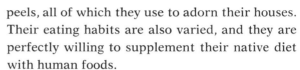

THE EVERYDAY LIFE OF MICE, SQUIRRELS, WOOD RATS, AND RABBITS

Like the deer, many of the smaller mammals of the forest seem to fare better now that the sun can reach down and give its energy to ground-level vegetation. A mature redwood or fir forest has little to offer for the brush rabbit, for instance, who thrives instead on terrain with a thick coating of bushes right next to the earth's surface that can provide it with both food and protection. Thus when the forests were logged, the rabbits quickly spread down from the high brush country into the former forests inadvertently opened up for their use.

Wood rats, likewise, took advantage of the logging activities to enjoy a more abundant life. Unable to climb very well, the wood rat builds its large, ground-level house out of loose sticks and other available debris, of which there is plenty to be had in a recently logged forest. The wood rat's house is quite an elaborate structure, sometimes measuring six feet high and twelve feet across. The extreme visibility of these houses requires several doorways through which the rats can escape invading predators. Wood rats are particularly fond of adapting abandoned buildings to their own use—another trait well suited to life in the wake of logging operations. They seem almost to enjoy proximity to human beings: one wood rat, for instance, shared an outhouse with us for several months, and another paid an occasional midday visit to our front door. The wide variety of objects humans bring into the forests is a particular attraction to the curious wood rats, which are great collectors of everything from trinkets to scrap metal to orange peels, all of which they use to adorn their houses. Their eating habits are also varied, and they are perfectly willing to supplement their native diet with human foods.

Mice seem to seek out human presence even more eagerly than do wood rats. They will eat almost anything people eat, and a single human household is a gold mine capable of supporting an almost limitless population of mice. The walls of a human habitation can be made into excellent, well-protected houses for mice, and even nesting materials, particularly cloth, are supplied by their hosts. Mice are extremely prolific (they have to be, considering the great number and variety of their predators), producing several litters a year with a good number of mice in each litter. Thus a family of mice can live on in a household even in the presence of the dangers that accompany cohabitation with people. Just as they have for the deer, the rabbits, and the wood rats, logging activities have amply increased the native food supply for the many mice that have not adopted a human household.

Tree squirrels, it seems, would have been hurt by cutting down the trees, but this is not the case. The loggers centered their attention on the fir and redwoods; however, the main attraction for the tree squirrels of this area is the acorn from the tan oak tree, and the tan oak is one of the first trees to grow up in a cutover forest. Thus although the tree squirrel population was probably hurt during the tanbark boom, the logging boom has proved, in the long run, to be a boom for the tree squirrels as well as for man. The squirrels of this area remain active throughout the year, storing some acorns in caches but supplementing their diet with tender twigs and shoots and various ground forage. They live in the trees, usually in holes they find in the trunks.

HOME AND HOARD: A PACK RAT NEST

Unlike the mice, they can survive perfectly well by producing only one litter a year.

Human presence has created new hazards as well as new benefits for the smaller mammals, however. Man has realized that these animals are competitors for his own food: they invade his gardens, feed off the graze he wishes to re-serve for his stock, and even raid his pantries. Modern man thus regards them as "pests" and does all he can to eliminate them. He puts out traps and poisoned bait, and employs his do-mesticated predators—cats and dogs—for their destruction. Thus, although man has eliminated many of their native predators (coyotes, wolves, wildcats, martins, fishers, etc.) and enriched their food supply, he has in some cases wreaked havoc on his small would-be beneficiaries. The large concentration of dogs and cats near my own home, for instance, has virtually eliminated the wood rats, who are less able to escape from the constant harassment of cats and dogs than are the mice, squirrels, or rabbits. In areas of extensive growing or grazing, large-scale trapping, shooting, and poisoning campaigns—intended to replace the functions of the predators who have also been trapped, shot, and poisoned —have taken their toll.

In just a few short years, the machine age has left its unmistakable mark on the back hills. For mankind, who invented the machines for his own benefit, it created first profit and then insoluble problems of unemployment. For the original trees and undergrowth of the forests it has meant instantaneous destruction, although new growth has taken their place. For the wildlife of the forests, it has meant a drastic change of living conditions, sometimes favorable and sometimes unfavorable, and the need for quick adaptation to a new age. For the land that supports the plants and animals, it has meant upheaval at the hands of the bulldozers, followed by the long-term effects of too much exposure: being parched by the sun in the summer and eroded by the rains in the winter. For the streams at the foot of the hills, it has meant more extreme seasonal fluctuations and increasing amounts of residue from eroded earth and fallen trees. For the salmon that swim up the streams, it has meant the elimination of most of their spawning grounds. It's not only trees that are killed by logging, nor the narrow strip of land that is altered when a road is built. All living creatures are being affected one way or another by man's domination of the earth.

IN BURRILL'S JUNKYARD

CHAPTER SEVEN.

THE PRESENT AS HISTORY

Did anybody ever homestead out in Whale Gulch?

That brush patch? Hell, wasn't nobody crazy enough till you come along.

—AN OLD-TIMER ANSWERS
A NEWCOMER'S QUESTION.

From the near extinction of the sea otter in the early 1800s to the depopulation of the salmon today, from peeling the tan oaks to clear-cutting fir and redwood, the depletion of natural resources has been quick and severe since white civilization first arrived in this area. As each new resource was discovered, a small civilization was founded around it; as each resource in turn disappeared, the civilization which depended on it vanished. A few decades ago, the maps of the northern California coast were dotted with towns that no longer exist: Needle Rock, Bear Harbor,

Usal. Whitethorn and Briceland, once thriving commercial communities, each of which supported several stores, hotels, dance halls, saloons, and stables, are now easily missed by an unattentive observer passing by in an automobile. At Ettersburg there is no more store, no more school, no more post office, and scarcely any people.

THE EVERYDAY LIFE OF THE ETTERS

Ettersburg was first settled in the 1890s by seven of the Etter brothers: Henry, George, Fred, Albert, August, Louis, and Walter. Because of its remote location and poor soil, the land they homesteaded had escaped development of any

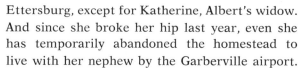

sort for the first forty years of white occupation. But the Etters were energetic pioneers, and within twenty years the firm called Etter Brothers was running a prosperous eight-hundred-acre ranch engaged in a variety of enterprises. On the rocky meadows, sheep were raised for meat and wool. The fir forests were cut down to provide wood for all the ranch buildings, and the trees were transformed into boards right on the premises by a steam-powered sawmill and planing mill. Since they operated a mill, the Etters received local contracts for lumber, and they also contracted out some of their tan oak forests for bark peeling. Forty acres were planted with apple trees and ten more with strawberries, and they ran their own evaporating plant in which the apples were dried. In addition to these commercial ventures, there were also all the usual homesteading activities, with the ranch raising all their own meat, milk, vegetables, and eggs. The Etter Brothers ranch was a sort of super-homestead.

With the Etters proving it could be done, more settlers moved into the area and eventually Ettersburg became a town large enough to support its own school, store, and post office. The town even gained some fame on account of the work Albert Etter was doing with his apples and strawberries. From the age of seven, Albert had been playing around with plant breeding. His extensive experimentation grew from a hobby into a vocation, and his thousands of crossbreedings produced several satisfactory new varieties of apples and strawberries—some of which are still being raised today by commercial growers.

Now the orchards have long been abandoned. Ettersburg itself is today no more than a couple of houses and there are no longer any Etters in

Ettersburg, except for Katherine, Albert's widow. And since she broke her hip last year, even she has temporarily abandoned the homestead to live with her nephew by the Garberville airport.

Past the "Etter Flying Service" sign, past some corrugated-tin hangars proudly announcing that they are the "Airport Cafe" and the "Pilots Lounge," over across the runway, and through the adjacent fields lined with parked private planes stands the house of Leo Etter. Katherine sits alone in the front room, with the gray and white midday TV shows as her companion. It's not the life she's used to leading. The phone rings, but she doesn't answer it. We turn the TV off, but the picture window looking out onto the airport takes over the function of Distracter. As we talk, we see N6168Y take off and then land, and then take off and land once again. "I wouldn't want to live here," she says. "It's too noisy."

Originally from New Jersey, Katherine was working in San Francisco when she met Albert. They got married when she was thirty-two and she joined Albert and his brothers on the homestead. By that time, the ranch had already been functioning for almost thirty years. Albert didn't want a woman just to take care of him, for he enjoyed taking care of himself. He loved to cook and is said to have made excellent sourdough bread. He took a special interest in canning and of course did much of the gardening, tasks usually relegated to the women on the homesteads. Katherine did take over the everyday cooking duties, however, as was the accepted custom. "They said I cooked very well. Had to say that, I guess. But they weren't hard to please."

When Katherine joined the family in the 1920s, they were, with the usual exceptions, still raising all their own food. For meat they had sheep,

IN AN ABANDONED APPLE ORCHARD

cattle, and pigs; they didn't do much hunting. ("I never cared for venison. Don't care for it now. Don't like the wild taste or something.") They had fresh vegetables all the time, since they planted a winter garden of carrots, kale, cabbage, and rutabagas. ("I used to eat them raw when I had my own teeth.") They did lots of canning, but they also had a storage cellar that stayed pretty close to forty-eight degrees the year round so they could eat many out-of-season foods without processing them. ("Don't like frozen food. Like it fresh. But I guess we're a country of frozen stuff now.") And of course there were loads of fresh apples and strawberries when in season, and dried apples all year. long from their own evaporating plant. "Yes, it's a great life. I think it's a good life. It's independent."

"What did you do when you got sick out there?" I ask.

"I didn't ever get sick. Not even as a kid. Maybe that's why I lived so long. But I remember once there was a little baby that died immediately. Albert took it clear up to Ferndale on horseback to be buried."

"Did you ever feel lost way out there? Didn't you ever want to get away?"

"No, I like the country. My family were farmers. The city—the wild city—don't give me any interest. I go into it and am glad to get out of it."

"How did the Etters first get started?"

"A lot of hard work, that's all it is. That place was a wilderness when they came. They cleaned all that land—chopped the trees down and everything. And all by hand. Even the roads were built by hand. And then, too, you have to feed the land before you get anything out of it. You know some people think that people who live on a farm or ranch live the life of Riley. They do like heck. You gotta work hard out there."

"Was there any particular trick to raising sheep?"

"No, nothing in particular. But after they get chased by dogs, they get so wild you can't catch them—at least for a while."

"Is there much usable timber left on the land now?"

"It's all gone like everything else."

Finally I get to the question that had puzzled me ever since I first heard the story of the Etters and Ettersburg. "How come Ettersburg became unsettled? What happened to everyone?"

"Couldn't make a living off that land."

"But the older Etters did."

"That was different. A dollar was a dollar then. And they were settlers—and set in their ways. The young people wanted to get away. They came to school in here and then went out to work. A man can't work out and work on his place both. Comes home at night and too tired to work.

"They want things that we did without. Those things weren't in existence then. People don't know how to do without things now. They want everything. Either that or it's 'Gimme, gimme, gimme.'"

In a few short sentences, Katherine had given a succinct statement of the Revolution of Rising Expectations. To satisfy the new needs, the younger generation of Etters took such jobs as delivering the mail or operating the airport. With the original Etter brothers all dead and the following generation (themselves now aging, some already deceased) all off working in the outside world, only Katherine is left on the ranch. She still lives there, under normal circumstances, in a cabin midst numerous cats and neglected orchards. "I live most of the time in the kitchen. Every once in a while there's a drip somewhere in the winter. You have to have a wood stove—can't stay warm without it." As soon as her hip is better, she'll be moving back out to Ettersburg. "After all," she says, "it's my home."

Not everybody left for the towns and the cities when life in the country became, or seemed to become, less profitable. Many of the old loggers, such as Frank, managed to acquire a little land at a time when land was cheap. The life they were used to living required little additional money; selling a few trees here and there and cutting a few shakes now and then supplied them with all they needed. Many of the old ranchers and homesteaders passed their land on to their children, some of whom tried to continue making a living off it just as their parents had done.

But times have changed. Taxes have gone up, and so has the cost of living. If the land has trees, the only feasible thing to do is to sell them—particularly since the value of the trees is itself subject to taxation. If the land is open, only sheep grazing will turn a profit and overgrazing is a great temptation—even at the risk of erosion. Whatever the shape of the land after logging and grazing, there is always the possibility of subdivision and development. In one way or another, the inhabitants of the back hills who have stayed on after the various booms have disappeared must find a way to make a living. If they own land, as most of them do, they must find a way of making the land work for them rather than against them. Cut it, graze it, develop it—or perhaps do all three. Somehow, some way, they've got to make enough money to survive in today's world.

THE EVERYDAY LIFE OF FRED WOLF
(PART 2)

"My folks started ranching out here in fifteen, but I haven't been here all that time. I been in and out of here. In my younger days, I was footloose and fancy-free and if the boss looked at me cockeyed in the morning I told him to kiss what he could and it wasn't his elbow and I'd take off, and maybe that afternoon I'd go to work on the same kind of a job only in another place. Wherever work took me. That's when I was single. I picked cotton, I picked grapes, worked in the Sierras in lumber, I tried everything. I went to work in the San Joaquin Valley. A big Swede came up and asked me if I was a skinner. I told him, 'Hell, yes.' So he told me to be there at two o'clock. Four bucks a day and you traded your blankets off for a lantern. All that saved me was I knew what 'Gee' and 'Haw' was, and the mules knew the rest of it. You was up four

o'clock in the morning taking care of them mules, six o'clock you was headed to the fields and you was there till six that evening, then you come in and unharnessed your team and put 'em in there and went in and had supper and then you come back out and fed 'em for the night. That's when you trade your blankets off for a lantern; you had so damn little time to do anything yourself.

"But I'd always come back here. Myself, I've been in the stock business since twenty-two. I got some sheep, and I built up a small place. Used to be hogs and goats and what have you, but now this whole country out here is in sheep. But ranching ain't like it used to be. It's gettin' so you can't hardly even butcher your own livestock and sell it. These butchers and what have you, they say it's gotta be cut and killed and federal inspected. So the only way you can get by there is sell it to 'em live. Years back, I butchered fifty, sixty lambs a year. Well, I butchered five this year and I got a tip that I better lay off. No, it was two years ago I was told to lay off, and I quit. Before, if you wanted a couple of lambs, I sold to you, and I had business built up. Some of 'em took one, some of 'em took two, some take three—it all depends. But now I gotta sell live through the auction.

"Dogs are my biggest problem now. My neighbor over here, this year he sheared just half the sheep what he sheared two years ago. I had two German shepherds come in and from the turn of the road to the orchard here they killed twelve of them, one right after the other. I found out who owned them dogs, and the woman was on welfare; you can't get blood out of a turnip, so I was just out. They just kill for the fun of it; they tear the throat out and get that one hot gush of blood and then go on to the next one.

141

I've lost a hundred and fifty head of sheep in the last four years by dogs. I build up my she-stock and get it back up there and the dogs come and knock it back down again. I've shot lots of dogs, and I'm gonna keep on shooting 'em. It's like one fella down here on the ranch—woman come along and says, 'If you shoot my dog, I'm gonna shoot you,' and he says, 'Lady, you better start shootin', 'cause I just shot the dog.' And I've done the same thing, but generally you shoot a dog and keep your mouth shut about it. The less you say about it when you shoot one, the less trouble you got.

"I don't do it here, but it helps if you can burn your timber off, on account of it brings up young sprouts and what have you for the summer feed. The longer they have green feed, the better they carry through. Like now, the grass is getting pretty badly sunburnt and there ain't much life to it.

"What's coming up now is these hunting clubs. If you got enough property, you can get ten guys in there and get a hundred dollars apiece. Well, a lot of 'em will pay that 'cause there ain't no other place to go. If you got ten guys, that's a thousand bucks, and you can't make a thousand bucks any easier. There's a lot of 'em that's doin' that, 'cause it's easy money, extry income. One ranch I know over here has got pretty near all doctors and they been comin' in there for several different years, but then you can get riff-raff in there too, you know. But you got to have it posted, you got to keep all the trespassers out. Another thing you got to watch is dogs run your deer out: they run 'em into the river, drown 'em, kill 'em, eat 'em, what have you. So you see dogs is not only a problem with livestock, but with deer too. You get the bunch in here huntin', they spending a hundred dollars and they don't get no buck, you're liable to have to find somebody else for the next year.

"I ain't gotten into this hunting club business, because there's only enough game here for me and my boys. But a lot of ranchers is doing it to pay off their taxes. In 1958, for this here seven hundred acres, I paid a hundred eighty-five dollars in taxes. I ain't got a bit more now than I had then, and taxes last year was six hundred dollars. They claim they don't raise the tax rates, but where they get you is they increase the assessed valuation all the time. Used to be, in this country here, you could buy forty acres, timber and all, for a hundred dollars. Now, the sonofabitch is more than a hundred dollars an acre.

"Keith Etter bought that whole goddamn Shelter Cove ranch for seventy-five thousand, and when he sold it, he sold it for two hundred and fifty thousand. He took all the timber off, too. Then the Jews that bought it from him held it a little while and then they sold it for seven hundred and fifty thousand. Then they subdivided it into what have you over there. But to make a living over there you got to have some kind of an income. If you don't, what good is it? You've got to live; you've got to eat.

"Now, there ain't a job in the country to be had. The sawmills are gone. The timber's gone. There's one or two left near the highway, but they're only hanging on by a whisker. They're hauling logs fifty miles to the mill; they're hauling from clear across the railroad. Downhill, uphill, and downhill, and then down the highway.

"Over the years, there's been some changes.

Only thing left for this country around here is when they strike oil. But even that—I remember when Briceland was all lit up with natural gas. Who knows what's gonna happen next?"

THE EVERYDAY LIFE OF THE DOG

With the virtual extermination of wild canines and felines in this area, domesticated dogs and cats have taken over their roles as predators. House cats are maintained primarily for the purpose of checking the population of rodents who would like to take advantage of man's overwhelming abundance. The situation with dogs is more complex. They are not employed specifically as predators, although the toll they take among both sheep and deer is immense. Originally domesticated for use as herders and hunters, dogs only rarely serve these functions today. Sometimes they are maintained as watchdogs, but more often, I suspect, their primary purpose is just to be around. Dogs are man's best friend, and everybody wants a friend.

Dogs inhabit two worlds: that of their masters and that of their peers. From their masters they learn tricks and civilized manners; they receive love and affection and, of course, food. They follow their masters around and obey their commands. When they meet other dogs, however, their orientation suddenly switches. Even with their masters pulling on the leash, they cannot resist sniffing each other out. Territory, dominance, sexuality, or friendly play—their instincts as canines transcend, at least momentarily, their roles as pets.

A dog is not just a dog; it is also a shepherd

or poodle, collie or pekinese, spaniel or beagle, or any one of the infinite mutations of the various breeds. No other animal species shows such a remarkable variety. But the breeds are the creations of people, not dogs. Through selective breeding, man has been able to emphasize some characteristics and suppress others according to his fancy. Dogs are bred to be hunters or herders, to have big noses or little noses, to be calm or nervous. Some of the creations are, in a word, freaks—creatures who never could have evolved and survived without the intervention of the human imagination.

Amadeus, a dog who upon occasion stays at my house, is a cross between an Australian shepherd and a Samoyed. His multicolored and asymmetrical markings give him the appearance of a circus clown. He is exceptionally mild-mannered, gentle with children, and unbelligerent toward other male dogs. He has a particular fondness for being rubbed on the belly. He barks at strangers, but is quick to accept them as friends. He obeys the few commands he knows and goes for walks with people at every available opportunity.

But there's another side to Amadeus. Often he disappears for days on end. The occasion for his journeys is sometimes a female in heat, and several pups have been born nearby with his distinctive markings. But his trips are more frequent than the number of females in the area would indicate. Sometimes, it seems, he just goes off on his own to be a dog. In his early days, he was once seen in a pack chasing deer. With all the male dogs in the area congregated around a female in heat, the formation of a pack after the sexual activity is over is not an infrequent occurrence. (Unlike most of their wild relatives, dogs do not form families and there

is thus no need for the father to stick around after the pups have been conceived. Indeed, how could domesticated dogs form families when both parties of a sexual union must return to their respective masters?) The dog packs apparently don't show the same degree of cooperation as do packs of wolves or coyotes, but they are still effective in tiring out the swifter but less enduring deer.

With age, however, Amadeus' taste seems to have become more modest. He is small enough to be bullied by other dogs in a pack, and he now prefers to hunt alone or with a trusted friend. The objects of his hunt have correspondingly shifted to the smaller mammals: squirrels, rabbits, wood rats, chipmunks. His choice of prey is a fortunate one, for he generally incurs man's favor for such activities rather than the wrath he would receive were he to focus his efforts on deer or sheep. On a backpacking trip we once took together, I had occasion to observe his technique. Upon sniffing or spotting a prospective meal, he would immediately chase it. Amadeus is quick, but more often than not his prey would easily escape. Sometimes, however, it would get cornered in a hollow log and Amadeus would impatiently await its inevitable emergence; and occasionally, it would get caught in a difficult position just long enough to be grabbed. Amadeus' percentage was bad, certainly no better than one in a hundred. But one or two successes each day were all he needed for both food and incentive, and the kibble I took along went untouched. When we saw a deer, Amadeus showed no interest whatsoever; he wasn't about to get involved in an all-day chase which, being alone, he most probably would lose. Squirrels, on the other hand, are less demanding and present very little danger. Aside from cornered deer and armed men, the only dangers a dog faces in the woods today are encounters with snakes and porcupines, both of which can be avoided once the dog has learned better.

In the summer, Amadeus' thick fur coat makes daytime activity uncomfortable. His normal schedule during heat waves is to sleep through much of the day and take off on his own from about two till ten in the morning. During this time he is undoubtedly sniffing and chasing squirrels and the like, but he can do so without any fear of failure: if his hunt is unsuccessful, he can always return to his bowl of kibble.

Amadeus' craving for human affection occasionally seems to get the better of him. For weeks on end, he sticks close to home, going for walks only with people. At night he even suggests that he sleep with the people, although he is good about accepting no for an answer. He is denied full participation in the human world, which has been his total orientation for weeks, and so, sooner or later, he gets himself together and goes off to be a dog again. By the time he returns, the delicate equilibrium between people world and dog world has been reestablished, and he is visibly happier.

Not all dogs are as capable as Amadeus in adapting to the basically schizophrenic nature of their lives. Many are neurotically attached to humans, while others, in attempting to reestablish their basic canine identities, act in such a way as to put them out of favor with the people upon whom they depend. The dogs in our area who chase sheep and deer are simply practicing, in a slightly confused form, what their instincts tell them to do. They know they like to hunt, but hunting isn't always well enough integrated in their lives for them to know what

to do with an animal once it is dead. Human ranchers and hunters, meanwhile, resent canine intrusions on animals they wish to reserve for their own use, and many of them think nothing of shooting the offenders. It is the story of Frankenstein, with human beings deploring the actions of the monsters that they themselves have created. Dogs, tamed by man to tend his herds, now hunt his herds instead.

THE EVERYDAY LIFE OF THE COYOTE
(PART 2)

With the sudden arrival of Western civilization, the world of the coyote was drastically altered. The newcomers killed off many of the coyotes' larger prey, but the game they introduced, particularly sheep, more than made up for the loss. When forced into close contact with the advancing civilization, the coyote quickly developed new tricks to take advantage of the situation. He waited patiently near bulldozers for small animals who were forced to flee. He patrolled the open highways for run-over carcasses. He looked for cooked remains in the wake of man-made fires. He savored the undigested milk in calves' dung. He followed irrigation water as it flowed into its ditches, flushing pocket gophers out of their holes. He tagged along after human hunters to feast on what they left behind or what they could not retrieve, just as the ancestors of domesticated dogs once had done thousands of years ago, which had resulted in the first links between canine and man.

Clever as he was, the coyote lacked the manners required by civilized man. His failure to treat livestock as the property of the ranchers earned him a bad name, just as it had done for the Indians who hunted the white man's animals. The coyote, like the Indian, was regarded as a competitor and therefore an enemy, and a ruthless campaign for his extermination was thus undertaken. The federal government hired trappers and paid bounties, and federally sponsored programs have accounted for the deaths of around three million coyotes since their initiation in 1915. Additional coyotes were killed by private parties, and even more were killed but never counted because their bodies were not retrieved.

In the early days, coyotes were killed primarily with traps. The presence of coyote trails or well-frequented haunts was determined by following their tracks and their feces. A trap would be set and sprinkled with a scent to lure the curious canines. Since no coyote can pass by the scent of another coyote's urine without some investigation, many a trapper found it worthwhile to maintain a captive in closely confined quarters to keep him supplied with the appropriate lure. When a trapper was fortunate enough to catch a nursing mother, he generally released her long enough to be led to her den. With a bared hook, the trapper would then explore the corners of the den and drag out the pups.

As time went on, poisoned bait became preferred over the cumbersome and sometimes inefficient traps. Strychnine would be added to a piece of meat and set out in a likely location. With advancing technology poisoning methods became more sophisticated, and the cyanide gun, or "coyote getter," became the main weapon in this war of extermination. An explosive cartridge containing sodium cyanide was concealed in wool or rabbit fur and appropriately scented. When pulled, the cartridge exploded and released the cyanide, often directly into the coyote's mouth. Death followed almost immediately.

The principal advantages of the "coyote getter" over earlier methods are that no coyote can escape long enough to warn his friends and the evidence of dead bodies can be easily retrieved. With both steel traps and strychnine, it was found that some coyotes who approached the bait seemed to avoid it as if they knew better. Perhaps they had been taught about the new dangers by those who had had close calls or who had observed less fortunate victims. The coyote's adaptability apparently applies to his own defense as well as to his food gathering. He quickly learned, for instance, how to double back on his own tracks when chased by dogs in order to confuse the scent. And despite the vigorous campaign which has virtually eliminated him from many areas, he has in recent years extended his territory farther east than ever before.

The effect of the anticoyote campaigns on the ecosystems in which they were waged has been profound. The traps, poisoned bait, and cyanide guns did not cease to function just because the animal who approached them was not a coyote. Several other species, particularly other carnivores, were thus endangered. With the predator population suddenly diminished, the population of rabbits, squirrels, rodents, and other small animals commonly considered "pests" by man consequently multiplied. These, in turn, were poisoned and trapped. Much of the poisoning of both predators and pests, furthermore, produced secondary poisoning in still other animals who fed on the carcasses. Sometimes it seems that modern man's at-

tempted **solution to an unbalanced ecosystem is**
no ecosystem **at all.**

With so many of the area's natural resources gone, it is harder than ever to make a living off the land—except, of course, by selling it. Glen, an old-timer who has been around, puts it bluntly: "You can't make a living off that land. You just can't do it anymore." But the fact that the trees are down and taxes are up does not imply that the region is economically depressed. Far from it. In fact, today there's a new but slightly different boom going on to follow in the footsteps of the tanbark and logging. The basis of this new boom is the simple fact that the back hills have not yet been consumed by the rapidly growing metropolitan centers. The new resource being exploited is not something that the land produces—it is the land itself.

Each summer hundreds of thousands of tourists travel up and down Highway 101 to explore the Redwood Wonderland. Roadside signs announce the competition for the tourists' attention and money: "World Famous Tree House—Believe It or Not," "Here It Is—the Living Chimney Tree," "Confusion Hill Mystery—Is Seeing Believing?" Individual competition is matched by competition among the towns: Garberville develops a "Squirrel" bus ride through the redwood forests to match the successful "Skunk" train in Willits. Whatever can catch the tourists' fancy is fair game: the towns in the nearby Siskiyou, for instance, offer themselves as the gateway to the land of the Bigfoot—legendary part-human creatures who mysteriously and elusively haunt the hillsides, leaving only their mammoth tracks as evidence of their existence. The coastline has its shipwrecks and the forest has its drive-through trees

and one-log houses, guarded by giant models of Paul Bunyan which look pretty impressive even next to the giant redwoods. The natural world is thus transformed into a supernatural freak show to satisfy the gawking customers, and money comes flowing in.

For vacationers who like it enough to stay, there are developments of retirement and summer homes with all the conveniences of modern living. Foremost of these is the multimillion-dollar project at Shelter Cove. "This wonderful place is called Shelter Cove Sea Park, California's finest recreational seacoast community unfolding between two worlds, the ocean-view spectacular and the park panorama, a master-planned seafront wonderland coming to life." These words, spoken dramatically and accompanied by constantly swelling background music, can be heard through any one of ten telephone receivers attached to a $7000 light-up plaster-of-Paris model of the development situated between the "Mermaids'" and "Neptunes'" restrooms in the on-site sales office. The main office for the project is in Los Angeles, because that's where most of the business is done. Up to ninety-six prospective buyers are flown up each weekend on three airplanes that land on the 3400-foot paved runway (which, the company proudly announces, cost half a million dollars).

Shelter Cove Sea Park is built on the scale of a small city. There are 4600 lots serviced by forty-three miles of paved roads and complete water, sewage, and electrical facilities. Four hundred of the lots have been sold, but, strangely enough, only thirty houses have been built, even though the development has been in operation for several years. No one knows exactly why Shelter Cove is still virtually uninhabited. It's a touchy point with company spokesmen, who alternately blame political hassles with the county and point to figures of how many people plan to build houses in the near future. At present, the roads, street signs, electrical wires, water tanks, and drainage pipes, in the absence of people or houses, give the Shelter Cove hillside a decidedly science-fiction appearance.

Roughly half the lots were purchased by investors. Many were bought sight-unseen, for anyone knows that you can't go wrong with land along the California coast. *The Beachcomber*, the company newspaper, suggestively quotes Will Rogers: "The way to make money in real estate is to find out where the people are buying, and buy land before they get there!" A list of buyers shows great numbers coming from such places as Las Vegas, Los Angeles, even Belgium and Germany—though the Germans, according to resident manager Jim Dawson, are more interested in retirement than investment. If and when Shelter Cove Sea Park does become populated, it will be as a retirement and recreational community. The tone is set by the "professionally designed" nine-hole golf course and by the horseshoe pit and miniature golf course outside the sales office, while the brochures proudly point out the hunting and fishing opportunities nearby. With Shelter Cove bordered on the south and west by the ocean and on the north and east by the newly created King Range Conservation Area, the promoters give a special pitch for future pensioners: "You are actually surrounded and protected from the entire world." For many of its prospective inhabitants, Shelter Cove will undoubtedly be a dream come true, a "seaside haven." In the words of one couple who have already settled down, "This is the end of the rainbow for us."

In contrast to the plush Shelter Cove Sea Park is the loose, shoestring development of the backcountry brushland by young refugees from the cities. Several years ago a man named Bob McKee, at one time the local schoolteacher and a descendant of the original McKees who first settled this area, started buying up large pieces of land, dividing them into ten, twenty-, and forty-acre parcels, and selling them with easy terms and practically no down payment. Young people seeking a "return to the land" started flocking to the area to buy up McKee's parcels and build houses tucked away in the woods where no one, not even the Indians, had ever lived before. In earlier times, human beings always chose the small meadows and valleys as the most suitable sites for their dwellings, but with the introduction of the Caterpillar and the widespread use of automobiles, there's no place in the back hills too inaccessible for settlement. The land that formerly provided deer and acorns for the Indians and tanbark and timber for the white settlers now provides homesites for the new pioneers. Much of the land boasts neither fields for grazing nor trees worthy of cutting—only brush cover; and much of the soil is far from desirable from an agricultural point of view. Yet the country is still country, and that's what counts.

THE EVERYDAY LIFE
OF THE NEW PIONEERS

PETER AND NANCY

NANCY: When we first came, it wasn't nearly so populated, that's for sure. When we drove the truck into the Meadow, we were the only

148

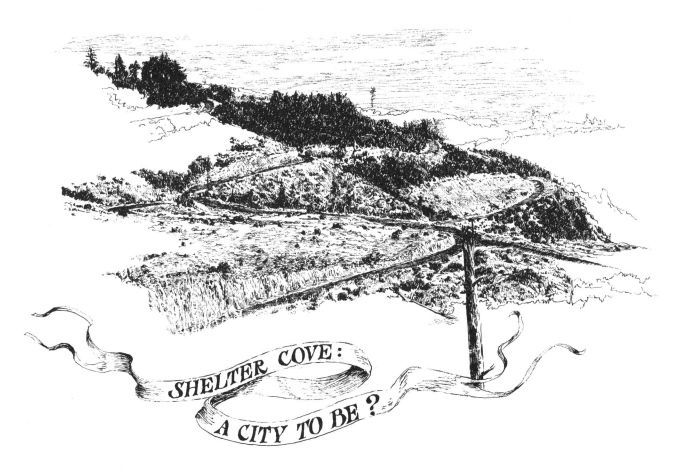

SHELTER COVE:
A CITY TO BE?

people here. The Sooters and Robert Quagliata had started their houses, but they were away. But it wasn't long at all before other people started coming—maybe a month or so. That was four years ago.

PETER: I started working for Bob [McKee], and we were building our house too, when we could. It was a really rainy winter, and I had hepatitis for about a month.

RAY: What did you do in the house truck during the rains?

PETER: Go crazy.

NANCY: Peter read the seed catalogue. I remember going for long walks to get out of the truck, and going over to clear land.

RAY: You worked in the rain?

NANCY: In the snow, and in the drizzle. Anything to get out of the truck.

PETER: When we first bought that land, it was all covered with cascara—there was hardly any cleared land there at all.

NANCY: Only one tiny little naturally cleared area, where there had been a big fir tree that was logged.

PETER: Then in the spring of that year, we were trying really hard to get the house done, because Nancy was pregnant with Jessica, and we wanted to move into the house before the baby was born. We didn't make it, so Jessica was born in the house truck.

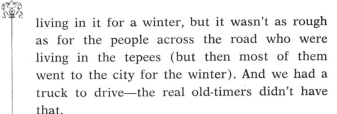

RAY: Were you scared when you came up here?

NANCY: It's pretty easygoing country. I think we would have felt a lot of tension if it were like Vermont, where you really have to get ready for the winter. But here you can let a lot of things go.

PETER: Like we've had plastic on our windows for three years. In Vermont . . .

NANCY: And we don't get in a whole winter's supply of wood sometimes before the rains, but you can always get it later.

PETER: I mean, there are a lot of times in February when you can go swimming almost.

RAY: Had you ever lived in the country before?

NANCY: Yeah, we lived on a little subsistence farm, I'd guess you'd call it, in Ohio; a garden and goats and rabbits and chickens and pigs and ducks. I think we were really fortunate to have had that experience, because we knew to look for good soil—so many people come here and look for a good view. But you can't eat a view. We had our pick of the land—Bob offered us all these different alternatives once we decided to buy.

PETER: It was a challenge, what we took on —a much bigger thing than we had ever done before. But on the other hand, it wasn't as hard as it was, like, thirty or forty years ago. What these old-timers went through is a whole different trip. We had the frontier scene with a lot of conveniences—like when Anna [their older daughter] got her finger cut off, we were able to take her to the doctor, and stuff like that. Or like our house truck—we had a gas stove in it, you know, and a sink. We had a nice, dry, warm little house. We just drove that right in and there we were, all set up. It was rough

living in it for a winter, but it wasn't as rough as for the people across the road who were living in the tepees (but then most of them went to the city for the winter). And we had a truck to drive—the real old-timers didn't have that.

RAY: But you still felt sort of like pioneers?

NANCY: For sure. I remember the thrill of first clearing the land and writing letters to people about that. It went back to something— it felt like something that maybe our ancestors had done—and I really wanted that connection.

One of the big differences between the old-timers and us is that they really had to make it, otherwise they died. But if our crops don't come through we can always go to Garberville.

PETER: Or if things get rough we can always go to the city for a month or two and make some bucks and then come back.

NANCY: And they didn't have welfare—no food stamps and stuff like that.

PETER: Of course they had more game, too. The country was more abundant and there were fewer people. That was sort of their kind of welfare. Their first years, I imagine, they got a lot of their food from the woods. The salmon would run up the rivers just like that. A lot of the old-timers still get a lot of their food that way.

NANCY: Like old Zumwalt. He says when he goes down to the garden to get his vegetables and sees meat in there, he shoots it.

RAY: Do you feel pretty settled here? Do you ever just feel like splitting?

NANCY: It would be hard. There are so many little things, like the garden—all these things that you'd have to break the connections with.

PETER: We've been trying; like last winter, I split for six weeks, and Nancy split for a couple of weeks. In the winter it's nice—there's not all that much work to do up here.

NANCY: And the fishing pretty much ties us down in the summer.

RAY: How'd you get into fishing?

PETER: I got tired of working for Bob, and started looking around for some other way of making a living. And right at that time Jay got a boat and was going to do some fishing, and André and Frank were going to fix one up, and then Peter Weisman and I got a little boat. And Nat the Fisherman had a big boat in Shelter Cove that summer. I got to know him and used to go out with him—I learned a lot from him. Then the next year I figured I needed a bigger boat, so I spent most of that season building the boat I have now. I had these visions of hundred-dollar days and stuff like that. Even when you make a hundred dollars a day (I made a hundred one day last year), you've earned every penny of it—maybe not that day, you know, but all the time and expense you've put into it.

NANCY: The preparation is as long as the season.

RAY: Are you depending on fishing for money?

PETER: Well, we're sort of trying to. That and other little things too.

RAY: Like what?

PETER: Like we have a house in Mexico that Nancy inherited, and she gets a thirty-dollar check a month. But we're trying to sell that house now.

RAY: How much food do you raise, and how much do you buy?

NANCY: We raise all our vegetables, except onions and garlic.

RAY: Why not onions?

NANCY: We grow them, but there are never

enough. And all our own fish and eggs. But we buy cheese and grains . . . and ice cream at Mrs. Marker's [the Whitethorn store].

PETER: We make a lot of our own ice cream, too.

NANCY: And we make all sorts of condiments to spice up the winter meals—jams and jellies and pickles and relishes—out of fruits that we pick.

RAY: Do you can vegetables?

NANCY: Some, but a lot of them grow through the winter. We smoke fish and can that.

PETER: Oh, and we make all our own wine.

NANCY: All the necessities of life . . .

PETER: That spices up the winter meals too, let me tell you.

RAY: What happened to your goat?

PETER: We sold it. Goats are a hassle. You have to be there every morning and every night, at a very specific time. And unless you have a billy goat, they're hard to breed: they come into heat one day, they're in heat one day, and they're out the next day. So you have to hustle your ass to find a billy goat.

NANCY: And the billy goats around here are half wild, roaming around the Ettersburg hills. Goatman Bob spent two days once looking for one, up and down, and couldn't find him.

PETER: They're really a trip—if you can get into them, they're worthwhile.

NANCY: So we decided later to get a cow, to make it really worthwhile. With a lot of people it would be feasible.

PETER: But it's such a tie-down.

NANCY: We finally decided to go easier on animals that take that much responsibility. Now we just stick to chickens and bees; bees just need attention in one part of the year.

PETER: The bees are doing pretty good. We

have four hives now—two of them are really strong hives and two are just starting out. So maybe in a few years we might make a fair amount of money off of that.

RAY: Do you have an extractor?

NANCY: No, not yet. Tony Tuck got his, though.

RAY: It seems like you have a lot of tools and equipment.

PETER: You have to. The only way you can possibly make it is with a lot of tools. Well, not the *only* way, but the way that we're doing it. Like all the accouterments of making boats and maintaining them. With all of my tools, and all of Keith's tools, and all of Nancy's tools, we can make almost anything now. When we were working on the boats, there were few pieces of hardware we had to buy—most of the hardware on the boats we made.

NANCY: We can make bolts with a threader.

PETER: We run a forge. Of course we can't make generators and water pumps, but we patch and repatch the exhaust systems over and over again.

NANCY: One of the arts to living around here, too, is scrounging. We were into it before Keith came, but he showed us some of the finer points. Keith's highlight of the day is going to the dump. He looks forward to that. For a vacation, he'll go to the Miranda dump.

PETER: He finds good shit, too.

RAY: What have you found in the dump?

PETER: Well, I've found two boats in the dump, right off, one of which I'm using as a tender for my big boat, and the other of which is a sandbox for the kids.

NANCY: And the tires . . .

PETER: Yeah, we find a lot of tires. Usually they're no good, but we take them anyway.

NANCY: Keith collects scrap metal—scrap brass and copper.

PETER: Old bed frames have really good steel. Or, like, springs from cars—you can make almost anything out of them, not to mention you can use them for springs. One day I found two toolboxes full of tools (I don't know if I should let this out!), including a three-quarter-inch pipe threader in perfect condition. I found three chain saws.

RAY: Did they work?

PETER: No, none of them worked, but I brought them home anyway. I kept them laying around for parts. Finally, I took one back to the dump, I traded another one for some records, and I gave the other one away to somebody for parts. Once we found a beautiful old washing machine. I've found, like, three or four electric motors off of washing machines. People just throw the whole machine away, and there's pulleys and belts and electric motors. So I've got about three or four electric motors that I can't even test because I don't have electricity.

NANCY: We found a set of children's books. Nineteen fourteen. Beautiful stories. All fairy tales with beautiful old color illustrations. And about a month ago there was a big haul when Gopherville threw away all their books and records because they were instruments of the devil, or something like that.

[At this point Peter, who gets up at 4:30 A.M. every day to go fishing, excuses himself to get some sleep.]

RAY: Is there any difference between the kind of work that you do and the kind of work that Peter does?

NANCY: When we first came up here, he did all the muscle work, and I did all the "cooking and cleaning and tendin' the childrens." When we moved onto the homestead back in Ohio, we pretty much took up the roles that had been laid down, right from the beginning. The day we moved in, I started the cooking and the washing. I remember Peter saying how nice it was to have somebody to do his laundry for him.

RAY: Did you really get into the spirit of Pioneer Man and Pioneer Woman?

NANCY: Oh, yeah. We got into it so far that we exhausted it. And it was good for learning the things that you learn, like learning to can. I guess we both learned a lot that way. It was exciting in the beginning. I remember when I baked my first pie and my first loaf of bread. They really stand out in my mind, they were such challenges.

RAY: You had never done that kind of thing in your childhood?

NANCY: Oh, no. I never did much cooking.

RAY: What did you do?

NANCY: I was a Mexican street kid—selling pop bottles for spending money and stuff like that.

RAY: How did things start to change?

NANCY: I've always had a really active imagination, and it didn't find enough outlet. I had already learned how to do well all the things that were the woman's role and I would have ideas going through my head while I washed the dishes, but I knew I'd never find time to carry them out because it was such a time-consuming thing being a housewife. So I just grew more and more frustrated, and envied Peter for being able to get into really fulfilling projects while I was still doing the dishes. I didn't really conceive of any change like what happened. It just happened all of a sudden when Toni came back with her women's literature from the city and

just started talking to people and started questioning things that I hadn't really thought to question. And all of a sudden, Peter and I found ourselves in an incredible whirlwind where changes were happening almost faster than we could assimilate. Every time I'd go to a women's meeting I'd come back brewing over with new thoughts and new feelings and new ideas. Peter was really shaken, but he went along with it, he was open to it, which a lot of men aren't. In their fear they'd just fight back.

We decided we'd have to set up some kind of a schedule to get ourselves into the new areas. We found that before we had a schedule, I would still have the consciousness of taking care of the small details: picking up after the kids, getting the dishes washed (Peter didn't like to wash dishes), and things like that. At first it was a daily schedule, where each day we would pick out two things to do: we'd either make breakfast or wash the dishes, and we'd either clean house or make dinner. That worked for some time, but Peter found it hard to really get into the cooking if he hadn't done the shopping. So Peter suggested after some time that we start doing it on a two-week basis: for two weeks one of us cooked and the other did the cleaning. And that's what we're doing pretty much now, except that Peter doesn't like to clean very much, and our standards are so different that I'm almost happier doing the cleaning and being in a house than I can live in. And Peter's really gotten into cooking, so for nearly two months now, Peter's been doing all the cooking, and I wash the dishes and clean house, and it's been working real well.

RAY: So you've more or less got a new role definition . . .

NANCY: Yeah, sort of. And we both do

153

things outside the house, like I've really gotten into carpentry. I was always really interested in building and shapes of things. Like I helped design the house and told Peter how I wanted it, but he was the builder and he always did it, and in the end he always did it how he wanted it, too. He was the builder, and you can't really build a house the way someone else wants it. I guess I didn't have much confidence in myself as a carpenter. The saw I'd always used was my grandfather's saw, and it was a dull saw and I didn't realize what a sharp saw was; it'd take me half an hour to get through a two-by-four. So I thought I really hated carpentry because of that experience. Then when Peter was in the city, I decided to build my kitchen—the counters and the drawers. He had his own ideas of how he wanted it, but since the kitchen was pretty much still my scene at that time, I wanted it how I wanted it, and I knew how it would be most efficient, and I thought he didn't since he didn't work there. It would be sort of like me building his boat. So the day that he left— I had just been waiting and waiting—I cleared everything out of the kitchen and started in. It was a really exhilarating experience. I'd work from the moment I got up in the morning, without eating breakfast even, until late at night, because I was so high on it. I'd just feed the kids scrambled eggs meal after meal after meal.

RAY: What else have you done since then?

NANCY: The stairs to the house. I got into cement and stonework. Now I'm doing the bathroom. It's sort of a tentative agreement that I'm doing the house while Peter's fishing. So I'm doing the bathroom by myself, but I imagine eventually we'll start working together and that'll be nice now that it's more equal.

RAY: Do you go out fishing?

NANCY: No. I went out once last year, but I don't really enjoy it. Eventually I see myself as contributing to the income, which Peter is doing now. When the workroom is built, there are all kinds of craft projects I really want to do—stained-glass windows, wood blocks—I've just got hundreds of ideas of things I'd like to make. But first we have to get it set up.

RAY: So the workroom is the big project now?

NANCY: First comes the bathroom. Taking the kids to the outhouse in the winter isn't much fun. And bathing is something that we've never been set up for yet.

RAY: What was the women's group like?

NANCY: In the beginning a whole bunch of women went through a great anger. There was like a hard core of us who went through more or less the same trip together: all the first realizations of how we'd been duped and what we'd accepted without really thinking about it and all the trips that society lays down on women. After that initial anger, we started to think about alternatives. Different people tried different things. Now, we feel that we've pretty much talked about all the things to talk about, except for changes that come up, but we know pretty much where things are at. So now we mostly do projects together: we put on Barbara's roof, we made a culvert for the lower road, we made an outdoor kitchen for Nina. We do things like that together. We talk while we work, and we have a good time.

RAY: Do you feel it's easier to work around other women than around men?

NANCY: Yeah, it is. You don't feel the pressure; there's nothing to live up to.

RAY: Were there any marriage breakups on account of the women's meetings?

NANCY: Yeah, but you can't call them bad ones, because they probably would have happened eventually. They just happened sooner.

THE EVERYDAY LIFE OF THE NEW PIONEERS:

TONY TUCK AND THE COMMUNE AT GOPHERVILLE

"We came up here four or five years ago looking for land. We were looking for some land with redwood trees fairly near the ocean, way out in the country, so when the real estate person showed us Gopherville, it seemed just perfect right away, and the land was pretty cheap then, too. The place was in terrible shape, but you could overlook that, knowing it could be cleaned up. What we wanted to do was live together with a dozen people or so and just really have a good family out in the country.

"Before we came, this was like a lumber mill. They had closed the mill down, but they still had all the cabins for the people that worked in the mill. At one time, I heard, there was about two hundred people living in this valley, and there were maybe seven or eight cabins left. The house up there on the hill used to be a bar, and the old-timers used to tell us about all the times that they'd had there dancing and drinking. A lot of times bottle collectors came by here and looked for old whiskey bottles or something. It was supposed to be a very rough area at one time; it would take hours for the police to come out from Garberville, so, knowing that, people who wanted trouble would really make a lot of it. We had a little hassle here ourselves with the people living in the houses, even though the real estate guy said he notified them. Still, when we tried to move in, they didn't want to move out. There were almost a few fistfights; it was really heavy. We didn't know what to do —we were so new and vulnerable up here. But eventually they all moved out.

"So then we had, like, five cabins and five families, all living separately. I had a house with my girl friend, and Bill and Katherine had their house, and so on. Then we put gardens in by the houses, and we all started building our own little things on our own little sections. We didn't come together too much except for a lot of social stuff—drinking beer and rapping. We played together, but we didn't work together. Everybody was just busy as they could be getting their cabins squared away: getting all the junk out, putting on new roofs, reworking the water systems. The place was really a mess. But we did work together on clearing—it took two years, because there was such a mess. We must have buried fifty cars because every house had an accumulation of cars that the old-timers would just keep around and use parts out of, and then when they were through with them, they'd just dump them in this field out here. There was no trace of any lumber mill anymore, just old cars and lots of logs. We had a Cat come out for two solid weeks to move all the junk into piles and bury it. Nature helped a lot too, after we did the heavy stuff.

"By the time we had the land all cleaned up, we were sharing more things—tools, vehicles. We were becoming this family that we really wanted to be, except we still had a lot of bickerings about the cars, a lot of hassles about the tools, and you're always expecting your neighbor to do more than he's doing. There was the opposite of that, too; a couple of fellows out

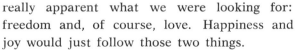

here just didn't want to do anything, and they expected other people to be like that, I guess. There were a lot of personality problems.

"We were all pretty spiritually conscious, like we knew that the real reason for being out here was to really love one another, to get it on with our brothers and sisters in a real fine way. But that was really hard. For a long time we never seemed to get anywhere—the same issue might come up over and over again. At the time I didn't know it, but I know now that a lot of dope and a lot of drinking didn't help any because when you're physically all messed up and your mind is cloudy, you can't really expect much from yourself. We all wanted to clean up more, but we never could; we were all really hung up in our habits and our desires.

"Meanwhile, more and more people were moving on. Starting off with eight, we got to fifteen or twenty in a couple of years. The more people that came on, the more we wanted to operate together. After about three years, we were sharing gardens, sharing cars, and sharing tools. We took one house and turned it into the Family House. We ate there and had a lot of meetings there. We had these Confrontation Groups once a week, where we'd deal with the personal problems of living together. Sometimes they were fun, and other times they were really terrible and they'd break your heart. You'd see a problem that you just couldn't settle, maybe a personality conflict that would repeat itself over and over again. A lot of jealousy trips came down. The different women that people were living with might fancy some other fellow (or even a wife—we were very loose in our morals), and we also felt that it was OK that this should be, that you shouldn't really be attached to your lover. So we tried to conquer jealousy. It was

really apparent what we were looking for: freedom and, of course, love. Happiness and joy would just follow those two things.

"Something comes into my mind right now. I remember when we first moved here, there were like only fifteen or twenty young people in the entire area, and everyone knew each other. When there was a party, everybody you knew was there. It was really blessed, a really close thing. But that's completely gone now that there are hundreds and hundreds of people in the area. Now, you can only reach to your own immediate family or a few close friends.

"Anyway, we saw that the material things that surrounded us were getting in our way. If there was a lot of hassle about the tools or the cars, then maybe they shouldn't be there. So we went through a period of getting rid of a lot of things, but it didn't last too long because our clutches were pretty heavy: we liked things. We liked good food, and we loved beer and wine. We were attached in a heavy way. So the next step was to accept all these things—have them all around you, but don't let them get in your way.

"By this time, we had about twenty-five people. We were eating together every night, and we didn't have quite so many meetings. It looked like we were really making it. Except some of us —myself, mainly—weren't really satisfied. Even though an outsider would come by and say, 'This is really perfect,' I could see that it really wasn't perfect. Almost daily, this big heavy selfishness trip would come into my life and show me that it wasn't perfect at all. There was this little space inside me that always showed me I was empty; all of us have had this empty space that you just can't fill. But at the time I accepted this emptiness as just being part of life, not knowing anything different.

"We had all these parties. About every other week there'd be a party somewhere in the community, and they were great. Physically, everything you wanted was there—everything you wanted to drink, to smoke, lots of men and women—but there was always this emptiness there. I think we were all getting more and more disenchanted with parties, and we started just staying at home more, working on the land and having our own smaller gatherings.

"Around this time I got into a conversation with a friend, and he asked me, 'What do you really want?' I've always had a pat answer for that: love. I've always wanted to be able to really love people, like all the saints and all the gurus that you'd hear about as being really heavy, high, spiritual beings. But that made me think, 'How am I doing on that?' It seemed that I hadn't really moved an inch; I was in the same trips that I was doing four years ago. What was changing was my environment, but deep down in my heart, I wasn't really loving my brothers and sisters that much more. This and a lot of other things set me off in a heavier kind of seeking, like, where is it really at? At this time six or seven of us were meditating through the Maharishi kind of meditation, so you can see we were trying to get into a place where we were really going to be spiritually content; we were going to fill up that void; we were going to find enlightenment or self-realization or whatever you want to call it.

"A couple of months went by, and an amazing thing happened to me. Out of the clear blue sky —I didn't read anything, no one came and gave me a rap about anything—I just started thinking about Jesus Christ. I didn't know what to make of it, because every time I'd ever heard about Jesus or met Christians, they really ap-palled me. I didn't like anything about them at all, but here I was thinking about Christ. I sort of just put it in a place in my mind, not really paying a whole bunch of attention to it, because like I say I couldn't make any sense out of it.

"I went to see a friend who had also begun thinking about Jesus. We were going to travel around together looking into Christian communes, but we never really did it. But more things were happening, because I did meet somebody in Colorado. They started talking about Jesus, and I started talking to them almost as if I was a Christian. By the time I got to San Francisco, I looked up an old friend of mine who I heard had accepted Jesus Christ into his heart. I asked him all the questions which, of course, everybody has when you first start thinking about the Lord, and he read a whole bunch of things from the Bible to me. I didn't understand any of them and I didn't like half of his answers. That night before I went to bed, his wife said, 'That happens to everybody, you know. No one really gets the answers that they want to get. The only way you can really get any answers at all is to ask Jesus into your heart.' So I thought about that. It astounded me that here I was hesitating on asking Jesus into my heart, when it might really mean the very thing I was looking for. But I finally did—I did accept Him that night. In accepting Him into your heart, what you're saying, I found out later, is that you want Him to take over your life for you. You're going to get off the bandstand, you're going to get off the chair where the ego's been sitting for all those years, and you're going to let Him sit there. You're going to let Him take over your whole life. So that was what was happening to me.

"When I came back here I was the only Chris-

157

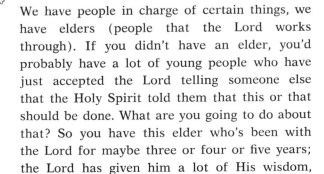

tian for a while, but soon Jim, the other brother who had been thinking about Jesus, also accepted the Lord, so I had some fellowship, and by that time a couple of girls accepted Christ into their hearts. A lot of other people were beginning to feel the spirit moving them; Jesus was knocking on a lot of people's hearts, and a lot of people here started accepting Christ, so here we had this small nucleus of Christians. We started praying together and reading the Bible, which all of a sudden was like this heavy, deep, powerful, eternal revelation. The whole thing is hinged around the Lord Jesus. By this time everybody was coming to discover these simple truths, and we started telling other people around the community about them. Hardly anyone can accept it at first; they think you're just pushing a trip on them, but what you're doing is telling them the Truth. The Bible says that man has a carnal mind, his mind is occupied in the flesh. The highest kind of thing you can imagine is still material, still flesh, if it's not Jesus. It's a lie if it's not Jesus.

"We had a big scene about those who still lived here but who did not know the Lord. Here's these people we lived with for two, three years, and all of a sudden a big thing, the biggest thing in the world, was missing. We didn't have any communication with them; it's not their fault they were in darkness, but they were. So there was a terrible time of strife, but after about six months' time most of the other people had left. Finally, now, this community is just all Christian people. It's like a total work just for one thing, and that's Jesus. Everyone who lives here is just living for Jesus Christ.

"It's not just that we're all thrown together and it all works perfectly. There are other things, for instance, like now we have an order.

We have people in charge of certain things, we have elders (people that the Lord works through). If you didn't have an elder, you'd probably have a lot of young people who have just accepted the Lord telling someone else that the Holy Spirit told them that this or that should be done. What are you going to do about that? So you have this elder who's been with the Lord for maybe three or four or five years; the Lord has given him a lot of His wisdom, and the Lord will work through the elder concerning the Flock. We all have all the respect in the world for the elders' authority in Christ.

"We have a schedule, too. Every morning we meet for prayer; we pray to the Lord and ask Him to bless our day. Then we work for a couple of hours together, eat breakfast, work again until about three or so, and then everyone does what they want to do for a couple of hours—maybe just pray or read the Word or just do nothing. Then we have dinner, and after dinner we usually get together again and study the Bible."

"What about economics? How do you make a living?"

"Well, before the Lord, it was completely on welfare, plus a few individuals would kick in. All this time of being here we've always idealized a place where we'd be making money through some other way besides welfare, and finally, through the grace of God, it's happening now. We're starting to make belts and leather crafts, which the Lighthouse already established —it's just us following through with it. That brings in quite a bit of money. We're also going to start doing split stuff with all the redwood around here. So the money thing is just happening—the Lord is really taking care of us in those respects."

"Are you going to cut redwoods?"

"Not fall them—just what's already down. We've been doing this all along for ourselves, like getting shingles, pickets, grape stakes, and things like that; now we're going to start doing it for the market. We're building a big truck that can just pick up any kind of log. And it's real good work for people who come here. A lot of young Christians come here who really need this steady kind of work to do during the daytime."

"Who do you sell belts to?"

"The Belt Ministry is in the Lighthouse right now. I don't know much about it; it hasn't really started operating from here yet. But that's going to be our income. In the last six months we've just sort of been living on our own money that we had. Certain individuals had a little money, and we just all threw it in a pot. When we came to the Lord, we just put everything together, even those little things that weren't before. Total sharing."

"Why did you go off welfare?"

"We just feel the Lord will take care of us, and we don't need that kind of dependence from the state anymore. We'll just depend on Him, knowing that He'll supply our every need."

"How do you feel about people from under-developed countries, Christians, about whom there's some doubt whether the Lord is adequately taking care of them?"

"I feel that it would be almost impossible for a Christian who really believes in Jesus to starve in another country. I've heard about starving people in other countries; I've seen them myself. But this was all before the Lord. I have a feeling that if I went anyplace in the world and met a spirit-filled Christian, let's say in India or China, they would just be happy and

they'd be taken care of. I would have a hard time to believe that there are Christians in other countries who are really miserable; if they're miserable, they're just not really feeling the fullness of Christ in their hearts. He *does* take care of you."

THE EVERYDAY LIFE OF THE NEW PIONEERS

AN EVENING BY THE CAMPFIRE
WITH ALDEN
AND HIS VISITING MOTHER-IN-LAW

(sort of)

"Let me tell you the story of the Great Dope Raid."

"Up here?" asks Alden's mother-in-law (sort of) innocently.

"A whole bunch of cops came."

"In this whole area?"

"Mostly Whitethorn and all the way out to the Gulch, too. They broke people's doors down . . ."

"Uh huh."

"And turned their houses upside down. They had no warrants."

"No warrants?"

"No warrants at all. There were sheriffs and sheriffs' deputies from Humboldt and Mendocino counties. They went to many houses and made people very angry."

"Sure. Frighten the children!"

"Oh, they didn't frighten the children. The children were ready to eat them. But in any case, the people were very angry. They decided to meet in Briceland, when the Briceland Store

AN AGE-OLD CUSTOM

was still there, which was a really neat store, a really nice place. It had a wood-burning stove in it and you'd come out of the hills every two weeks or so and you'd sit there all day next to the wood-burning stove, drink apple wine out of a paper cup, and meet everybody that you know. It was a big social trip."

"How nice."

"The store was still going on then, so everybody decided to meet at Briceland. There was a whole bunch of people in front of the old garage, the thing that burned down, where the A-1 truckers were staying. Tuna Jackson, Mayor Jackson, was making a speech up on the pedestal. That's why we call him Mayor: he loves to make speeches.

"So he was making a speech; he was contemplating being a law student or something like that. He was informing everybody of their rights: how you should behave in front of a police officer and blah blah blah. People all around were really uptight. I started to try to say something kind of quietly, and he went right on. I tried to interrupt him again, and he went right on. Then I finally just went . . . [Alden sighs] . . . and he heard that, and he stopped. So I said: 'Why don't we follow them?' They were out here again. that day, doing the same trip again. There was a little bit of discussion, and finally everybody decided: let's do that. So everybody piles into the pickups and cars and shit like that and files out of Briceland in a caravan fourteen cars long. There was a whole bunch of people and kids and everybody. I was in the second pickup, sitting in the back drinking wine, waving my wine bottle. "

"But you were very serious about the issue!"

"So we were coming down to the Shelter Cove Junction, and these two cars are coming back up the road, and I think it was Captain Trips in the first car—he kicked their car as it was coming by—bang—real hard. So the cop slams on the brakes, furious, and opens up the door: 'You kicked my—' And then he sees thirteen other cars coming out of the hills, with people piling out of them like an Indian ambush. They must have read somewhere in a manual that when confronted with such a situation you form a line. There were two more cop cars coming along after that, and they were all stopped by the blockade: fourteen cars, seventy or eighty people, kids, knives . . . Those dudes were terrified, you know. The people started rapping to them, and the rap was so intense that they forgot about their defense line—they all got surrounded eventually. Trips was out there screaming at this cop face-to-face: 'I know you, and I know where you live, and I know your old lady, and by God if you do this again I'll off you and I'll fuck your old lady.' And all the while the cop is standing there with a gun, turning red with rage, his hands trembling, wanting to reach for his gun. And straight people coming down the road from Shelter Cove, wanting to come through, and there's this mass of cars and people and cops and hippies. So while the cops are standing there, the hippies are directing the traffic through.

"The second car contained three plainclothes narcotics agents, thoroughly terrified, sitting in the back seat looking straight ahead. Wouldn't move their heads right or left. People are passing by on both sides, saying: 'What's your name? Where are you from? What are you doing here? Oh, Eureka? That's a long ways away.'"

"Politely?"

"There were so many mind games going on, it was incredible. So we held them there for about half an hour. They were just paralyzed. Finally we decided it was time to let them go before the National Guard comes. But there was this one fat dude that had a shotgun that got so engaged in conversation, and the rest of the cops were in the car saying, 'Come on, come on, come on! Let's get out of here!' But the dude was into this rap, thoroughly seduced by the rap, couldn't tear himself away. So he was the last one to get into the car, and then they split.

"Then Big John went to the telephone booth and called Sheriff Cox in Eureka, and said this is what happened and we want to see you and we want an explanation. He didn't say it then, but later he said you can send three or four people up. At first we wanted to send twelve people, but he didn't know how to deal with twelve people."

"That's a lot of people."

"So we sent four people up there with a tape recorder, and we were granted a two-hour interview with Sheriff Cox."

"Oh!"

"So he's sitting at his desk with *his* tape recorder, and there we are with *our* tape recorder. It was really neat. I wasn't there, but I heard the tape afterwards. He said such incredible things, like, 'One should not object to illegal search and seizure if one has nothing to hide.' Outrageous. Maybe it'll get him votes, I don't know."

"That was his explanation?"

"That was Humboldt County. Then the Mendocino County sheriff's deputy, narcotics agent, and probation officer were invited up for dinner and a town meeting at Gopherville (that was before they were Jesus freaks). So they came up here and Tuna Jackson wanted to get 'em into an argument right away, before we had even eaten dinner. We were going to have plenty of fuckin' time to argue, so we should digest the meal, I thought.

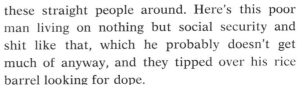

"It just **so happened** that the day before I had shot a salmon with my crossbow in the Mattole. Strictly illegal, any way you look at it. So we broiled it and were feeding it to them, and they knew it was poached salmon. I was sitting next to them and kept offering it to them: 'Won't you have some more salmon?' They politely ate a few bites. It was fun."

"Aren't you allowed to go fishing up here?"

"Well, it's illegal to use a crossbow, and it's illegal to hunt salmon when they're spawning."

"Oh, I see."

"And I didn't have a fishing license. But they ate it anyway. Then afterwards we had the town meeting—the only town meeting we ever had up here. A whole bunch of people were there —a bunch of hippies and a bunch of straight people too."

"What'd they have to say?"

"The cops had made the unfortunate mistake of breaking into some straight peoples' houses too, thinking they were hippie houses. Mostly old-timers. This one old dude, this old-timer— I remember I was really attracted to him first when I met him under the Drinking Tree. He said, 'This is a forty-year-old drinking tree. It's got a long history. I've drunk more shit under this tree than you've ever seen.'"

"The Drinking Tree?"

"Yeah, that's the stump in Whitethorn. But the thing that impressed me most was he came up one day talking to us hippies and said, 'You people call them pigs. In my day we called them rich men's dogs.' So anyhow, he was there at the town meeting. They had ripped off his fucking cabin, overturned his rice stash and shit like that, and he was saying: "Why do you destroy food? Why do you destroy food?' And they're getting red and embarrassed because there's all

these straight people around. Here's this poor man living on nothing but social security and shit like that, which he probably doesn't get much of anyway, and they tipped over his rice barrel looking for dope.

"The deputy sheriff gave an apology. He said, 'This will never happen again. We weren't aware that there were no warrants issued. We were asked to participate by Humboldt County.' Bullshit like that. Then Tuna Jackson got up and made this incredible speech. He makes speeches you don't listen to because they're so fucking dull. So I was sitting there being very bored by this speech, and there was a gallon of Red Mountain on the other side of the room, so I just stood up and pointed at it till somebody passed it over. Sit there with my gallon of wine, people smoking dope and stuff like that, with the sheriff right there. So I was just drinking my wine and looking at the fire with Tuna droning in the background. Finally, he said something like, 'One day the police and us will be brothers too.' And somehow that caught my ear and I bolted up and screamed, 'What?!' And a whole bunch of people started laughing. It was the only thing that caught my ear during the whole speech. I said, 'Listen, let's not go *too* far.'

"You know, we knew about the raid before it happened."

"You did?"

"We always know before it happens. They don't know how, but we know. Then a couple of months later some cop came to the post office on the first or the fifteenth, I forget which one it was, on the day the welfare comes in. He positioned himself in front of the post office and set about checking IDs. And John the Candlemaker **was wandering by** (John's a philosopher for sure) and he starts a rap **with** the cop. The cop says, 'Every time we come out here, we're met by an army. You people always know when we're coming. How does that happen?' So John looks at him, with his long gray beard flowing. He smiles, and points upward."

"What time should I yell for you?" asks Alden's mother-in-law (sort of) as she prepares to go to bed. After her departure, we play back the tape to make sure it's working.

"Damn, that sounds so academic," says Alden. "I had six years of college, but I try to hide it. Two years at Wesleyan in Connecticut, a very fancy men's school."

"So you are academic after all," I say.

"Yeah, right."

"What road led you out here?"

"101. I was just hitchhiking through on the way to Canada, and Jay and Toni picked me up. They said they could use some help on their house, so on my way back I thought of their offer and came on out. I stayed there all winter, working—helping to put on their roof and stuff and they put me up and fed me. Meanwhile I met some of the people in Tepeetown and got to like it, and I decided I didn't want to live anywhere else but here. Then I started helping Richard on his dome, and I stayed in one of the tepees no one was living in. When it came time to put the sticks together on the dome, we had a big party—a whole bunch of people came and we had a lot of booze and dope and chicks were out there cooking and there was music playing and we were climbing all over this thing. It was like a big jungle gym—all the sticks were cut and all we had to do was bolt them together. A barn raising, twentieth-century."

"Do you have any more stories about famous historical happenings from around here?" I ask.

"Oh, yeah. The Briceland Truk Stop Story.

The A-1 Truckers—they were established somewhere south of here, and then they came up here and started a garage. It was a big open place, with gas pumps in front of it. Their trip started out pretty good: they had all kinds of automotive repair equipment and shit like that, and they were gonna have a free trip where you could come in and use their tools and fix your car. It sounded really great. I had an acetylene torch and a couple of tanks, and I turned them onto that—because I wasn't using it. But as time went by, I don't know how it happened, they got into ripping off Larry's store—calling him capitalist and bullshit like that. Money is free, they said. They were complaining that Larry didn't have any good enough organic food, and then they'd break into his store at night and rip off all his tobacco and booze. Kinda weird, you know? So they broke his front window first, and I heard about it after that. I got really angry because I really dug the Briceland Store. It was one of my favorite trips; you didn't have to go to Garberville to get all your shit, you'd just go there and meet all your friends and everything like that. So I was really pissed—he got ripped off day after day and no one was doing anything about it. Finally he got people to guard the store, the most violent-looking dudes around, the kind of people you don't fuck around with. I did it a couple of nights, stayed up all night there. Larry said drink all the wine you want, so I could just be drinking wine, feeding the fire, sitting there with my crossbow in one hand and a Mauser in the other—it wasn't loaded, but it was a Mauser. They didn't know me at all, and I was looking very wild, just out from the hills.

"One day I needed an ax to cut up the firewood, and they were next door chopping wood. So I unbolted the door and walked over there.

163

I came up to them and said, 'Oh, that ain't the way to do that—let me show you.' So the guy lets go of the ax and I grab it and run back into the store and bolt the door. So they came rushing over. 'Bring back the ax when you're through!' It turned out to be the ax that belonged to the store—they had ripped it off. Larry came the next morning and said, 'Oh, you got my ax back.' I said, 'Oh, sure.'

"So, anyway, the thing finally burned down. Nobody knows whether it was rednecks or hippies that burned it down."

"Oh, I know who burned it down," I add.

"You do?"

"Yeah, I watched the whole thing."

"I was in jail at that time. Who burned it down?"

"The Truckers burned it down."

"They burned it down themselves?"

"Sure. I happened to be there that whole last day; I was just sitting outside watching them get it together to split. It was quite a scene. I was at a folk dance nearby, so I just walked over to check the scene out."

"What was their reason for doing that?"

"They were just into this trip: they were breaking stuff first, and taking all the remains out of the store. They were getting back, throwing rocks at all the windows and finally setting fires."

"I missed all that. I was staying at Tom and Natashia's for the winter; I didn't have nothing built, so they invited me to stay for the winter. I got into some really heavy drinking. Started out in the morning with a bottle of port wine before I even went to work at McKee's and got really strung out. Every once in a while I figured I was too strung out, so I'll try to dry out. But sometimes drying out is kind of weird. With me, it tends to put me in a real classical paranoid position. I hadn't drunk anything in a day, and I started having these paranoid hallucinations. Like I was flashing on the electricity that comes into their house from P.G. & E.; the CIA has tapped those things and they can hear every fucking word you say. I was going on all sorts of paranoid trips like that. This is in the middle of the Briceland trip, and I was rapping with Tom and Natashia, and I was getting angry that they weren't as angry as I was at the Truckers. I was pissed that they were complacent, that they'd sit there and watch Larry's store being trashed. They had some friends with the A-1 Truckers, I guess, or something like that. Anyhow, I got in an argument with Tom that night about all this. I decided I was going to put my backpack on and split—I was getting paranoid about the electricity, the CIA, and I was sure there were narcotics agents among the Truckers. I still think that's true and not just my paranoid—there must have been 'agents provocateurs,' or whatever you call it, among them. I couldn't make sense of it in any other way.

"Anyhow, I was getting my backpack all packed, putting a bag of rice in there, and I was gonna take my crossbow and go out into the hills and stay out there. And also I was going to go to Briceland in the middle of the night with my crossbow and put one bolt—bang—in their door. Just this one arrow right through their door in the middle of the night. That's what I wanted to do, but Tom got freaked out by my freak-out—they thought I was really going to kill somebody because of all my dramatic gestures and shit like that, so Tom ripped off my crossbow. I got so paranoid about my crossbow being ripped off that I split. I was gonna go up Thompson Creek, up to the Gulch, stay with some friends, cool down, something. I had never gone that way from their house to Thompson Creek, but the moon was out and I knew that somehow if I went in that direction I'd find the Creek and cross it, and then I could find the trail. So I was walking through this beautiful meadow, and the redwoods . . . wow . . . beautiful place. And then I saw all these cabins . . . wow . . . 'I wonder who lives here—I never saw that before.' I started really walking slowly in the dark, nightwalking, not making a sound. At first I thought, 'Wow, I found Bigfoot's hideout!' I thought I knew all the houses around here, but I had never been at this place. I thought, 'Bigfoot, wow!' I always wanted to meet Bigfoot."

"Who's that, a local character?" asks Alden's mother-in-law (sort of), who has just re-emerged from the plastic tent.

"No, it's a legend, an Indian legend."

"You wanted to meet Big *Foot*?"

"Yes, it's a legend."

"Oh, it's a legend."

"Yes, it's a legend about a seven- or eight-foot-tall hairy animal, sort of semihuman or something."

"The passionate one, with the heavy footsteps?"

"Yeah, that's it."

"Yeah, somebody tried to scare me with that the first night I was here."

"Well, Bigfoot captures people, you know, he keeps them for three days, and nobody knows exactly what he does in those three days . . ."

"And you never see them again?"

"No, after three days he lets them go."

"Oh, he lets them go."

"Yeah, something like that."

"Are they zombies or something?"

"I don't know that much about it."

"So it's an actual legend?"

"Of course. An Indian legend."

"Do you have Indians up in this area?"

"Do *I* have Indians?"

"Oh, you know what I mean."

"Yes, *I* have many Indians."

"Seriously, are there any Indians living in this area?"

"A few . . . Well . . . so here I am creeping around this building, this huge building with no windows, and there's this noise inside, an electrical kind of noise . . . bzzzz . . . that kind of thing. And there's this great big antenna out there, about twenty feet up from the ground. I thought, 'Wow, Martians!' And on the door of this building with no windows, which is padlocked from the outside, is this little rag doll and some things hanging from a string, shells and things like that. It looked like a hippie thing, you know. So I knock on the door and say, 'Howdy.' The machinery shuts off—thunk. So I figured there were people in there, but there weren't of course, because there was a padlock on the outside. Maybe they were slaves, I don't know, I went through all these trips. Hippie slaves making things for Martians! Good Lord!

"I went over to the other house. It was getting cold by now, and I really wanted to get warm. So I come up really quiet to the steps and onto the porch, not making a sound. I open the door, and it's dark inside. I say real loudly, 'Howdy, anybody home?' I expected Bigfoot, or Martians, or hippies, or whatever. But instead, it was Mr. Look, flashing on the electric light— boom—standing there with his pants on, no shirt, with a pearl-handled .38, pointing it right at me from ten feet away. He says, 'Get out! Get out!' I say, 'I ain't gonna draw my knife.' I just finished the sentence, and he goes: bang! It felt

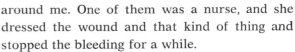

sort of like a ball peen hammer hitting me. It went through my hand and into my groin. I just sort of bent a little at the impact, standing in this doorway. I couldn't think . . . I didn't want to say nothing. I just turned around and walked out, real slow. My hand was in my pocket; I didn't want to move anything 'cause it really felt like something had happened. I was walking down his trail to the county road (I found out later he was following me) and I was looking at the redwood trees. If I wasn't hallucinating before, I sure as hell was hallucinating then. I saw these huge redwoods; I thought, 'Those have all been cut down; they've grown up again. Wow! Oh, I've been killed! I'm going to a different world. It's just like this one, only the redwoods haven't been cut down.' It was beautiful, you know . . . I got this whole conception in my mind that I was in a duplicate world that was identical in geography but had not been raped. So I was walking down the road, and I knew there would be a Whitethorn and there would be people like I knew, but they would be people of . . . a slight difference! I got as far as the Monastery and I was getting weak. I didn't think I could make it all the way to Thorn, so when I saw the Monastery sign, I said, 'Shit, I'll go in there.' I figured they'd help me; I knew them, and they're really fine people. So I walked in there, still flashing on all these trees, and I come up to there and they have a little **buzzer** outside their door, an electric button. I was just leaning on that . . . bzzz . . . five o'clock in the morning . . . bzzz . . . and these nuns come out. I said, 'I've been shot.' I didn't know what to do; I figured they'd help me, whatever needed to be done. So they invited me in and they all got their clothes (I had gotten them out of bed). There were a whole bunch of them, all hovering

around me. One of them was a nurse, and she dressed the wound and that kind of thing and stopped the bleeding for a while.

"So they took me to Garberville Hospital. They put a big plank in the back of a van and made sort of a stretcher thing; I could have sat up, but they were doing all this elaborate stuff so I thought, 'Fuck, I'll lie down.' So I was just lying on my back in the back of the pickup, watching the dawn come, the hills rolling by, and listening to the nuns rap. We got to Garberville Hospital, and the doctor called the cops because of the gunshot wound. The cops came there and took all my clothes away and put them in a plastic bag and sent them to Eureka jail—without me being under arrest, they just took my clothes and sent them to jail."

"They put your clothes in jail!"

"So all I had was this fucking smock. I'm not saying nothing, I'm not into talking; I'm just watching with amazement what's happening to me. They took X rays, and sure enough, there's a bullet there. The doctor starts probing it: 'Yep, sure enough, it's there. But it can't be treated here.' The reason was that the police wanted to hold me; they were sure a crime had been committed, but they didn't know what happened, so they couldn't arrest me on any charge. They couldn't hold me in Garberville Hospital, because it's a private hospital—I could walk out legally—so they wanted to take me to a hospital where they could hold me. They took me from there one hundred miles south, with the bullet still in me, to Ukiah, to the Community Hospital. There, they did a really weird trip: they put me on an X-ray table, and I said, 'Don't you have the X rays with you that you just took in Garberville?' And this nurse *pretends* to take X rays —I was just in an X-ray machine, I know what

166

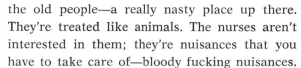

it sounds like when you press the button. She didn't even put the plates under the bed. She's pretending, occupying my time while the doctor is talking to the cop. I thought, 'My God! These people aren't interested in my welfare!'

"Then they take me to the Admitting Doctor's office in the General Hospital. I sit down in his office, and he's out rapping with the cop. He comes back and pulls out a big sheet of paper and starts writing. I did not say one word; he did not ask me one question; and he goes on writing and writing. Then when he finished writing, he said, 'Will you sign this?' By this time I'm enraged. I looked at him, with blood all over my fucking smock and the bullet still in me, and said, 'Have you ever heard of Hippocrates?' He pretended like he didn't hear me. I said, 'Have you ever heard of Hippocrates?!' He said, 'My hands are tied.' So I didn't sign the papers.

"The only place the police can hold a man without any charge is the mental hospital, so they took me to Napa. Well, they figured I was nuts in the first place, for sure. And by that time I *was* freaking out with these paranoid hallucinations; I was really figuring these people were out to get me, and they got all the power to do it. I stayed there a month and a half. It took me a while to get over my hallucinations, which were just growing and growing into really classical paranoia.

"I kept asking the social worker what my legal trip was about: 'Am I under arrest? What's happening?' He said, 'There's an investigative hold on you.' Investigative hold—I had never heard of that. Then, after that, 'There's a burglary charge out.' Burglary is five-to-life in San Quentin! So that's what they finally charged me with, and here I am trying to get over my paranoia!

"They put me on the orthopedic ward with all the old people—a really nasty place up there. They're treated like animals. The nurses aren't interested in them; they're nuisances that you have to take care of—bloody fucking nuisances.

"Finally, the wound healed. I had a good surgeon for my hand—the only dude in the place that was interested in me. He really did a lot of delicate work on my hand—the bones were all smashed up. So when the hand had healed, I figured why the fuck do I have to lie in bed all day? So finally I said, 'I think it's time . . . my hand is healed, you know . . . I think it's time for me to go.' Well, they transferred me back to the admitting ward, which is mostly young people, mostly longhairs. There's chicks and there's dudes on this ward, and there's a big dayroom with a TV that went on from morning till night. Shit, those fucking TVs on all the fucking time—that's what was driving me nuts. But anyhow, the admitting ward was a little more lively than the orthopedic ward. There was this chick, the President of the Ward. They pretended they had a democratic ward; they had the patients have these meetings, and one patient would be elected President of the Ward, who had absolutely no powers whatsoever. So the President, of course, was the most beautiful chick on the ward: long red hair, beautiful, sexy . . . Oh, man! Seductive too, you know. So one day this friend of mine came and turned me on to a couple of bucks, and the nuns at the Monastery had sent me a whole basket of fruit. The gates were open (we had freedom of the grounds), and it was a nice day, and there was this pretty chick and this other dude I had met that seemed groovy, so I said, 'Let's have a picnic.' So we went outside the gates to the liquor store and bought two bottles of wine— I hadn't drunk nothing in a month and a half.

VITA BREVIS

We came back and had our picnic and we all got really drunk and ripped and I ended up balling this chick, the President of the Ward, in view of the front gate and half the fucking hospital. So the next day there's a meeting in the ward, and I never saw so many psychiatrists and psychiatric social workers before. All these dudes, about five or six of them that I had never seen before, were lined up in chairs at one end of the dayroom. 'It has come to our attention that there's been a violation of the rules.' And they did such incredible trips, like asking the young chick, 'Why do you feel you have to escape into alcoholism?' I said, 'What do you call your cocktail parties?'

"The next day a uniformed cop with a crash helmet came and took me away to jail. I stayed there eight days, before I got released on my own recognizance. There's a really neat public defender there, Joe Allan. And all the people around here finally found out where the fuck I was. For a while, nobody knew what happened and stories were running rampant: I had raped Look's daughter (he doesn't even have one)—it was really getting wild. So anyhow, I got a whole bunch of letters from people who I had helped with their houses, and from the Monastery too, and McKee wrote a letter saying that I was working there, that I had a job. So here I had all these letters—God on my side and employed too—a pillar of the community! Here I am, all scroungy-looking, a wild man from the woods, a madman for sure—but I looked so good on paper, they had to release me on my own recognizance.

"But I had to go back to court a whole bunch of times, trying to make those fucking appointments hitchhiking from the Gulch to Ukiah. So finally it comes time for the jury selection—I was going to have a full jury trial for a felony. Joe Allan and I are sitting there just before it starts, and the telephone rings, and it's the D.A.: 'I've just read the transcript from the last hearing.' He was talking about the preliminary thing. I was on the stand and Frank Look was on the stand. I told them what happened and then they put Look on the stand and he told the same story. I have to say, he could have put me in San Quentin for ten years by just changing the story a little bit, but he had some sense of honesty in him somehow, so he told the same story. But the prosecutor is not listening to any of this—he's thinking of things in his head, strategy and shit like that. He doesn't even

168

listen to what the fuck is going on. So he just reads the transcript the day before the trial, and it blows his fucking mind. He says, 'I can't do that for burglary; I'll make a fool of myself.' So he says, 'Trespassing.' Trespassing—what's that? But Joe Allan tells me, 'Plead guilty to trespassing.' I said, 'No, I want a jury trial.' 'You'll never make it, no way, jury trial or nothing. You were trespassing.' Well, I guess that's the way it was: I was trespassing. So I plead guilty to that.

"So it came time for my sentencing, and I had to go all the way out from the Gulch so I was late as usual. They already had a bench warrant out for me as I ran into the courtroom, and they had to go through this trip of canceling the bench warrant because I was there. The judge asks me, 'Are you ready for sentencing?' I said, 'Yes. For the misdemeanor of trespassing I got shot through the hand and in the groin, and I spent a month and a half in the hospital. Anything additional that you think just, I'm listening.' He frowns at me: 'Thirty days!' Bang! I look at Joe and Joe looks at me, and we both said, 'Thirty days?!?'—screaming at the top of our lungs, simultaneously. So I spent thirty days in jail. They wouldn't give me road-crew jobs unless I cut my hair, so I spent the whole time inside. I kept doing architectural drawings the whole time I was there.

"Fuck, that's a pretty long story. I don't know whether it's really relevant, except I guess it shows how things can happen."

Homesteaders with automobiles and welfare checks, Indians of the space age, settling on land that no other human beings have ever settled, gathering wild foods and drinking soda pop, living a semisubsistence life on the fringes of the complex and abundant American economy— the situation of the new pioneers is filled with ironies. The social movement of which they are a part is scarcely five years old, but it already has a history of its own. The former home of the Briceland Truckers, a garage with a brightly colored sign "A-1 Truk Stop—Gypsies Welcome," is now nothing more than a pile of scrap metal with two disconnected gas pumps in front. The Briceland Store is boarded up once again, just as it was after the logging boom of the '40s and '50s. Just down the road stands the empty foundation of the Briceland Free School, which folded before the school was ever built. History lives in the present with these ruins of a movement which has hardly yet begun.

Many of the old-time residents feel threatened by the most recent invasion of newcomers, just as they did by the arrival of the Okies in the late '30s. But resentment against the hippies is based more on social belief than economic interest, for the hippies, like the tourists along the Redwood Highway or the investors and pensioners at Shelter Cove, are bringing money into the community. Stores which might have folded haven't; cabins which might have been vacant are rented; jobs have opened up in construction-related fields due to the increased demand for housing and housing materials.

With money flowing in from tourists, from refugees from the cities, and from the long-time residents of the surrounding countryside, Garberville, a town without an industry, is kept in prosperity nonetheless. To folks within a radius of thirty miles, Garberville is "town." That's where people go to do their business: shopping, laundry, doctor's visits, banking. Several shops carry most of the essentials needed for life in twentieth-century America, while the taverns, cafés, movie theater, and bowling alley provide some of the basic amusements. Of course, it can't match up to big-city amusements for variety and electric stimulation, but it serves the function of making all the conveniences of modern living easily accessible to the backcountry folk. Garberville also serves the function of providing rest, food, and fuel for the yearly pilgrims to the Redwood Wonderland. Neon signs, far taller than any of the buildings, tower overhead so as to be easily visible to motorists from the freeway. Garberville is a creature of the highway, which perhaps explains why in recent years it was Garberville that came to be "town" for the area—instead of Briceland or Whitethorn, which in former times were its equal in size. In appearance, pace, and mood, Garberville is much the same as the thousands of other small towns that service the highways of America.

Beneath the glitter of the neon, tucked away where tourists never go in the back streets of Garberville and neighboring Redway, are people —just plain, ordinary people living their everyday lives. Despite the reign of modernized and standardized America, despite the all-pervasive power of TV, many of the local residents seem to live in a timeless space only possible in the back hills. At Burrill's junkyard and Meimi's luncheonette the pulse of the community can be felt.

EVERYDAY LIFE AT BURRILL'S

Just outside town, down behind the highway maintenance yard where nobody can possibly find it, is a large red warehouse with "New and Used" painted on the roof. This is Burrill Keating's junkyard. Rusted metallic forms of every conceivable size and shape, ruins of a machine-age civilization both past and present overflow the warehouse onto an acre or two of land. There are also sinks and toilets, office cabinets and windows, along with countless items of dubious utility such as the disembodied red letters from a huge TEXACO sign. A million different objects— discarded, lifeless remnants of a fast-changing world—wait for years in Burrill's junkyard until someday the right person comes along. For us it's like a museum, but for Burrill it's like home.

Standing with his characteristic half-smoked cigar, Burrill greets his customers: "What's your problem?" The customer states the problem, and Burrill finds the solution somewhere in the yard. It's like a game.

"I need to lift the fire up in my heating stove so I can boil water on top. There's not enough heat up there now."

Burrill listens attentively. Without a word, he walks slowly, determinedly to a remote corner of the yard and comes up with two iron spirals. Whatever their use in the past, they would now serve to hold up a grill in a wood stove. A few moments of thought, and Burrill moves on to another pile of scraps and comes up with an adequate semblance of a grill. "I used to know where everything is," he says, "but I'm slipping with age."

The problem solved, Burrill turns to a bearded young man who has helped himself to the use of his hacksaw and vise. "What'cha doing to that re-rod?"

"Just making me a jig for catching ling cod."

"Why don't you use a torch?"

"Don't have one."

"Well, use mine."

"A-1 TRUK STOP – GYPSIES WELCOME." –RANSACKED!

"Sure, thanks." A pause. "Ah, by the way, Burrill, do you want to buy some fish?"

"I don't eat fish. Maybe my son wants some." He yells across the yard, "Hey, Dick, want some fish?"

"Yeah."

A little mental tabulation soon reveals that three dollars' worth of re-rod and other hardware, minus two dollars' worth of fish, leaves a bill of one dollar. The young man pays the bill, but something is still on his mind. "Look, ah, Burrill, this is kind of an undercover operation. We don't have a commercial license."

"Oh, that's OK. Anything illegal I like."

The tone is set. When the next customer asks, "Do you have a vise?" there is only one possible response: "I have many vices."

"What are these?" asks a young woman.

"Chain-saw parts. Why?"

"I'm gonna use them for jewelry. How much do you want for them?"

It's hard to throw Burrill, but this does it. "Jewelry? These? Maybe I should pay you for them." A fair price is finally agreed upon: nothing.

The rush of customers subsides and Burrill

returns to the business at hand, which is moving a six-foot-long metal box into stock. "What's that?" I ask.

"Used to be an army box, I guess. I don't know exactly what it is, but I like it." While admiring his new acquisition, he takes out a magnet from his pocket and holds it up to various places on the box. "Seems like mostly tin, but there's some iron in the clasps. Maybe somebody will use it to hold tools or guns in the back of their pickup."

"How'd you get it?"

"Trade for a chair and a frying pan."

"How do you get all the rest of this stuff?"

"Oh, we bring it in by the truckload. Buy up old hotels and things like that. But we don't have much. Sometimes people come in and want something and we don't have it. Can you imagine that?"

"I can't imagine what it is you don't have."

"No money, no whiskey. Of course if we had money, we'd have both. And just yesterday someone came in wanting a rocking chair. I had to tell 'em no. We brought in twenty-five rockers a couple of years ago. Only one stayed here overnight, and that needed work. Came in the next morning, and there was a woman sitting in it. She wouldn't move until she bought it."

"How do you remember everything that's here?"

"I take inventory every morning. There's only a couple of million entries."

"How'd you get into the junk business?"

"I've always liked junk. A while back I worked as assistant steward for the Transportation Club down in the Palace Hotel. It was easy to get connections with the salvaging companies, so on my days off I'd buy and sell things on the side. Wasn't long till I was in business on my own."

"Has business here picked up since the hippies moved in?"

"Oh, yes. Fella came in here the other day and wanted some screen for his compost. I took him over here and said, 'Is this OK?' 'Sure. Do you have one with slightly bigger holes, too?' 'Sure.' So he says, 'You know, you got the weirdest things, and we ask for the weirdest things.' So things work out."

"Burrill, would you mind being in a book?"

"It doesn't cost me anything, does it?"

"Nope."

"Then I don't mind. Say anything you like. You don't have to say anything good about me. Well, you don't have to say anything bad, either."

EVERYDAY LIFE AT MEIMI'S

Walking through the doors of the Post Office Fountain, one is greeted by Ronald Reagan, in full western attire, drawing a six-shooter from the hip and announcing, "We tax everything," by means of a comic-strip bubble emanating from his mouth. To the left are a psychedelically colored poster of George Harrison and a jukebox, while to the right are situated a television set, a pinball machine, and a magazine rack filled with ten-year-old gardening rags and cheap mysteries. The counter itself is a mixed-period piece: in one section there are wrought-iron chairs of the type found in mod-antique ice-cream parlors, while in the other section there are plain round stools, fixed to the floor but with movable tops. Two chalkboards hanging to one side of Ronald Reagan announce the current prices, while two chalkboards on his other side function as a sort of classified ad directory:

Blood Hounds!
Baby Sitting
Wanted JIG SAW
Male Goat—Good!
Walnuts—3-3334
Roto-Tiller 2 for 45
Lawnmower (Red)
Truck with A-Frame

If you're interested in any of the items listed, or, indeed, in anything at all, the idea is to just ask Meimi and she'll give you the rundown.

A house to rent, a ride to Eureka, the weather, the local news—just ask Meimi. "Most every day," says Meimi, "someone is looking for another. It is a challenge. We get all the clues we can and, almost, never miss. The last one was for a young lady who was to be the recipient of five thousand dollars. There was very little to go on, except she was supposed to be in the area. The Evergreen Store was suggested and connection was finally made. Once a woman came in and asked, 'Can you help me find my son? He's tall and has long hair.' That didn't give us much to go on either, but this son was found near Tepeetown and has, since, given up the carefree hippie life and is happily married, with a teaching position out of state."

Today the contacts to be made are less dramatic. "Meimi, I have a question to ask you. Do you know the people in Redway who make the little bird feeders? He wears a crazy hat and they drive a blue bus."

"Let me see. There's the ones over on Madrone who do arts and crafts. Maybe they'd know." If it turns out they don't know, Meimi will be sure

to think up another clue. Meanwhile, she returns to her business of the day, which is simultaneously to prepare three cheeseburgers and to telephone the highway patrol concerning a car that has been left stranded outside.

"Want me to win you a few games?" says a young woman with a baby to two twelve-year-olds at the pinball machine. She turns to her companion. "Give me a dime, Bill. I'll win you some games."

A new customer enters. "Meimi, who's the guy who drives in every day from Shelter Cove and his wife works at the bank and he drives a blue pickup? I think his name is Buster."

"Oh, Buster. Yes. Why?"

"I hear he rents chain saws."

"Well, he used to run that chain-saw business where Sears is. He has a few at home now. Comes in here every morning."

"What time does he come in in the morning?"

"You never know about him. He has many irons in the fire."

"Guess I can just reach his wife at the bank."

"Well, she doesn't know the business end. Better talk to him. Try him at home tonight."

The young mother is up at the pinball machine, giving it some friendly encouragement. Meimi addresses the father: "Bill, I think if you give your tomatoes a shot of fish fertilizer, it will give them a shot in the arm. I have some in the car. If you're lacking something in your mixture and they don't look strong enough, it'll really help them."

"Think I'll do that."

It's not hard to get Meimi talking about plants. "Much gardening is done over the counter," she explains. Her green thumb expertise focuses most often on trees.

"When we were kids—I'll get that soon as I

read my letter—Why don't you sit over there too, and then we'll get that quick-like—Oh, yes, we moved so much when we were little kids that there wasn't much time for flowers. We planted sweet peas and then maybe we'd move again, but we were there long enough to see the sweet peas bloom. Nothing elegant and elaborate. The foolproof things. And then . . . I think it all started with the old apples. I wanted always to carry on the old apple that was there at Blue Lake on our property—the Gloria Mundi —which was so big. I just went to the old apples, collecting the unusual, not just the apples you find today. I have a Wolf River, about the largest apple going, but of poor quality. My Alexanders came out very large this year, too. You don't see the Alexanders listed anymore. I got the Cornell, which the fellow said he couldn't reorder on 'cause he said it wasn't available. I was collecting the old ones and keeping them going. And I have trouble keeping myself going. Write about that—how we oldies want to keep everything going and ourselves most of all. I get better mileage out of everything, yet . . .

"Oh, I was reading . . . I wrote to this woman how I was so sorry about her husband's death (letters should have been written before). The way I learned of her husband's death (I have no time to read the papers), when I lay the papers on the floor I look at part of them and I happened to look at the page with the obituary and there was our neighbor, who had been hale and hearty when we last saw him. Then I was lamenting that none of my family, the kids, have any interest in the trees and plants. The older Etter, the one who liked the trees, no one followed along there either. The fruit trees—they're just about all lost. None of them knew about the trees after Albert Etter died. I have grafts from several of the Etters' apples. The Alaska came out very well. I have two of the Pink Pearls, the pink ones, down there but the deer bit them back so far. But I kept them alive. People have said that once they're mutilated by the deer they never recover, but they will, if you give them a boost of fertilizer. And they're looking real good and lush and tender and nice, and pretty soon a deer's going to think, 'Oh, what a nice apple.' "

"How quick do plum trees grow?" I ask. Meimi knows of my fondness for plums and is saving me some shoots to plant.

"They are small, but you're young. You have all the time in the world for your trees to grow. Now, I go for the dwarf trees which bear fruit quicker. But I hope to go another twenty years for sure, and, with luck, thirty. I'll fight it all the way. But, oh, let's not think so far ahead."

Meimi's, like most luncheonettes, has its regulars. There's Mr. Kennedy, the mineral man, who will readily show his gold and talk of his mines to the newcomers. There's Eldon: "One Christmas Eldon came in with Santa's Ho! Ho! Ho! This went on and on and through the summer. He became known as Mr. Ho! Ho! We've been doing this for twelve years now. He's a gracious host for his corner of the shop. 'How do you get an elephant into a pack of Camel cigarettes?' he asks. 'You've got to get the Camels out first.' Never fails to draw a laugh, though we tell him he'll have to come up with some new ones."

Then there's Earl, the Coke man. Several times each day—once as many as sixteen times, it is told—Earl pulls up on his bicycle, wearing a cap and a shoulder bag, both fashioned of cardboard coated with masking tape. He walks in the door with an air of determination, goes behind the counter, takes from his masking-tape bag a masking-tape container, places a glass in the container, opens the refrigerator, and pours a bottle of Coke into the glass. "It's one of my habits," he says by way of explanation.

Several candy-seeking kids are also regulars. Because of a constant danger of petty thefts, Meimi was forced to institute a rule: only one customer at a time at the candy rack, which is strategically situated behind the counter. Meimi is tough on young hoodlums, but she's willing to give the kids a chance. "Can I charge this, Meimi? I'll pay tomorrow." "Well, OK, but it took sixteen months last time . . ." The kid walks up to the rack and picks out nineteen cents' worth of gum and Tootsie Rolls.

The Post Office Fountain plays a unique role in community life: it's about the only place where hippies and straights, youngsters and old-timers can all come and feel at home. "Intro-ductions," as Meimi says, "are made whenever possible." Eldon is sitting near a hippie, and Meimi helps break the ice: "This is Mr. Ho! Ho! He comes in the door and says 'Ho! Ho!' so we call him Mr. Ho! Ho! Mr. Ho! Ho! this is Pagan." Not knowing the exact meaning of Pagan, Meimi looks it up in the dictionary. Once a group of hippies came in to serenade Meimi with a song they made up about her and found themselves serenading the uniformed deputy sheriff as well. And once a straight couple and their son were chatting casually, watching "The Newlywed Game" on TV as if they were in their own living room. "Hit the Road, Jack" started playing from the jukebox, causing Meimi to remark: "That always reminds me of the day the Briceland revolutionaries left. They came and played that tune, singing and moving around with the music. It was really very nice. Though they left in a hurry, all bills were paid later."

PERSPECTIVES:
DANCING WITH HISTORY
& LIVING WITH MOTHER EARTH

Funny how things happen.
—AN OLD-TIMER

Changes. Spring turns to summer and summer to fall. A sweet smell of diffused smoke fills the air. The tomatoes are beginning to ripen. The leaves of a few isolated maple trees in the stream beds are yellow. The surffish seem to have stopped running, and the salmon are no longer congregated in schools off the coast. The fishermen are taking their boats out of the water until next year. The deer are almost ready to mate; the hunters wait by the roadsides at dusk. The summer tourists have returned to the city, and the school year has started.

The smoke must be coming from a controlled burn up north. Or is it from a real fire? Will it spread? Will the tomatoes mature before being hit by frost, which might come any day now? Will the rains stay away long enough for people's houses to be completed? Or will they come soon enough to fill the diminishing springs and prevent the autumn fires?

Alden is dead. He died four days after his picture was taken for this book, a month after our evening by the campfire. Since that night, I've felt quite close to him. He liked being in a book, and I liked spending several hours by the tape recorder transcribing his stories. He had been drinking a lot lately, and at the same time he was trying to fight off a staph infection. He passed out one night just as he had done many times before, but he never woke up. The exact cause of death seems uncertain.

Alden was, in many ways, a genius. He had plans for several houses: domes on top of domes, ovals made of stone, delicate Japanese frames. He loved to work with wood, carving whales on the beams of bridges and erotic scenes on the frames of waterbeds. His hand-split shakes and other personal touches adorn many houses in the area. His personable openness and his unforgettable laugh affected all who knew him. What happens to a new community when such a well-loved member suddenly disappears?

In talking with the old-timers, I've been painfully aware of death as an imminent possibility. With age, people begin to experience their own death more as a reality than an abstraction. Since many of the old-timers talked of their days being limited, I began to fear that by the time my book was finally finished some of the participants might not be around to enjoy it.

At no point can the world stop spinning on its axis long enough for us to say with certainty, "This is the way it is." The only constancy is change. Within the present chapter of history there is still movement. Our new community in this particular "somewhere" has already experienced several births, a few deaths, and many changes in mating partners. Each year we notice that the stream beds have altered their courses and the ocean has taken sand from the beaches or caused new slides along the bluffs. Numerous buildings and roads and gardens exist today that didn't exist a few years ago, and several abandoned cars and campsites give witness to our fluidity.

An everyday history is the story of life and death, of things coming and passing. Learning the everyday history of anywhere is like feeling the pulse of the cycle of life.

Changes. The changes in the natural world come even quicker, now that man dominates the environment. With one scoop of the shovel, ten plants die in order that a plant we prefer might live. With a single sweep of the Caterpillar blade, a hundred plants die and a thousand insects are left homeless. Some changes are obvious: no one, for instance, could mistake a mature redwood forest for one that has been clear-cut, or a dead deer for a live one. Other changes are subtler, and not often seen: an introduced weed called *Senecio* grows profusely on old skid roads and in burnt-over areas, giving off fluffy white seeds that stick to the spider webs and make them highly visible. To the spiders the *Senecio* plants are a pest, while to the flies they are a welcome addition to the environment. The webs of the funnel spiders who live by the roadsides are likewise covered with dust throughout the dry summer months. The fates of the spiders and the flies were probably not a consideration when the roads were being built.

All living creatures use their immediate environment as a source of livelihood. Each organism has certain requirements and tries to shape the space around itself as best it can to suit its own needs. Man is no different, except that he now has so much power that in transforming the world according to his own desires, he transforms everyone else's world as well.

There is an obvious source of conflict here, for different organisms have different conceptions of what the world should be like. Man

SEAWARD OVER THE GULCH: THE FOG

wishes to make the redwood trees into houses, but the redwoods themselves probably prefer to remain trees. The deer, meanwhile, don't mind the absence of the redwoods but don't particularly appreciate the ubiquitousness of man. Among men themselves, conflicts develop over how to shape the world: some people prefer to turn an orchard into a freeway or an airport, while others would rather leave it as it is.

Despite the arrogant use of power that West-ern civilization has applied to this area, the land here is still fantastically beautiful. Some-times it seems as if nothing man does can stop the surging force of life. When the trees are cut down, new trees grow, or perhaps a different set of plants grow in their place. An old skid road is not a forest, but it has a life of its own. Even in the towns, living organisms force their way through the cracks in the pavement.

And as much as I might dislike what has been

179

done to the land, I love many of the individuals who took part in it all. When the old-timers tell of life in the days of the tanbark boom, they often radiate far more gentleness and humility than arrogance. They were not, in themselves, destroyers of the forest, but simply decent people making an honest living. They, like the redwoods or the deer, were living organisms functioning as best they could within the world that was given to them.

Changes. People come and go; civilizations come and go. If we think of the millions of years that have passed in the history of this "somewhere," the events of the past few centuries seem to fly by in quick succession. Telescoped time shows a parade of different men and different societies filing through this backcountry in a matter of seconds: Indians, Spanish seamen, Russians, Kodiak fur hunters, American trappers, prospectors, soldiers, merchants, homesteaders, bark peelers, ranchers, loggers, fishermen, tourists, hippies. Each new wave seems to disappear almost as soon as it arrives, but each wave leaves its mark. Sea otters are speared and coyotes are poisoned, but sheep and cattle are introduced. Ceanothus brush flourishes where fir trees once stood, while squirrels and oak moths enjoy the acorns that used to support the Indians.

The legacy modern man has left to this piece of earth is not one to be proud of. But, like it or not, I am a part of modern history. I am a participant of the latest wave of humanity to flow through this area: the movement of city émigrés seeking a return to country life. What mark will we leave on the land and its non-human inhabitants? Will we continue with the illusion of mobility, so common among Americans, which permits us to treat Mother Earth

more as a house than a home? Will this book itself leave its own mark on the everyday history of somewhere? If so, will its effect be to attract still more tourists and newcomers to the area? I hope not. Or will its effect be to sensitize people both here and elsewhere to the delicate relationship between man and environment and to give readers a sense of their own involvement in the historical process? I hope it will. For myself, learning the everyday history of where I live has had a most significant impact: it has added to my feeling of being alive on earth, and to my sense of respect for the world which is in my hands.

BIBLIOGRAPHICAL ESSAY

THE INDIANS

My main source on Indian life was Harry Roberts, who was raised as a Yurok and taught the traditional "man's medicine" directly by Robert Spott. Spott, the adopted son of the last great Yurok "high man," Captain Spott, was a close friend of anthropologist A. L. Kroeber and the principal informant for Kroeber's extensive work on the Yuroks. What I learned personally from Harry and indirectly from Robert and Captain Spott carried an authenticity and excitement that can't be found in books.

As I studied with Harry, I began to wonder about the Indians who had lived right around my home. A little research in the library at the University of California taught me that they were a virtually unknown "tribe" called Sinkyone. The material on the Sinkyone is necessarily sketchy, since only a handful of them survived the early white massacres.

180

1 KROEBER, A. L. *Handbook of the Indians of California.* California Book Co., Berkeley, 1925, 1970. This is the bible for students interested in California Indians, but only a few pages are devoted to the Sinkyone.

2 NOMLAND, G. A. "Sinkyone Notes." *University of California Publications in American Archeology and Ethnology (UCPAAE),* vol. 36. The only work dealing exclusively with the Sinkyone, but based solely on three very elderly informants who had spent only their early childhoods in Indian society.

3 BAUMHOFF, M. A. "California Athabascan Groups." *Anthropological Records,* vol. 16. The information here is primarily geographic and linguistic, not ethnographic.

According to the anthropologists, the Sinkyone were the southernmost people to share the northwest California Indian culture. The most influential "tribes" on the Sinkyone in this culture area were those living along the Klamath and Trinity rivers: Yurok, Karok, and Hupa. The Sinkyone also had much in common with their neighbors to the south, the Yuki and Pomo, who belonged to the central California culture area. With the data available about their neighbors, I began to piece together what life must have been like for the Sinkyone. In addition to information gained from Harry Roberts and the extensive data on the Yurok in Kroeber's *Handbook,* I learned much about the lives of the Indians in this general area from the following enthnographies.

4 GODDARD, P. E. "Life and Culture of the Hupa." *UCPAAE,* vol. 1.

5 GIFFORD, E. W. "The Coast Yuki." Sacramento Anthropological Society. Paper no. 2, 1965.

6 NOMLAND, G. A. "Bear River Ethnography." *Anthropological Records,* vol. 2.

7 LOEB, E. M. "Pomo Folkways." *UCPAAE,* vol. 19.

Other sources with general information concerning nearby Indians include:

8 THOMPSON, LUCY. *To the American Indian.* Eureka, 1916. Unique among early books because it was written and published by an Indian woman on her own, with no help or inspiration from the anthropologists. A free-flowing account of the life and culture in which she was raised, complete with lively incidents from her personal experiences and several legends from her people.

9 AGINSKY, B. W. and E. G. *Deep Valley.* New York, 1967. A novel based on intensive anthropological research. The style is a bit forced, but it gives a good picture of Pomo Indian life.

10 GIFFORD, E. W. "Composition of California Shellmounds." *UCPAAE,* vol. 21.

11 MERRIAM, C. HART. *Studies of California Indians.* U. C. Press, 1955. Of particular interest for its pictures of the houses of central California Indians.

12 HEIZER, R. F., and WHIPPLE, M. A., eds. *The California Indians: A Sourcebook.* U. C. Press, 1960.

Detailed studies of specific areas of Indian life include:

13 HARRINGTON, J. P. "Tobacco among the Karok Indians of California." *Smithsonian Institution Bureau of American Ethnology Bulletin (SIBAEB),* no. 94, 1932. A book-length work with exhaustive information regarding the

cultivation, curing, and smoking of tobacco (the Indians' only agricultural product), the manufacture of pipes and baskets intended for tobacco storage, and a wealth of tobacco-oriented folklore. Much of the monograph is accompanied by a phonetic rendition of the spoken Karok words of the informants.

14 KROEBER, A. L., and BARRETT, S. A. "Fishing among the Indians of Northwestern California." *Anthropological Records*, vol. 21. Another exhaustive study, complete with numerous pictures and diagrams.

15 O'NEALE, L. M. "Yurok-Karok Basket Weavers." *UCPAAE*, vol. 32. It is awe-inspiring just to look through the 100-plus pictures and diagrams, even if you can't understand how the baskets were actually made.

16 PURDY, CARL. *Pomo Indian Baskets and Their Makers.* Mendocino County Historical Society.

17 BARRETT, S. A. "Pomo Indian Basketry." *UCPAAE*, vol. 7. Another detailed study, reprinted in book form by Rio Grande Press.

18 ALLEN, ELSIE. *Pomo Basketmaking.* Healdsburg, Calif., 1972. One of the few books on basketry written by a real basketmaker. If you want to try it yourself, this is the book to start with.

The myths and legends of the nearby Indians are available from the following sources:

19 CLARK, C., and WILLIAMS, T. B. *Pomo Indian Myths.* New York, 1954.

20 GIFFORD, E. W., and BLOCK, G. H. *Californian Indian Nights Entertainment.* Glendale, 1930.

21 WARBURTON, A. D., and ENDERT, J. F. *Indian Lore of the Northern California Coast.* Pacific Pueblo Press, 1966.

22 MASSON, M. *A Bag of Bones.* Naturegraph, 1966.

23 KROEBER, T. *The Inland Whale.* U. C. Press, 1954.

24 SPOTT, R., and KROEBER, A. L. "Yurok Narratives." *UCPAAE*, vol. 35.

25 "Yuki Myths." *Journal of American Folklore*, vol. 50.

26 HARRINGTON, J. P. "Karok Indian Myths." *SIBAEB*, no. 107.

27 GODDARD, P. E. "Hupa Texts." *UCPAAE*, vol. 1.

28 GODDARD, P. E. "Kato Texts." *UCPAAE*, vol. 5.

29 GODDARD, P. E. "Chilula Texts." *UCPAAE*, vol. 10.

30 REICHARD, G. A. "Wiyot Grammar and Texts." *UCPAAE*, vol. 22.

A number of excellent films are available from the University of California Extension Media Center in Berkeley:

31 *Basketry of the Pomo.* A three-film series: *Introductory Film, Forms and Ornamentation,* and *Techniques.* The films give a basic understanding of how it's done, but to make the baskets yourself you would require extensive personal instruction.

32 *Acorns: Stable Food of California Indians* and *Beautiful Tree—Chishkale.* Two films dealing with the elaborate process of leeching and preparing the acorns.

33 *Pine Nuts* and *Buckeyes: Food of California Indians.* These foods were used only slightly in this region, but the films are interesting.

34 *Obsidian Point-Making.* A simple, not too helpful demonstration of a difficult craft.

35 *Hupa Indian White Deerskin Dance.* There are several articles in the anthropological journals dealing with this and other religious ceremonies. I have not included these articles in the bibliography because I feel their academic attitude is not in keeping with the mood of their subject matter. The

films are less informative, but at least they are more alive.

36 *Dream Dances of the Kashia Pomo* and *Kashia Men's Dances.* Some of the original form is preserved by these films, but the spirit seems gone.

37 *Sucking Doctor.* The spirit is very much alive in this cinema-vérité documentary of a Pomo curing ceremony. Essie Parrish, the doctor, is not trying to retrieve a lost culture but is practicing the medicine she still believes in.

38 *Sinew-Backed Bow and Its Arrows.* Homer Cooper gives an impressive demonstration of his craft. The day before I first viewed this film, I had seen a movie on old folks in America which showed people spending the last of their days as childlike vegetables in old-age homes. Seeing an old man so energetically engaged in a difficult and almost forgotten craft was a refreshing change. The film had been made several years before and in it Homer appeared already well advanced in years, but I asked around and found out that he was still living in the hills above the Klamath River.

THE EVERYDAY LIFE OF AN INDIAN CRAFTSMAN

HOMER COOPER

"Nobody home but the old bachelor" was the greeting Homer gave us when a friend and I appeared at the door. We let it be known that it was he whom we wished to see, and without further ado Homer took us into the house and started talking. No more introduction was needed. He appeared pleased to have company, and, no doubt due to all the attention anthropologists had given him, he seemed accustomed to strangers coming to ask him questions.

Because of his age, Homer had recently moved in with his daughter. The house was fairly modern, with easy chairs, thin wall paneling, and a large woven picture of a deer on the wall directly facing the door. Also hanging on the walls were expertly made bows and arrows and beautifully woven Indian baskets. It was slightly confusing as to which culture we were in, or what period of time.

Homer started by talking about his bows and arrows. "I learned this from an old Indian when I was a little boy. The others would shoot at wild pumpkins, and I wanted one too. I wanted to be a big boy too." He asked his mother if he could have a bow, so she worked it out for him to hang around the old man and "be handy." In this way he learned how he could make his own bows and arrows.

When he got older, Homer was sent away to live on a ranch. In his eyes, this was broadening his education: "and I learned those things, too." He learned how to feed and care for the animals, how to swing a rope, how to shoe horses, etc. Soon he "graduated" and went to work on a ranch herding stock. He married a woman "who could swing a rope," and together they made a sort of homestead-ranch in the back hills, where "it snowed so much your toenails fell off—I won't forget it." They ranched for a number of years, but when his wife died, Homer was left alone and had to start life anew. He went to work on the roads and as a blacksmith. "I learned those things, too. I was still getting educated." All of life, for Homer, is a continual education.

Homer met his second wife as she was roping a calf—he was always impressed with a woman "who could swing a rope." She was interested in the old Indian ways and turned him on to pursuing the crafts he had learned as a young boy. Since then he's devoted much of his time and energy to making the various wooden artifacts used by the Indians, although he sometimes employs modern rather than Indian tools. At this point in his story (his life history had been simply but elegantly introduced: "Let me tell you my story . . . "), Homer went into his room and returned with the fruits of his labor: all sorts of bows and arrows in various stages of completion, pipes, gambling sticks, stools, drums, an elk-horn purse, and a toy boat. There used to be lots more, he said, but many had been lost to fire and theft, and many had been sold. He explained in some detail how he made the bows and arrows and showed us some of the raw materials, such as deer sinew, he had on hand. As a sort of climax to his story, he played the drum and sang a gambling song he learned as a child. It was the only "authentic" song he knew, but he also sang a song he made up when his second wife died.

When the anthropologists discovered someone with a thorough knowledge of Indian woodcraft, they were understandably excited. They wanted Homer to come down to Berkeley, where he could make a valuable contribution to the education of anthropology students. The thought of giving up his home and his way of life to move to the city to be studied did not particularly appeal to him. "I have work to do up here," he told them.

SPANISH AND RUSSIAN EXPLORATIONS

Written history starts with the arrival of the Europeans. The following sources include and/ or are based on primary texts of the first whites to take an interest in this area.

39 WAGNER, H. R. *Spanish Voyages to the Northwest Coast of America.* California Historical Society, 1929. Included are the translated texts of the ships' journals.

40 HEIZER, R. F., and MILLS, J. E. *The Four Ages of Tsurai.* U. C. Press, 1952. Excerpts from Spanish, Russian, and American documents describing a Yurok Indian village on Trinidad Bay. An excellent source for early white-Indian relations.

41 OGDEN, ADELE. *The California Sea-Otter Trade, 1784–1848.* U. C. Press, 1941.

42 *The Russians in California.* California Historical Society, 1933. Articles concerning the establishment and abandonment of Fort Ross, and an article by Adele Ogden titled "Russian Sea-Otter and Seal Hunting on the California Coast, 1803–1841."

LOCAL HISTORY SINCE THE ARRIVAL OF THE AMERICANS

For the period before 1900, oral history is largely unavailable. The settlers in the nineteenth-century, however, had a sense of their own historical importance and compiled much material concerning the first settlements. The libraries are a gold mine of fascinating information dealing with life before the turn of the century.

43 *Humboldt Times.* First published in 1854, the *Times*, along with other papers that have come and gone, serves as the basic primary source for the area surrounding Humboldt Bay. Occasionally news is reported from the back hills of southern Humboldt County.

44 *History of Humboldt County, California.* Wallace W. Elliot & Co., 1881. The first local history, written only thirty years after settlement.

45 BLEDSOE, A. J. *Indian Wars of the Northwest: A California Sketch.* First published in 1885 and reprinted by Biobooks, Oakland, in 1956. A detailed history of white-Indian conflicts written by one of the pioneers who lived through it all.

46 EDDY, J. M., and the Humboldt Chamber of Commerce. *In the Redwood's Realm.* San Francisco, 1893. A promotional book extolling the rapid advance of civilization in the area, and encouraging more of it.

47 IRVINE, LEIGH H. *History of Humboldt County, California.* Los Angeles, 1915. Several hundred pages of too-flattering biographies of prominent individuals and families of the region. To finance the book, Irvine sold space to those who wanted to write their own portraits.

48 THORNBURY, D. L. *California's Redwood Wonderland: Humboldt County.* San Francisco, 1923. A sort of historical travelog with a personal touch.

49 COY, OWEN. *The Humboldt Bay Region, 1850–1875.* California State Historical Association, 1929. A very scholarly secondary source based largely on the material listed in this section.

50 GENZOLI, ANDREW M., and MARTIN, WALLACE E. (a) *Redwood Frontier,* (b) *Redwood West,* (c) *Redwood Bonanza,* and (d) *Redwood Cavalcade.* Eureka, 1961, 1965, 1967, 1968, respectively. A series of booklets with interesting anecdotes from the past. Genzoli is a local historian-in-residence who writes a daily column for the *Eureka Times-Standard.*

51 HAYDEN, MIKE. *A Guidebook to the Northern California Coast,* vol. 2. Los Angeles, 1970. A travelog with interesting historical notes.

52 *Humboldt County Historical Society Newsletter.* Like a yearbook for old-timers, with columns like "Down Memory Lane." A personal, human approach to history.

53 CARRANCO, LYNWOOD. "Chinese Expulsion from Humboldt County." *Pacific Historical Review,* Nov. 1961. Another detailed account of this episode appears in Genzoli's *Redwood Bonanza.*

54 CARRANCO, LYNWOOD. "Three Legends of Northwest California." *Western Folklore,* July 1963. The legends about the Bigfoot and the Spanish galleon treasure near Kings Peak are described and examined.

55 HOOPES, CHAD L. *Lure of the Humboldt Bay Region.* Dubuque, Iowa, 1966. Included are the journals of L. K. Wood's exploration and Indian agent Redick McKee's mission, as well as an interesting section on the uninteresting lives of the soldiers at Fort Humboldt.

56 HYMAN, FRANK J. *Historic Writings.* Ukiah, Calif., 1966. The history of the Mendocino coast as seen by an old-timer from the Fort Bragg area.

There are hundreds of sources on the gold rush and thousands of books and articles on general California history, many of which contain small gifts of information concerning this area. I'll mention only those cited in this book.

57 CAUGHEY, JOHN and LAREE, eds. *California Heritage.* Los Angeles, 1962.

58 LEWIS O., and DENEVI, D., eds. *Sketches of Early California.* San Francisco, 1971.

59 ATHERTON, G. *California: An Intimate History.* New York, 1914.

60 "Reminiscences of Mendocino." *Hutching's California Magazine*, Oct. 1858. (Author unknown.)

The history of logging is a subject in itself. Good sources include:

61 ANDREWS, R. W. *This Was Logging!* Photos by Darius Kinsey. Seattle, 1954. Kinsey made a living by charging loggers to have their pictures taken on, or sometimes in, their fallen trees; his photographs are recognized as classics. The book is humanly fascinating but ecologically frightening.

62 MOUNGOVAN, T. O. and J. L., and ESCOLA, NANNIE. "Logging with Ox-Teams: An Epoch in Ingenuity" and "Where There's a Will There's a Way: Unusual Logging and Lumbering Methods on the Mendocino Coast." Mendocino County Historical Society, 1968. Included is a complete vocabulary of old logging terms.

63 FINNE, RON. *Natural Timber Country.* A fantastically alive and informative documentary movie about old-time logging and old-time loggers in Oregon. Original still and moving pictures that fortunately have been saved are shown on the screen while the loggers tell in their own words how it all was done. The loggers give an impressive demonstration of skill and courage, but they also display a profound ecological consciousness as they mourn the loss of the majestic forests in which they once lived and worked. Distributed by Ron Finne, Rte. 1, Box 43, Springfield, Oregon 97477.

ORAL HISTORY

Practically all the information concerning the twentieth century was obtained directly by word of mouth from the old-timers. The oral histories speak for themselves. The interviews were recorded on tape and edited slightly for purposes of continuity and clarity. In many cases what might appear as an editing job really isn't. The interchange between Roy and Mabel Cathey, in which they feed each other so well, took place just as it appears in the book, and the life stories of Fred Wolf, Glen, and Blackie appear without the presence of an interviewer because no questions had to be asked—they just took off on their own. Some of the old-timers, however, preferred to answer questions rather than tell the stories themselves. In such cases (Ernest McKee and Katherine Etter) I have sometimes summarized their remarks rather than repeat them verbatim, since to record the interview word for word would have necessitated devoting too much space to the interviewer's questions. The names I have used for the people interviewed are those by which they are most commonly known—in some instances a full name, sometimes a first name, and occasionally a nickname.

As I was asking around for people who knew something about the local history, everyone kept sending me to Mrs. Margarite Cook of Cook's Valley, who is more or less the local historian-in-residence of the Garberville area.

Mrs. Cook started talking to the old-timers when she first moved here in the 1920s, so much of her information goes well back into the nineteenth century. Mrs. Cook says of her work, "The geodesic survey comes down here to ask me how to spell names on their maps. Like that sign outside of town saying 'Sprowel Creek'— it should of course be 'Sproul Creek' since it was named after the Sproul brothers. The Chamber of Commerce gets a hundred and one letters from people named Garber wondering if they're related to the founder of Garberville—and they give all the letters to me. Then people keep writing me about their families, and every time I find out something new, I have to change it all. Some people just came up from San Diego to tell me about their family from around here. And then I chase all over the country doing research—down to Santa Rosa and up here to Eureka to the Recorder's office. Why, I could take my sleeping bag and stay a month in the Recorder's office, there's so much to do. It's damn near an education itself to learn how to go through all those books and follow the procedure up."

NATURAL HISTORY

Some of the information concerning plants and animals was learned from personal observation, some from Harry and the old-timers, and some from books. Once I had decided to do an "every-day life" section on a particular species, I'd go to the library in search of anything and everything I could find: encyclopedias, textbooks, popular books, scientific articles, etc. The research I did in this field was admittedly not too professional, but it was certainly fun. The most interesting pieces I came across were from books based on extensive personal observations:

64 DOBIE, J. FRANK. *The Voice of the Coyote.* Boston, 1949.
65 HOOVER, HELEN. *The Gift of the Deer.* New York, 1966.

OLD-TIME AMERICANA

The more I learned about what life was like in the old days around here, the more I became interested in the past in general. I became fascinated with all the old things which filled the local junkyards and which in New England would be called antiques: washboilers, broken furniture, logging tools, farm implements. I visited New England briefly while writing this book and found that the people there took a much keener interest in the past than did people out west. Antique stores lined the roads. Every town had its own historical society, and many had their own museums. In almost every house I visited I found some of the excellently illustrated books by Eric Sloane (of particular interest are *A Museum of Early American Tools*, *ABC Book of Early Americana*, *A Reverence for Wood*, *The Little Red Schoolhouse*, *American Barns and Covered Bridges*, *Our Vanishing Landscape*, *American Yesterday*, *An Age of Barns*, and *Diary of an Early American Boy*) and/or Edwin Tunis (especially interesting to students of Americana would be *Colonial Living*, *Colonial Craftsmen*, *The Young United States*, and *Frontier Living*).

Perhaps the most fascinating books dealing

with life in the old days are those written by Laura Ingalls Wilder: *Little House in the Big Woods, Little House on the Prairie, Farmer Boy, On the Banks of Plum Creek, By the Shores of Silver Lake, The Long Winter, Little Town on the Prairie, These Happy Golden Years, The First Four Years.* They are written for children, but most Wilder fans these days are adults. The detailed accounts of her own childhood in the pioneer days of the midwest are unparalleled.

Today there is a renewed interest in Americana, with the most significant recent work being *The Foxfire Book*, an attempt to capture and preserve in print the practical folk wisdom of Appalachia. My own book can be seen as part of this resurgence, and I suspect there will be others.

The information is there: in these and other books tucked away in local libraries; in old letters, pictures, and newspapers; and in the memories of the old-timers themselves. Wherever you live, an everyday history, no doubt as fascinating as this one was to me, is waiting to reveal itself.

THE DRAUGHTSMAN'S APOLOGY

SPEEDWELL

Gently misled Reader! Ray has kindly lent me these pages in closing his book—the making, meeting-of-partners, and picturing of which have been altogether as unlikely, and so as *Everyday*, as possible. And oh my, the temptation is mortally great to just go on about how I'm no artist at all, but, say, some fleshed-out ghostwriter; how these aren't authentic, original, or bona-fide drawings, but only a hand-cranked homogenization of good old ingredients; how, to compound deceptions, the whitecaps of the Chesapeake might as well be the Pacific surf, for all I (being of Virginian stock, Yankee veneer, and a very staid grain) ever saw—well, you see, don't you now, how it could run on, till I'd bored the ink clean off the page. But I shan't.

I will say this much. If you've taken a fancy to what Ray and I have patched together here out of odd, but quotidian, motives—uncoerced, I mean, by any professional, or careerist, or academic, or some-such need—then Amen: may it give, as it was got with, all the more pleasure.

If, contrariwise, you've come this far and aren't the least bit caught up in it all, what then? Say, if these drawings, in endless repetition, seemed altogether too picayune, too spidery, and, to be plain, dull as all get-out. Far be it from me to take exception to your saying so: unlike Artists' drawings, these didn't come busting out, like Athena from Zeus' brow, in greased flashes of inspiration, and I didn't much expect they'd go down smooth as sipping whiskey either.

But I will say this. There is something in this hairline sort of drawing that peculiarly befits Ray's original notion in making his *History*. Just, you see, as he musters his ranks (and his heroes)

from among all the most ordinary places, creatures, contingencies and events, so these drawings spin, out of mere ranked-and-filed India-ink filigrees, the grander forms and lightings of the world at large. Surely *there* is some cause for delight.

Our claims withal are modest. Like everyone else between these covers, Ray and myself (if I may speak for him) are devoted amateurs following the ground rules of Life. Accordingly, neither of these lives nor their depictions may be, in the first degree and strictest sense, Imaginative. If I were to face a firing squad of Critics and Creators on that score I might just, for last words, recite those lines by which Wallace Stevens dignifies the humdrum and minutiae of "An Ordinary Evening in New Haven," which he calls

Flickings from finikin to fine finikin
And the general fidget from busts of
Constantine
To photographs of the late president, Mr.
Blank,

These are the edgings and inchings of final
form, . . .

Like an evening evoking the spectrum of violet,
A philosopher practicing scales on his piano,
A woman writing a note and tearing it up.

It is not in the premise that reality
Is a solid. It may be a shade that traverses
A dust, a force that traverses a shade.

On that premise, I expect, Ray and I both might rest our case: predicated in whimsy; conspired in fellowship; prosecuted in happenstance; and judged, we humbly pray, by the same imponderable logic—we trust it *is* a logic—that everywhere holds sway.

Thanks abounding, for my part, are owing to the kind people at Williams College, and to their pleasantest *Somewhere*, on whose many graces I've drawn so heavily; to Ray, of course, who said yes and never, in good faith, thought twice about it; and to our Friends who thought of us both team-wise in the first place; and to you, gentle Reader, thanks and farewell!

MARK LIVINGSTON

Williamstown, Massachusetts
March, 1974

192

A NOTE ABOUT THE TYPE

The text of this book was set on the Linotype in Aster, a typeface designed
by Francesco Simoncini (born 1912 in Bologna, Italy) for Ludwig and Mayer,
the German type foundry. Starting out with the basic old-face letterforms
that can be traced back to Francesco Griffo in 1495,
Simoncini emphasized the diagonal stress by the simple device of extending diagonals
to the full height of the letterforms and squaring off. By modifying the weights
of the individual letters to combat this stress, he has produced a type of rare balance and vigor.
Introduced in 1958, Aster has steadily grown in popularity wherever type is used.

This book was composed by Cherry Hill Composition,
Pennsauken, New Jersey;
printed and bound by Halliday Lithograph Corporation,
West Hanover, Massachusetts.

The book was designed by Earl Tidwell.